GOVERNING MEDICINE:
Theory and Practice

GOVERNING MEDICINE: Theory and Practice

Edited by

Andrew Gray

and

Stephen Harrison

Open University Press

Open University Press
McGraw-Hill Education
McGraw-Hill House
Shoppenhangers Road
Maidenhead
Berkshire
England
SL6 2QL

email: enquiries@openup.co.uk
world wide web: www.openup.co.uk

and Two Penn Plaza, New York, NY 10121-2289, USA

First published 2004

A catalogue record of this book is available from the British Library

ISBN 0 335 21435 5 (pb) 0 335 21436 3 (hb)

Library of Congress Cataloging-in-Publication Data
CIP data applied for

Typeset by YHT Ltd., London
Printed in the UK by Bell & Bain Ltd., Glasgow

Contents

Acknowledgement

This book is the third and final publication produced by a series of five seminars on clinical governance held at various locations in the North of England in 2000 and 2001. The previous publications were both special issues of journals: 'Clinical Governance' in *Journal of Management in Medicine*, 2002, 15/3, and 'Clinical Governance: Early Studies' in *Clinical Governance: An International Journal*, 2003, 8/1. Both were also edited by Andrew Gray and Stephen Harrison. They and the participants wish to acknowledge the support of the Economic and Social Research Council which sponsored the series and the then Bradford, County Durham and Darlington, Leeds, Manchester and Stockport health authorities for accommodating the seminars.

Contributors

Dr Marian Barnes is Reader in Social Policy at the University of Birmingham. She is author of *Building a Deliberative Democracy: An Evaluation of Two Citizens' Juries* (Institute for Public Policy Research) and numerous other books and articles.

Dr Andy Bilson is Professor of Social Work in the Department of Social Work at the University of Central Lancashire.

Professor David Byrne is Professor of Sociology and Social Policy at the University of Durham. He is author of numerous texts on theory and research methods, including *Complexity Theory and the Social Sciences: An Introduction* (Routledge) and *Social Exclusion* (Open University Press).

Barbara Coyle is Research Associate at the Centre for Clinical Management Development at the University of Durham.

Professor Pieter Degeling is Professor of Clinical Management and Director of the Centre for Clinical Management Development at the University of Durham. He has published widely internationally and is currently engaged on extensive research and development projects funded by the NHS on clinical management.

Dr Tracy Finch is Senior Research Associate in the Centre for Health Services Research, University of Newcastle upon Tyne.

Professor Rob Flynn is Professor of Sociology at the University of Salford. He is author of several books about NHS management and professionals, including *Structures of Control in Health Management* (Routledge) and (with Gareth Williams and Sue Pickard) *Markets and Networks: Contracting in Community Health Services* (Open University Press).

Professor Andrew Gray (Editor) is Emeritus Professor of Public Sector Management at the University of Durham and, among other freelance positions, Visiting Professorial Fellow at the Centre for Clinical Management Development at the University of Durham, Vice Chairman of Durham and Chester-le-Street Primary Care Trust and Editor of the Blackwell Journal,

Public Money and Management. His other publications with Stephen Harrison on clinical governance include two special issues of journals: *Journal of Management in Medicine*, 2002, 15/3 and *Clinical Governance: An International Journal*, 2003, 8/1, both of which (as with most of the chapters of this volume) drew on an ESRC seminar series organized by the editors in 2000–01. Other recent publications include *Collaboration in Public Services: The Challenge for Evaluation* (Transaction).

Professor Steve Harrison (Editor) is Professor of Social Policy at the University of Manchester. He was formerly Professor of Health Policy and Politics at the University of Leeds. His academic interests are in health policy analysis, medical–managerial politics, and participation and democracy in health care. He has published widely in books and articles. His other publications with Andrew Gray on clinical governance include two special issues of journals: *Journal of Management in Medicine*, 2002, 15/3 and *Clinical Governance: an International Journal*, 2003, 8/1 (described as 'unputdownable' by the Deputy Chief Medical Officer), both of which (as with most of the chapters of this volume) drew on an ESRC seminar series organized by the editors in 2000–01.

Rick Iedema is Senior Lecturer, Faculty of Medicine and Centre for Clinical Governance Research, University of New South Wales.

John Kennedy is Research Fellow at the Centre for Clinical Management Development at the University of Durham.

Dr Fergus Macbeth is Consultant Oncologist, Velindre NHS Trust, and Director National Collaborating Centre for Cancer.

Professor Frances Mair is Professor of Primary Care Research and Director Mersey Primary Care Research and Development Consortium, University of Liverpool.

Sharyn Maxwell is Research Fellow at the Centre for Clinical Management Development at the University of Durham.

Professor Carl May is Professor of Medical Sociology in the Centre for Health Services Research, University of Newcastle upon Tyne.

Professor Michael Moran is WJM McKenzie Professor of Government at the University of Manchester. He is author of numerous books on health policy, including *Governing the Health Care State: A Comparative Study of the United Kingdom, the United States and Germany* (Manchester University Press).

Dr Maggie Mort is Senior Lecturer in Health Studies at Lancaster University. Her publications include *Building the Trident Network* (MIT Press).

Dr Nancy Redfern is a Consultant Anaesthetist at the Newcastle upon Tyne Hospitals Trust, Associate Postgraduate Dean of Medicine at the University of Newcastle and an assessor for the Commission for Health Audit and Inspection.

Chandra Vanu Som is a PhD research student at the University of Durham investigating the human resource implications of clinical governance.

Jane Stewart is Lecturer in Clinical Education, University of Newcastle, specializing in the design and delivery of postgraduate medical education. Her interests include the recognition and management of risk.

Barbara Telfer is a Physiotherapist and Research Assistant, Centre for Clinical Governance Research, University of New South Wales.

Dr Stephen Watkins is Director of Public Health, Stockport Primary Care Trust and author of *Medicine and Labour: The Politics of a Profession* (Lawrence and Wishart).

Professor Sue White is Professor of Health and Social Care at Huddersfield University. She is co-author (with Carolyn Taylor) of *Practising Reflexivity in Health and Welfare: Making Knowledge* (Open University Press).

1   Governing Medicine: An Introduction

Andrew Gray

There has been a good deal of beating on the clinical governance drum since the Labour government's White Paper of 1997 (Department of Health 1997). If we have heard this partly as a call to lance various NHS boils, including paediatric cardiac surgery at Bristol, cancer screening at Canterbury, organ retention in Liverpool and even, at its most extreme, serial murder by a general practitioner, we have also picked out the rhythm of a more systemic campaign to install a regime for improved clinical care. Yet the tenets and provisions of clinical governance have been based on only a limited conceptual elucidation and empirical research. So, what does it mean in theory and practice for troops on the ground? This book is an attempt to provide a set of answers to this question through an exploration of the historical, conceptual and practising elements of clinical governance. As a prelude, this chapter portrays the policy context and prepares for the exploration that follows.

Formal definitions of clinical governance are unhelpful

The government's first reference to clinical governance, in *The New NHS: Modern. Dependable* (Department of Health 1997), defined it as an instrument:

> to assure and improve clinical standards at local level throughout the NHS. This includes action to ensure risks are avoided, adverse events are rapidly detected, openly investigated and lessons learned, good practice is rapidly disseminated and systems are in place to ensure continuous improvements in clinical care.

Later, *A First Class Service* (Department of Health 1998) elaborated it as:

> a framework through which NHS organizations are accountable for continuously improving the quality of their services and safeguarding high standards of care by creating an environment in which excellence in clinical care will flourish.

If these definitions are not notably endowed with practical precision, they served to emphasize the quality assurance aims of clinical governance. As the government rolled out its plans through circulars and guidance, however, it stressed the central role of clinical governance as an instrument of the government's wider policy to 'modernize' health policy and management. The emphasis here was on new institutions, processes and incentive structures to manage medical quality proactively and minimize risk. The thrust was a break with the traditional assumption that professional self-regulation has operated in both the public and professional interest and a challenge to professional autonomy and medical–managerial relationships. Lugon and Secker-Walker (1999: 1) were perhaps the first to pick up this policy delivery instrument role in:

> the action, the system or the manner of governing clinical affairs. This requires two main components; an explicit means of setting clinical policy and an equally explicit means of monitoring compliance with such policy.

These definitions already show differences in usage of the term clinical governance. However, they share a focus on explicit structures and processes. These may be labelled as formal clinical governance. None of the definitions, however, elucidates what is involved on the ground in the relationships that make up the governance of clinical practice. As part of a Joint Research Programme in Clinical Governance between the Nuffield Institute for Health (Professor B.W. Ferguson and Dr J. Lim) and the University of Durham from 1999 to 2001, the author held informal discussions with clinicians and managers in both primary and secondary care within the old Northern and Yorkshire Region. The aim of these discussions was, as a prelude to more extensive work, to identify practitioner conceptualizations and images of clinical governance and thus throw light on both the way the government's clinical governance initiative was being perceived and the tensions that are inherent in the governance of clinical practice. Although these respondents in no way constituted a statistically significant group their responses expectedly fell into two broad groups – those who resisted and those who accepted what was on offer. The **resisters** saw clinical governance as a device for 'blaming' clinicians (as part of a general blaming culture) and 'bouncing' them into new ways of working with other health professionals and managers, or as a 'source of fear' and 'need for reassurance'. This group also tended to conceptualize clinical governance as a 'formal' arrangement, specifically as a managerial set of corporate 'plans', 'structures' and 'processes' somewhat distant from clinical practice but which the trust made provision for through designated committees and personnel. The **acceptors**, in contrast, recognized how it could be a way of 'identifying' and 'preventing adverse forces', an opportunity to show that 'clinicians can perform' and work effectively in 'multidisciplinary teams' through 'collegial effort'. This group tended to regard clinical governance more as a 'method' than a structure, a way of developing and applying new ways of working (such as through teams and evidence-based medicine) and therefore a matter that was indeed much more central to clinical responsibility.

Even in this limited informal selection of clinicians, however, there were acceptors who were formalists (i.e. accepted the need for new managerial structures) and resisters who were methodologists (i.e. it was the new method they were resisting). Perhaps such a mix of understandings may be attributed to the usual culprits of poor communication (by government of its intentions) or vested interests of the medical professions. They might also, however, be derived from the manifest contemporary lack of an authoritative elucidation of governance, both in general and in the specific sense of clinical governance, and the overlooking in the elaboration of the latter of the relationships that constitute the reality of delivering clinical care. All these factors will be addressed to some extent in the remaining chapters of this book: the nature of the governance inherent in the government's modernization programme for health care by, for example, Chapter 2, the history of government–medicine relations by Chapters 3–5, the differentiation of the medical professions by Chapter 6, and the realities of the working relationships that define the evidential base used in clinical practice by Chapters 7–10. The remainder of this Introduction, however, will concentrate on our central concept, governance, and set out the basis of what might be implied by it for clinical practice.

The concept of governance

A project (with Professor Bill Jenkins at the University of Kent) on the nature of governance and administrative politics in British government has involved a search for a conceptualization of governance to use in the investigation of, for example, the changing roles of public service professionals, the machinery of government, the policy and practice of public expenditure, programme evaluation and evidence-based policy, and service relations with consumers. This search led to membership of the Economic and Social Research Council-sponsored seminar series on *New Public Management* and *Public Policy Implementation*, in addition to that on *Clinical Governance* from which most chapters in this book are drawn, and to *Evaluation and Collaborative Government*, a project of the International Policy and Programme Evaluation Group (INTEVAL) that explored the implications for evaluation of different collaborative forms and processes.

A striking feature in all these forums (and, indeed, experience as a non-executive director of a Primary Care Trust) has been the vagueness of the notion of governance employed. To escape this ambiguity, we ought to be able to seek refuge in the political science literature on governance. Yet it reveals a similar confusion, well set out by Rhodes, who has provided prob- ably the most complete survey thus far (1997). He identified several usages in the literature including:

- minimal or enabling (rather than providing) state;
- prescriptions of 'good governance' embracing independence, effi- ciency, accountability and rule of law;
- policy-steering models of 'new' public management;
- instruments of corporate (financial) control;
- systems of 'interacting interventions' (Kooiman 1993: 258); and
- self-organizing networks.

To this, we can now add, from the notion of clinical governance:

- quality assurance.

That the idea of self-governing networks is perhaps the most recent common usage of governance (in part perhaps because of Rhodes' very endorsement of it) does not help us very much. In common with the other notions, it is a *form* of governance rather than an expression of its *essence*. Indeed, to redefine governance as any one of these usages may allow the particular to take over the genus and thereby impoverish our analytical instruments and consequent understanding. Yet, if these various elaborations of governance are not helpful as definitions, they do comprise some common elements. Most striking are the arrangements for the exercise of authority and function and for ensuring that rights and obligations are established and maintained. Moreover, the very practices of these arrangements draw attention to the relationships that underpin these forms of governance and bind the en- gagement of participants.

From such common elements it is possible to elucidate an initial working definition of governance as the arrangements by which authority and func- tion are allocated and rights and obligations established and regulated and through which policies and practices are effected. It is the underlying nature of the relationships by which participants engage in the collective arrange- ments that not only gives governance its essence but also its modes. Rhodes' own exposition of various usages of governance indicates that, for example, the relationships may take many forms depending on the mix of styles or modes of relationship. Again, reflecting on the commonalities in these re- lationships, we may draw on earlier work (Gray 1998) and postulate three ideal types or modes of governance: command, communion and contract. The **command mode of governance** is based on the rule of law emanating from a sovereign body and delivered through a scalar chain of superior and subordinate authority. The legitimacy for actions under command governance lies in their being within the bounds prescribed through due process by the institution. The strength of command lies in the efficiency and effectiveness of control and accountability and its weakness in rigidity and conservatism in the face of changing environments. The **communion mode of governance** is a relationship based on an appeal to common values and creeds. In this mode, the legitimacy for actions lies in their consistency with the understandings, protocols and guiding values of a shared frame of reference. The strength of this governance lies in the guidance afforded by its shared values through different environments, and its weakness in its insularity from those environments and a consequent failure to adapt its normative order. Third, the **contract mode of governance** is based on an inducement–contribution exchange agreed by parties. Here the legitimacy derives from the terms of the agreed exchange, i.e. the contract, or at least its interpretations. The strengths of contract as governance lie in the predetermined life of the contract, the motivation to perform up to contract expectation and the consequent high probabilities that planning assumptions will be acted on. The weaknesses can be traced to a tendency of contracts to reduce behaviour to a common denominator (that specified in the contract) and the difficulty in the face of changing circumstances in effecting alterations to specification without undue cost.

An essential view of clinical governance

When applied to clinical governance, both to help clarify what it embodies and identify the challenges in realizing it, this elaboration of governance promotes clinical governance less as a formal arrangement of structures and processes for quality assurance (expressed perhaps in 'upper case' Clinical Governance) than a relationship of authority and function through which clinical policies and practices are effected and rights and obligations regulated (perhaps expressed as 'lower case' clinical governance or, more strictly, the governance of clinical practice). No doubt, the government is seeking to shape the latter through the former. But the rolling out of Clinical Governance, the policy, is being informed very considerably by the practices, qualities and values already espoused by practitioners as part of the governance of clinical practice.

This broader perspective suggests that clinical governance now comprises **the arrangements of command, communion and contract relationships by which authority and function are allocated and rights and obligations established and regulated and through which clinical policies and practices are effected**. Its realization has to meet both strategic and operational challenges. The **strategic** include (a) the determination of appropriate emphases on the modes of governance (command, communion and contract) in particular circumstances, (b) the provision of an ethical framework for individual and collective action and (c) the creation of a learning culture. The **operational** include (a) the design of contingent structure and process, (b) the forging of appropriate relationships with beneficiaries, (c) the elaboration of protocols for integrating operational and resource decisions, (d) the building of evaluative mechanisms, and (e) the development of the roles and capabilities required of practitioners. If all this seems far removed from the apparently more limited 1997 notion of clinical governance as quality assurance, it is both implied by the original and is more consistent with established usages of the term governance.

An outline of chapters

In this essential conceptualization, clinical governance is not new, of course, but intrinsic to clinical practice. How far it has always been and remains dynamic and how far the balance of advantage within it has been in flux and exclusive will be addressed by later chapters. On the face of it, the nature of modern medicine pulls this flux in two contrary directions: one, based on the development of technical expertise, appears to lead to the fragmentation of ever more exclusive sub-specialties; the other, based on the recognition of the need to treat patients in context, appears to lead to the development of more inclusive supply chains and integrated care teams.

The first group of chapters explore these and related issues that necessarily arise in the relationship of medicine and governance. How far the emphasis in the realization of clinical governance on command (structures, formal plans, external inspections) rather than communion or contract renders clinical governance a ('soft') bureaucratic instrument is explored in Chapter 2 (Flynn) through a sociological approach to governmentality. Chapter 3 (Moran) provides an examination of the emerging regulatory British state and through it an explanation of how clinical governance came to be introduced at this time in this form. Chapter 4 (Watkins) investigates historically the commitment of the medical profession to state health care provision in an account that seeks to explain the current distancing of the medical profession from the government. Chapter 5 (Harrison) examines this relationship in the more direct terms of medical autonomy and managerial authority. And Chapter 6 (Degeling *et al.*), in an empirical investigation, explores the extent to which different occupational groups of health care staff have distinctive or similar perceptions of clinical governance.

The second group of chapters focuses on the enhancement of the evidence base for medicine (a central tenet of clinical governance) and how far it is challenged by the context of the development and application of evidence in clinical practice. Chapter 7 (Byrne) questions whether the intellectual appeal of methodologies that test single interventions in whole populations is limited by the context in which practitioners have to apply combinations of interventions to single patients. Chapter 8 (Bilson and White) explores the extent to which such patients may be constructed by clinical interactions into cases for treatment and Chapter 9 (Mort *et al.*) questions whether experimental interventions or technologies such as telemedicine may not all be equally amenable to established notions of the highest tests of evidence. Finally, Chapter 10 (Barnes) demonstrates the kind of grounds upon which patients do not necessarily relate to clinical practitioners in terms of scientific rationality but in terms more personal to their condition and context.

Since *Tomorrow's Doctors* (GMC 1993), more attention has been paid to the whole patient, whole context and whole system of care. A final group of chapters considers some prescriptions for realizing clinical governance that are consistent with this direction. Chapter 11 (Redfern and Stewart) reminds us that education and socialization of doctors figures prominently in the agenda for change. Yet this chapter questions whether prevailing notions of education and training, however conducive to technical proficiency (and even this might be more limited than we have assumed), are consistent with the context and culture in which medicine now has, for both technical and policy reasons, to be practised. Although health care commissioners may have little influence on the education of their medical providers they might indeed have interests in the extent to which their care-providing organizations explicitly manage other aspects of their human resources. Thus, Chapter 12 (Som) discusses the requirement of clinical governance for human resource management to be transformed from a one-dimensional (usually legal) reactive function into a purposive proactive strategic instrument if only for NHS organizations to have some hope of matching capability to need. Commissioners might also be interested in how providers are organizing the management of clinical production and specifically whether they are responding to government policy with traditional functional or more innovative and integrative mechanisms. Chapter 13 (Degeling *et al.*) provides an argument and illustration of an innovation that seeks to bring together not only the potential for new structures, but enhanced self-governing professional processes of systematized care that proactively manage quality and resource variances.

The chapters that follow provide, therefore, a variety of detailed explorations of the theory, practice and prospects of Clinical Governance and the governance of clinical care. We might expect them to show, both in the practice of governance in medicine and the development of its scientific underpinning, disjunctions between exhortation (rhetoric) and practice (reality) and between public and private rationalities. We might also expect them to confirm that when it comes to realizing clinical governance there are dilemmas to be managed as well as techniques to be fixed.

PART 1
MEDICINE, AUTONOMY AND GOVERNANCE

2 'Soft Bureaucracy', Governmentality and Clinical Governance: Theoretical Approaches to Emergent Policy

Rob Flynn

The introduction of clinical governance into the National Health Service (NHS) in England represents a fundamental shift in the relationship between the state and the medical and other health care professions. It is a state response to increasing problems with the regulation of expertise in an era of heightened consumer awareness of risk. From the inception of the NHS, various institutions and systems have been used to regulate professional medical education and training, clinical practice, resource use and standards of performance. Many measures have relied upon extensive self-regulation by the professional bodies (e.g. General Medical Council and Royal Colleges), whilst others have imposed direct and indirect bureaucratic and managerial controls (Harrison 1988; Flynn 1992; Harrison and Ahmad 2000). During the 1990s, the application of quasi-market competition further transformed the relations between medical professionals, patients and managers, particularly because of the explicit focus on cost-efficiency, effectiveness and quality of service in the contract negotiations between purchasers and providers (Flynn and Williams 1997; Ham 1999). Following the 1997 election of the 'New Labour' government, all health care professionals were required to be more responsive to patients' needs, and to take greater responsibility for securing improvements in quality (Department of Health 1997). From 1998 a statutory duty was placed on NHS Trusts to demonstrate quality assurance, and new agencies for setting national clinical standards and performance monitoring were then established, linked through a new system based on the concept of 'clinical governance' (Department of Health 1998).

This chapter examines the emergence of clinical governance as an example of 'governmentality'. The purpose is analytical and theoretical, not normative: it critically scrutinizes the assumptions underlying clinical governance, examines their implications for the regulation of the medical profession, and sets these in a much broader context. Like all policies, clinical governance has its advocates, zealots and critics, but it must be investigated not merely as a discourse but also as a set of real practices with real effects. The approach adopted here is not a 'de-bunking' or nihilistic exercise. To 'de-construct' clinical governance does *not* mean that the author does not ap-prove of better standards of medical care, or greater professional accountability to patients and other service-users. Rather, it stresses that the assumptions underlying the concept of clinical governance are themselves contestable and value-laden, and some procedures are methodologically problematic (for example, the measurement of outcomes and effectiveness). The arguments discussed here are thus concerned with the analysis *of* policy rather than analysis *for* policy (Gabe *et al.* 1991; Ham and Hill 1993; Sibeon 1997); the focus is principally at the meso- and macro-levels of analysis, or-iented towards what Turner (1995: 5) referred to as the 'societal organization of health-care systems'.

The chapter first outlines official NHS definitions of clinical governance, and places these in the context of other policies to subject the medical pro-fession to increased surveillance and control. It discusses briefly the links between public sector managerialism and governance, connecting these de-velopments with sociological arguments about bureaucracy, professionalism, risk, trust and the regulation of professional experts. It is argued that the Foucauldian concept of 'governmentality' provides a useful heuristic frame-work for understanding the nature of these issues and the increasingly complex modes of state intervention and public policy. Finally, recent de-bates about 'post-modern', 'post-Fordist' and 'post-bureaucratic' organiza-tions are outlined, and clinical governance is described as entailing a shift towards 'encoded knowledge' (Lam 2000) through the use of 'soft bureau-cracy' (Courpasson 2000).

Contextualizing clinical governance

Official NHS definitions of clinical governance are ambiguous and varied. According to the Department of Health (1998), clinical governance: is 'a process' designed to reduce inequalities and variations from good practice (para. 1.1.2); is 'a framework' of accountability (paras 3.2 and 3.14); is ap-plicable to all health care workers (para. 3.7); requires partnerships (para. 3.9); is 'a programme' of continuous quality improvement (para. 3.27); is a 'new mindset' (para. 3.27); is based on the principle that health professionals 'must be responsible and accountable for their own practice' (para. 3.42).

This new 'model' for marrying clinical judgement with national stan-dards is contrasted with previous systems of central control of clinical judge-ment and patient needs (late 1970s), and laissez-faire competition (early 1990s). The political objective is to reduce inequalities in clinical practice (and outcomes), or variations in care, by ensuring adherence to national standards and evidence-based guidelines by medical professionals. Clinical governance is described as a process 'by which each part of the NHS quality assures its clinical decisions' (para. 1.16), and is later defined as:

> a framework through which NHS organizations are accountable for continually improving the quality of their services and safeguarding high standards of care by creating an environment in which excellence in clinical care will flourish.
>
> (Para. 3.2)

The document repeatedly stresses the necessity for improvements in quality, linked to stronger mechanisms for professional self-regulation. Professional self-regulation is outlined as health professionals having the ability to set their own standards of professional practice, conduct and discipline. However, it is noted that in order to justify this freedom and to maintain patient trust, professionals 'must be openly accountable for the standards they set and the way these are enforced' (para. 3.43).

New agencies to coordinate the setting of clinical standards, or 'yard-sticks' [sic] were set up. NICE (National Institute for Clinical Excellence) specifies how services can best be organized for particular conditions as well as the standards such services must meet, issues guidance for clinicians about which treatments work best for certain types of patient, and evaluates particular drug therapies for their clinical and cost-effectiveness. National Service Frameworks (NSFs) also set standards and prescribe models for specific services or care-groups, including performance measures against which progress can be assessed. The Commission for Health Audit and Inspection (CHAI), the successor in April 2004 to the Commission for Health Improvement Inspection, monitors standards within a Performance Framework, carries out local reviews of services, and can take on a 'trouble-shooting role'. CHI's role, always changing (Patterson 2002), has been expanded by CHAI resolving perhaps CHI's Janus type position dealing with competing and paradoxical functions (Rowland 2003).

Clinical governance was introduced as the best way of achieving the devolution of responsibility combined with accountability for performance. For Donaldson, one of its original champions, it is a progressive development building on a succession of previous reforms designed to enhance quality within the NHS and explicitly a means of preventing the failures in standards of care and medical disasters such as those which occurred at hospitals in Bristol and Canterbury, where there were excessively high rates of death in a paediatric cardiac unit and numerous mistaken diagnoses in a breast and cervical cancer screening service respectively (1998, 2000). He regarded it as a major improvement on the previous system of clinical audit and characterized it as the most ambitious quality initiative that will ever have been implemented in the NHS (Scally and Donaldson 1998). He later noted the fragmented evolution in the 1980s of medical audit, general management, clinical guidelines, performance indicators, patients'/consumers' rights, and the rise of evidence-based medicine and observed that the post-1997 'modernization' of the NHS required a coherent and long-term programme necessitating the transformation of NHS organizational culture (2000). Thus clinical governance became a statutory duty on health authorities and trusts to assure quality and continuously improve it.

The elasticity of the term clinical governance may be a factor which eventually contributes to its widespread acceptance, but may also lead to misunderstanding and disagreement. Maynard (1999: 5) noted that 'There is no satisfactory definition of clinical governance: those offered in government statements are generally ambiguous.' But he went on to argue that the purpose of clinical governance is to 'manage health care activities [that is, clinical services] with a vigour and discipline similar to that exercised over NHS budgets for more than fifty years'.

In tracing the genealogy of clinical governance, several features stand out. First the proliferation of mixed metaphors (umbrella, model, framework, culture, mindset, etc.) indicates its inherent ambiguity. Second, clinical governance involves fundamental changes in medical professionals' accountability. Third, in practice, clinical governance embraces a complex and diffuse *combination* of different processes and activities (see Swage 2000). Moreover, empirical evidence about the implementation and impact of clinical governance properties has emerged only slowly. Hackett *et al.* (1999) observed that clinical governance challenged clinicians' power, and they also noted that 'cultural' and 'behavioural' barriers presented real threats to chief executives and Trust boards trying to implement clinical governance. Hackett (1999) found that doctors perceived clinical governance as threatening their clinical freedom and increasing the risk of conflict between clinicians and managers. A larger scale study (Latham *et al.* 1999; Walshe *et al.* 2000) found a 'spectrum' of attitudes to clinical governance among clinicians: the most enthusiastic groups were nurses, paramedical professions and psychologists; the most sceptical groups were doctors, but with physicians more positive than surgeons. Wallace *et al.* (2001b) confirmed 'ambivalent' attitudes towards clinical governance among clinical staff. Walshe (2000) found considerable variation in the adoption of clinical governance, but concluded that it had involved a shift in power from individual clinicians to managers. Nicholls *et al.* (2000) also described the implementation of clinical governance as entailing a 'whole system cultural change'.

In short, clinical governance emerges as a multi-faceted policy instrument generating mixed reactions in the health economy. However, as we shall see below, it shares a lineage with many other aspects of today's management of public services and invites analysis of it in terms of governmentality.

New public sector managerialism and governance

Other chapters show how clinical governance evolved from successive government attempts to control NHS costs and improve the quality of services. It forms one part of a long-term programme of reform in the public sector, and may be seen as the latest phase in the expansion of managerialism and the new public management (Pollitt 1990; Gray and Jenkins 1993; Clarke *et al.* 1994; Hood 1995a, 1995b). The genealogy of clinical governance can be traced back to these generic aspects of managerialism, and specifically to total quality management and similar approaches to quality assurance in industry and consumer services.

As both Gray and Moran point out elsewhere in this book, the terminology of governance also represents an important shift away from government or public administration conceived of as a homogeneous central state allocating resources to passive clients by administrators or expert professionals, towards a system in which the state is only one element in a mixed economy of funding and provision, clients are active consumers, and professionals' expertise and autonomy are subject to increased managerial control. Kooiman (1993) described this growth of new processes of 'steering' and regulation of complex interdependent networks, and noted that public management had become the sphere of 'governance'. Rhodes (1997) identified various meanings of governance – ironically noting that there are too many meanings to be useful – but then proposed a working definition of governance as referring to a new process of governing based on 'self-organizing interorganizational networks' (Rhodes 1997: 52). For Rhodes such networks are broader than government; indeed 'Governance means governing without government and is the ultimate in hands-off government' (Rhodes 1997: 110). Evidently this does not correspond with the current system of NHS clinical governance, but the crucial point is that the concept of governance is necessary in explaining dispersed and devolved systems of policy implementation.

The concept of governance is also connected with management theory about excellence in organizations (see Peters and Waterman 1982; Du Gay 1993, 1996). Companies and organizations were advised to encourage all employees to recognize their individual responsibility for work performance and quality, and a commitment to excellence. 'Entrepreneurial governance' was also a solution for allegedly unresponsive and inefficient welfare services (Osborne and Gaebler 1992). These ideas spread rapidly and extensively throughout the British welfare state, and were adopted in the NHS discourse of clinical governance. In order to indicate their importance for the re-definition of accountability in health care, it is necessary briefly to review the centrality of risk and regulation.

Risk, regulation and trust in bureaucracy and professions

The development of 'modern' society rested on the growth of scientific knowledge and the application of rational thought in technological innovation and capitalist industrialization. Weber identified bureaucracy as the most efficient and rational way of organizing complex tasks, ensuring precision, reliability, standardization and speed. He also anticipated that the expansion of control through bureaucracy (the 'iron cage') potentially threatened individual freedom and innovation as well as democracy (see Ray and Reed 1994). Dandeker (1990) points out that Weber's model of bureaucracy (rational administration) in practice depended on the fusion of knowledge (professional expertise) and discipline (authority grounded in rules). However, 'modern' organization continually faces problems in coordinating individual action with collective objectives, and reconciling tensions between decisions governed by formalized rules and procedures, and action determined by tacit knowledge and individual expertise.

The latter is crucial for the concepts of 'profession' and professionalism. The sociological literature on professions focuses on how specialized occupations acquire state-licensed monopoly of particular forms of knowledge and practice, and how far they are able to determine the training, content of, and rewards for their work, and the degree to which public trust in their expertise allows them to operate a system of self-regulation (see Abbott 1988; Crompton 1990; Freidson 1994; Dingwall 1999). The dominant theme is the question of professional 'autonomy'. Most definitions of autonomy stress the individual professional's capacity to make decisions based on internalized norms and expert knowledge (rather than conforming with instructions or codified rules) and professionals' insistence that their work is only subject to evaluation by their peers. Trenchant critiques of professional autonomy, and demands for increased state regulation, stem from a number of factors: anxiety about the risk of possible harm to clients because of incompetence or malpractice; potential financial exploitation of clients or third-party payers; monopolistic dominance of a market; risks that there may be profession-driven excessive expenditure; and the fact that clients are less deferential and have become critical consumers increasingly challenging experts (see Moran and Wood 1993; Kelleher *et al.* 1994). All have contributed to cultural, social and political questioning of professionals' autonomy and power, and the expansion of institutionalized regulation, particularly in the health care system (see Freidson 1986; Elston 1991; Flynn 1992, 1999; Harrison and Pollitt

1994; Harrison 1999a; Moran 1999; Harrison and Ahmad 2000). Consequently a very complex notion of 'autonomy' is necessary to account for the
variation in the relationship between the medical professions and the state,
and the fluctuating boundary of bureaucratic and managerial control (see
Dent 1995; Light 1995).

Theoretically, as Johnson (1995) has stressed, advances beyond a simplistic dichotomy of the state *versus* professional autonomy are needed. He
emphasizes that we must recognize that modern professions and the state
were, and are, inextricably interconnected, and that we should use a Foucauldian approach to understand the dynamics of power. The use of a theoretical framework derived from Foucault (1991) enables us to understand the
institutionalization of expertise as integral to the operation of systems of
power. As argued below, the Foucauldian framework also offers a distinctive
way of rethinking aspects of risk and trust connected with professional expertise and regulation. Numerous theorists have focused on risk and the
fragility of trust in 'post-modern' society, identifying it as a perplexing problem in economic transactions and also linked with political disenchantment
with state institutions and public policy-making (see Fox 1974a; Luhmann
1979; Giddens 1991; Fukuyama 1995). The recurrent theme is that complexity, fragmentation and uncertainty all place severe pressure on individuals' and groups' capacity to collaborate and their willingness to trust
others. It is suggested that global capitalism and post-modern society have
intensified the precariousness of such trust, and this is reflected in different
institutional responses (for example the emergence of the contract culture,
and the audit explosion – see Power 1997). Beck's notion of a risk society
(Beck 1992) highlights the multiplication of risks from biological, ecological
and technological developments, creating new forms of hazards and anxi-
eties, and new relations of power between populations, experts and governments (Kemshall 2000). Distinctive risk regulation regimes have emerged
with variations in the means by which state agencies and other bodies
manage the different hazards and risks associated with particular sectors
(Hood *et al.* 1999).

Whatever the mechanisms (or regimes), it is clear that expertise and
professional knowledge are simultaneously important channels or means
through which macro regulation of the economy, technology and public
policy (including health policy) is exercised, but are also regarded in themselves as posing questions for accountability and scrutiny. This ambivalent or
paradoxical nature of the relationship between expertise, risk, trust and regulation (see Turner 1995, 1997) can be usefully explored through the Foucauldian framework of governmentality, which we now consider in greater
detail.

Governmentality

Foucault's theory of governmentality rejects a simple concept of power as residing in the state and political institutions, or social classes, or individuals (Foucault 1991). Instead, Foucault sees power as embedded in social relations, discourses and practices. Contemporary society is conceptualized as pervaded by a system of regulation concerned with 'the conduct of conduct'. Government, for Foucault, is not merely the state apparatus, but political rationalities defining issues for action and prescribing goals and values, as well as technologies comprising 'the complex of mundane programmes, calculations, techniques, ... documents and procedures through which authorities seek to embody and give effect to governmental ambitions' (Rose and Miller 1992: 175).

Governmentality is about disciplining the population without direct or oppressive intervention. It is about achieving 'action at a distance', so that actors come to perceive problems in similar ways *and* accept a responsibility to seek ways of transforming their position themselves. Turner (1997: xv) observed that governmentality is a regime which 'links self-subjection with societal regulation'. In this regime, however, experts play a strategic role in producing knowledge (discourse) and schemes of action (practice). As Johnson (1995: 23) describes it, professionals become crucial in the 'exercise of power, systems of technique and instrumentality; of notation, documentation, evaluation, monitoring and calculation', and so render society governable. According to Foucault, in a disciplinary or 'carceral' society, surveillance becomes institutionalized and routinized in every aspect of economic and social life. This affects all groups and organizations, and is especially visible in the activities of managers and professionals (see Rose 1993; Burrell 1998; Clegg 1998).

Rose (1999) noted the limitations of the governance perspective because its focus is restricted to organizational processes and networks. Instead he argues convincingly for 'analytics of governmentality' which uncover the relation between knowledge and power, and which examine 'the invention, contestation, operationalization and transformation of more or less rationalized schemes, programmes, techniques and devices which seek to shape conduct so as to achieve certain ends' (Rose 1999: 20). As an example of governmentality, Rose emphasizes the enormous impact of the trend in advanced liberal (that is, contemporary capitalist) society towards audit of all kinds. Audit has become a large-scale activity for governing at a distance and especially for judging the activities of experts: it consists of the control of control processes (Power 1997). According to Rose (1999: 154), 'Rendering something auditable shapes the process that is to be audited: setting objectives, proliferating standardized forms, generating new systems of record-keeping and accountancy.' Moreover, this intensification of audit and its concern with transparent accountability and standardization potentially displaces conventional expertise by establishing new norms and objectives. The audit system necessarily challenges trust in professional and experts, and the proliferation of audit both amplifies doubt and multiplies the points at which suspicion arise. Rose notes an ever-increasing spiral of distrust of professional competence which prompts yet further demands for more complex technologies of surveillance.

Dean (1999) stressed that governmentality is not merely the exercise of authority over others but is also how we govern ourselves. The Foucauldian 'analytics of governmentality' approach is thus concerned with how we govern and how we are governed within different regimes. Dean notes that in neo-liberal states, the combination of responsible and disciplined autonomy for actors and agencies is a characteristic feature. This is linked with the new prudentialism (associated with increased risks) and an expanded role for professional expertise. It is also connected with the growing importance of technologies of audit and performance which presume – but which also in turn generate – a culture of mistrust.

Yet the most important aspect of this culture of audit is that individuals become co-opted into it: they are required to participate in its routine implementation, accepting individual responsibility and embracing accountability. Osborne (1993) pointed out that rather than disempowering doctors, new methods of governing the medical profession entailed the *alignment* of managerial and clinical rationalities, so that doctors are enrolled into a system of governance. More broadly, in organizational terms, bureaucratic and Taylorist principles of regulation are potentially redundant once managers and professionals routinely engage in self-assessment and performance appraisal (McKinlay and Starkey 1998). Deetz (1992, 1998) argued that this movement towards self-surveillance and self-control is particularly prevalent in so-called 'knowledge-intensive' industries, and may result in new forms of domination/subordination among professionals. Significantly Rose (1999: 50) also argued that 'Rule "at a distance" becomes possible when each [agent] can translate the values of others into its own terms such that they provide norms and standards for their own ambitions, judgements and conduct.'

This approach is especially relevant in analysing clinical governance. Swage (2000) provides clear examples of placing the responsibility on clinicians and incorporating them as active participants in their own (self-) surveillance, and distancing this process from conventional notions of bureaucratic or managerial control. However, Hackett (1999) found that hospital clinicians simultaneously displayed two contradictory and different paradigms: one maintained the importance of clinical freedom whilst the other recognized that unacceptable variations in clinical practice justified closer scrutiny and control of their performance. Similarly, Walshe *et al.*

(2000) stressed that clinical governance comprised a whole systems approach to quality improvement, and that their interviews with clinicians showed the latter's acceptance of a need for changes in their organizational culture. Llewellyn (2001) has shown that the new cadre of clinical directors act as 'two-way windows' between medicine and management, creating new forms of professional–managerial discourse. Brown and Crawford (2003) have described how mental health team members are self-regulated by a subtle 'deep management'.

This illustrates what Dean (1999) and Rose (1999) have termed mentalities of rule, which are a reflection of a political rationality. For Rose (1999: 24), political rationalities 'have a distinctive *moral* form, in that they embody conceptions of the nature and scope of legitimate authority'. Similarly, Dean describes mentalities of governmentality as the organized practices through which we are governed and through which we govern ourselves. These mentalities and practices:

> contract, consult, negotiate, create partnerships, even empower and activate forms of agency ... On the other hand, they set norms, standards, benchmarks, performance indicators, quality controls and best practice standards, to monitor, measure and render calculable ... performance.
>
> (Dean 1999: 165)

Clinical governance can therefore be seen as an example of a mentality of rule. It has emerged as another technology of governmentality applied to professional expertise, which 'whilst apparently devolving more decisional power to those actually involved in devising and delivering services ... renders those activities governable in new ways' (Rose 1999: 153).

Post-modern organizations, governance and soft bureaucracy

Clinical governance is thus seen here as a particular form of governmentality, where audit is linked with regulation, accomplished through new forms of self-surveillance. It also reflects trends identified by Hoggett (1996) for the public sector, and mirrors the development of 'loose-and-tight' private sector organizational management systems (see Du Gay 1996). The latter is clearly connected with a broader development within contemporary capitalism towards post-Fordist organizations and management: a shift away from a Fordist economy (and society) based on mass-production of standardized products and services, and bureaucratically centralized companies with hierarchical management, towards a post-Fordist economy (and society) where global competition demands flexible specialization in production, rapid innovation, differentiated consumers, flatter organizations and decentralized management. Hoggett (1994, 1996) and Jessop (1994) suggest that these tendencies have been paralleled in the welfare state and public services, but in a highly uneven way. For Hoggett (1996), control at a distance is facilitated by the conjunction of autonomy and regulation: new post-modern types of organizational governance are based on the principle of regulated autonomy. However, such a system has not yet been fully implemented in the British welfare state. In the public services, a combination of intensified performance management with limited professional discretion is necessary because the services are highly politicized, monitoring enables the centre to retain control whilst insulating itself from frontline responsibility, and trust in professional standards is uncertain.

This fundamental question – how, in the new context, can decentralized and flexible organizations and professionals be governed? – is addressed by Courpasson's (2000) concept of soft bureaucracy. Courpasson disputes the conventional view that the domination previously found in bureaucratic and hierarchical governance has given way to 'gentler' forms of management. He asks: 'How can rules be imposed on members of professional elites whose system of rules is based largely on autonomy?' (2000: 146). His case studies indicate that organizations dependent on professionals evolve systems of self-governance based on a number of elements. First, responsibility (particularly in instances of failure) is clearly assigned; second, professionals orient their behaviour to maintain their reputation; third, professionals adopt standardized criteria of performance, but they initiate and influence their definition, in order to 'preserve a grey area around success and failure' (2000: 151); fourth, professionals practise a kind of flexible corporatism – they exchange more controls over their autonomy in exchange for recognition of their expert effectiveness. Conversely, senior managers develop strategies to exercise more control over professionals by instrumentalizing success and failure (for example, new tools for appraisal); and by objectifying personal responsibility (for example by explicitly linking objectives and tasks with specific personnel) thereby 'attributing initiatives, decisions and therefore possible mistakes to individuals' (2000: 153).

Courpasson argues that this system of control is soft because the standardization of performance achieves legitimacy among professionals in an 'entrepreneurial' and decentralized organization without external coercion. Soft bureaucracies are 'organizations containing managerial strategies which are oriented towards the construction of political centralization' (Courpasson 2000: 155), 'where processes of flexibility and decentralization co-exist with more rigid constraints and structures of domination' (2000: 157). Soft bureaucracy, then, is a form of organizational governance which, particularly in the case of professionals, attempts to fuse internal and external legitimacy. It is a highly appropriate and relevant concept for extending Hoggett's analysis, and for describing clinical governance in the NHS. It also bears a close correspondence with Foucauldian notions of governmentality and action-at-a-distance.

Soft bureaucracy is primarily a method of dealing with the indeterminacy implicit in expert knowledge. However, there may be different matrices of organizational form and types of expertise. Lam (2000) proposed an ideal-type of different sorts of knowledge:

- *embrained knowledge* is individual, explicit, depends on cognitive and conceptual skills, and can be represented in abstract formal knowledge;
- *embodied knowledge* is individual, tacit, action-oriented and practical, and is context-specific;
- *encoded knowledge* is collective, explicit, codified, enables organizational control, but fails to capture individuals' tacit knowledge, skills and judgement; and
- *embedded knowledge* is collective, based on shared norms and routines and understandings, dispersed but organic.

Lam argues that all organizations contain a mixture of types but that the dominant knowledge-type is associated with specific organizational configurations (see Figure 2.1). She observes a close affinity between embrained knowledge and professional bureaucracy. In professional bureaucracies, highly trained experts, acquiring knowledge and skills through formal education and training, and having a high degree of autonomy, experience standardization from professional bodies and external institutions. Individual professionals are regarded as authorized experts who apply knowledge in their specialist areas. There is also a separate and distinctive link between encoded knowledge and machine bureaucracy. Here, there is a clear division of labour and specialization, close supervision, and continuous efforts to codify knowledge and skills to reduce uncertainty (and variation), and an emphasis on managerially generated rules, monitoring procedures and performance standards. A machine bureaucracy tries to minimize the use of tacit knowledge, and corrects mistakes through performance monitoring. A third configuration is that which combines embodied knowledge with what Lam describes as an operating adhocracy. In this arrangement, there is little standardization of knowledge or the work process, the stress is on problem-solving and know-how, individuals have high levels of autonomy and discretion in their work, the experts are creative but collaborate in project teams, and the tacit knowledge has to be acquired fast and be constantly renewed. Operating adhocracies usually provide non-standard services in experimental and fluid ways. The final pattern described by Lam is the combination of embedded knowledge with a J-form organization, i.e. the idealized Japanese-style firm or organization relying on teamwork, flexibility, a strong corporate culture, flat or no hierarchy, and a stress on innovation, where knowledge has been diffused throughout the organization in its operating routines and relationships. In J-form organizations, multidisciplinary non-hierarchical project teams cooperate through shared values.

KNOWLEDGE AGENT
(autonomy and control)

	Individual	Organization
High	Professional bureaucracy	Machine bureaucracy
STANDARDIZATION OF KNOWLEDGE AND WORK		
	Operating adhocracy	J-form organization
Low		

Figure 2.1 Typology of organizational forms and knowledge-types
Source: Lam (2000: 494)

It must be emphasized again that this is an ideal-type schema and, empirically, organizations may have elements of some or all of these knowledge-types and organizational forms. Theoretically, they can be reinterpreted in Foucauldian terms as mentalities and technologies of governmentality. Lam's typology offers an interesting and useful meso-level comparative framework in which to locate clinical governance in the NHS. Thus it is argued here that medicine combines aspects of both embrained and embodied knowledge, and that current schemes of clinical governance represent a drive to transform medicine into encoded knowledge (especially through the promulgation of clinical guidelines by NICE; Jankowksi 2001). Some of the rhetoric of total quality management and collaborative working contained in accounts of clinical governance suggests an affinity with embedded knowledge, but the nature of scientific medicine and the structure of the medical profession may make this unlikely or impossible. It is also argued here that, with the full implementation of clinical governance, the organization of medicine (and the control of medical professionals) in the NHS is increasingly moving away

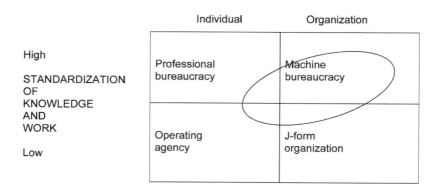

Figure 2.2 The implementation of clinical governance

from a system of professional bureaucracy towards a machine bureaucracy (see Figure 2.2).

To recapitulate, encoded knowledge places a premium on codification, rules and procedures, generates 'unified and predictable pattern[s] of behaviour and output' (Lam 2000: 492) and facilitates centralization and control in organizations. A machine bureaucracy depends on encoded knowledge, and is designed to achieve efficiency and stability, relying on management information systems. The objectives and machinery of clinical governance are very similar to, and highly congruent with, encoded knowledge and machine bureaucracy. Theoretically, the emergent policy and system of clinical governance displays many of the aspects of governmentality described earlier, but the additional intermediate concepts of soft bureaucracy and encoded knowledge are useful to understand the specific nature of changes in organizational control occurring in the NHS.

Conclusions

Clinical governance is geared towards modernizing professional self-regulation, so that whilst clinicians (and the professional bodies and Royal Colleges) will help set standards, the system will also identify lapses. The Commission for Health Audit and Inspection (CHAI) can intervene in local Trusts where it decides medical practices vary unacceptably from the National

Service Framework guidance, which is used to judge how well or badly clinical services are delivered. The National Institute for Clinical Excellence (NICE) can challenge variations from good practice, and issue authoritative advice and national guidance about good practice to be implemented consistently across the NHS. Medical professionals are required to become more open and accountable for their clinical performance: individual hospital doctors will have their performance compared with national averages, and will be required to share the results with their Trust medical director and clinical governance lead. Such data will also be independently evaluated by doctors from CHAI. The drive for quality improvement and modernizing professional accountability is to be managed in a comprehensive and systematic way, and has statutory force (Department of Health 1999, 2001c).

From a theoretical perspective, clinical governance is evidently *not* the governance defined by Rhodes (1997) as 'governing without government', based on self-organized interorganizational networks having significant autonomy from the state. In the NHS, the central state is dominant precisely because the NHS is politicized and collective, so clinical governance is another method of strengthening state control over quasi-autonomous professionals in a decentralized system. However, clinical governance *is* different from hierarchical (Fordist) models of bureaucracy. Equally, it certainly does *not* conform to a post-Fordist, post-bureaucratic, hands-off model of organizational management linked with high trust in devolved collaborative networks. Instead, it is a peculiar *hybrid*, combining in different institutional forms a mixture of rationalities and strategies designed to establish and codify explicit clinical standards and to achieve a rigorous method of performance evaluation through the co-optation of medical professionals in ways which give some semblance of delegated autonomy. It displays many of the features of Courpasson's soft bureaucracy, but also has elements resembling Lam's machine bureaucracy.

Clinical governance is thus a specific example of governmentality in practice. Medical professional expertise is an essential aspect of the management of health risks, but its regulation requires that clinicians engage in their own surveillance and self-management. Injunctions to accept responsibility for improving quality and accountability for performance demonstrate the adoption of discourses informed by total quality management and excellence in organizations. But these discourses and practices are different from modern bureaucracy precisely because they entail discretion, entrepreneurship, flexibility, normative commitment and self-discipline, rather than obedience to rules and management directives (see Knights and McCabe 2000). Ironically, the former attributes are conventionally synonymous with professional autonomy. However, in the NHS, the state's obligation to control total expenditure and health risks, and to secure improvements uniformly across the system, has led to increased attempts to intensify performative control in which service provision and performance are driven by measurable indicators of output (see Webb 1999). In seeking consistency, reliability and standardization, clinical governance is therefore impelled to adopt a bureaucratic mode of control whilst appearing to incorporate professionals in the design and implementation of the quality assurance process. It is precisely because of this incorporation that clinical governance has also been officially recognized as a central mechanism in reducing poor clinical performance, and as an element in the modernization of regulation of health professionals.

Acknowledgement

This chapter is a much developed version of Flynn (2002), drawn on with the permission of Taylor & Francis Ltd (www.tandf.co.uk).

3   Governing Doctors in the British Regulatory State

Michael Moran

The government of medicine has changed greatly in the UK in recent decades, and at the centre of these changes have been profound alterations in the government of the medical profession. How far these latter changes have diminished or enhanced the power and influence of doctors is a matter on which there can be debate. But there can be little doubt that the changes have transformed the political environment and the regulatory setting of the profession. Two features mark out the government of the medical profession in the new millennium, as they mark out the wider government of medicine. The first is that the domains of contestation are much wider than was the case even in recent historical time. The exercise of power by doctors depends much more than in the past on winning open adversarial contests. It can rely much less certainly on 'constitutional silence' – Foley's vivid image of arrangements where areas of government are simply shut off from open political contest by customary assumptions that they should be controlled by professional communities (Foley 1989). The second new feature is that doctors, like the rest of the health care system, now live in an age of hyper-innovation. There has been greater change in the government of British medicine in the last thirty years than occurred in the preceding century; and there is no sign that this era of innovation is over. The government of medicine, and the government of the health care system generally, has moved from a period in which governing settlements were stable, to one in which governing settlements are subject to constant change: from an era of stability to an era of hyper-innovation.

In this chapter I take the changes as given and ask the obvious following question: why have they occurred? To anticipate: my argument is that answers to this question that derive from the domain of the health care system alone are inadequate. These 'health-specific' answers are well rehearsed: that there are profound issues of resource allocation and power distribution within health care systems, and that changes in the government of the medical profession reflect the outcome of the struggles about these issues. The government of doctors, in other words, is a function of the government of medicine.

I do not deny the partial truth of these answers, but I argue that they are indeed partial. They are partial because they neglect an important insight:

that the government of doctors, whilst it cannot be separated from the government of medicine, also cannot be separated from other systems of government. The government of the medical profession evolved in particular historical and political settings. These settings had nothing directly to do with medicine. The way doctors were governed historically reflected these settings, and the way their government has changed is necessarily a function of the way these wider settings have also changed. Patterns of medical government in Britain closely resemble patterns elsewhere in the British governing system. In particular, the great changes in the government of doctors in recent decades reflect more than stresses within the profession itself, or even within the wider health care system. They reflect the working out of a profound crisis in the British system of government.

That crisis was due to two forces: the collision between systems of rule developed in pre-democratic settings and a modern set of institutions and cultural patterns that presupposed democratic and open ways of doing things; and the particular effects of a crisis of competence in the governing system which was a product of the great failures of economic management that led to national economic decline and the economic turmoil of the 1970s. For much of the twentieth century British government was organized according to a nineteenth-century template. It reflected the great bursts of institutional innovation that accompanied the creation of the first industrial society in history. Because government was the product of an era of oligarchy, deference and social elitism it was a government of clubs. Club government has been famously described by Marquand: 'The atmosphere of British government was that of a club, whose members trusted each other to observe the spirit of the club rules; the notion that the principles underlying the rules should be clearly defined and publicly proclaimed was profoundly alien' (Marquand 1988: 178). It is this club system which has been destroyed in recent decades. The government of doctors was patterned on the club system; and the crisis in governing medicine is therefore a product of the wider crisis of club government.

Doctors and the Victorian regulatory state

The modern government of doctors begins with the era that produced a Victorian regulatory state designed to meet the challenges of the new industrialism. Many of the regulatory innovations of that state – for instance in factory regulation and the regulation of financial markets – were entirely novel creations. But by the height of the industrial revolution medicine was already an 'ancient' profession with the defining English marks of the ancient: an emphasis on the importance of social rather than technical skills as a condition of qualification; roots in the ancient universities; and, in its most prestigious parts, a set of institutions – notably the Royal College of Physicians dating from 1518 – enjoying close connections with the metropolitan state elites (Berlant 1975: 130–8). The Medical Act of 1858 was the defining moment of reorganization. It shaped a modern profession to take advantage of the opportunities (and threats) posed by the new markets in medical consumption, and the new technologies of medical care, created by industrialism. It did this through the device of registration and through the creation of an institution (originally, the General Council on Medical Education and Registration, but universally abbreviated to the General Medical Council), which controlled registration. Legislation was both instrumentally and symbolically the sign that state power now stood behind those who controlled the Council. Control over registration also gave control over the title of doctor – the key sign of competence to clients – and by extension gave control over the terms of qualification (by supervision of the medical curriculum) and control over professional ethics, breaches of which were the grounds for being struck off the register (Waddington 1984: 135–52, 1990).

This system rapidly settled down to a pattern, which lasted for a century, until the profession entered a new period of turbulence in the 1960s. Having invested the Council with statutorily backed powers the state withdrew from the regulatory arena. There were virtually no interventions in the regulatory system for a century, and those few occurred only on the rare occasions when the Council itself requested them: the inquiry by the Merrison Committee into the regulation of medicine in 1972 was the first for a century (Merrison Committee 1975: 2). Although the rules of nomination to the Council could in principle have allowed external institutions (the universities and the central state) to impose a majority of lay people on the Council, it was in practice dominated by doctors and not until 1950 was there any statutory provision for lay membership (Stacey 1992: 23). The composition of the Council itself institutionalized a collegial system of regulation in which the Council refrained from any attempts at detailed control over the institutions under its surveillance. Thus the Council was formally responsible for supervising and approving the medical curriculum in the universities; but even in the 1970s the Merrison Report found that it had virtually given up the business of inspection (Merrison Committee 1975: 13–14).

The Council extended this collegial culture to the formulation and enforcement of ethical codes on individual practitioners. The rules of professional conduct and misconduct were dominated by a concern with how doctors should treat each other, rather than with their conduct towards patients. Thus the rules governing the etiquette of relations with other medical professionals – concerning, for instance, the conditions under which doctors could give a second opinion on a medical diagnosis – were detailed and strongly enforced (Stacey 1989a, 1989b, 1992: 203–55). Nor was this surprising. It was entirely consistent with the collegial conception of professional regulation, which developed from 1858. Professionalism in medicine involved the organization of an elite college of equals, and in this collegial culture detailed control over the professional judgement of the doctor, once admitted to the collegial community, was inappropriate. The fundamental purpose of regulation was to regulate relations between members of the collegial community and to preserve its solidarity. And as in any collegial conception of social life, regulation depended on harmonious, cooperative relations.

'The atmosphere of medical government was that of a club': this rephrasing of Marquand's famous characterization of the wider system exactly catches the character of the government of doctors as it was practised for more than a century after the founding legislation of 1858. And club government in medicine was nested in a surrounding series of similar clubs that regulated domains as various as higher education, the City of London and the workings of the metropolitan civil service elite itself.

It is worth reflecting for a moment how extraordinary it was that this pattern of medical government persisted into the second half of the twentieth century. It was born in a society marked by deference to social, economic and professional elites; by a system of politics from which the mass of the population were excluded from official politics; by a system of government dominated by an alliance of bourgeois and aristocratic interests; and by a state with neither the means, nor the inclination, to practise intervention of the kind that became common over the course of the twentieth century. It survived extraordinary changes: the rise of a well-organized labour movement with industrial and political wings; the development of formal democracy; the waning of deference; the shattering cultural and economic impact of two world wars; and the rise of a modern interventionist state. What was nevertheless remarkable until well past the second half of the twentieth century was the extent to which the Victorian regulatory settlements for medicine 'held'. The successful embedding of the Victorian pattern of professional regulation is all the more remarkable in view of the fact that many of the occupations which had originally developed as liberal professions – that is, small entrepreneurs making a living from cash transactions with individual clients – in the twentieth century began to derive all, or a substantial proportion, of their incomes from the state. Medicine was emblematic of the change. The economic setting of the medical profession had been transformed by the foundation of the National Health Service in 1948. Yet over a quarter of a century later the report of the Merrison Committee into the regulation of the profession still faithfully defended the Victorian ideology of professional self-regulation (Merrison Committee 1975: 5, 13–14).

The striking endurance of the Victorian settlement in medicine was due to three factors. The first might best be summarized, quite simply, as spillover from the wider system of regulation: from club government, in other words.

The ideology of self-regulation that developed to legitimize the Victorian regulatory settlement both contributed to, and benefited from, the wider British regulatory ideology. Medical government remained stable because the wider club system remained stable. A second factor was the ability of the profession to function as a political lobby in defending its interests. That is an obvious and well-documented feature of the settlement won by the medical profession when the National Health Service was established. Not only was the nineteenth-century structure of regulation organized around the General Medical Council left largely intact; both general practitioners and consultants were also able to establish an 'arms-length' relationship with the state, for instance through a special employment status that preserved the traditional independence of the liberal professional (Webster 1988: 107–20 for this history).

The success of doctors in preserving much of the Victorian regulatory settlement at the foundation of the National Health Service also sprang from a third factor, the most fundamental of all: the central role that professionals came to play in the world of the interventionist state in the twentieth century. The new world of the interventionist state created dangers for professional autonomy, but it also offered opportunities. Perkin has charted the way the discourse of professionalism – of impartial expertise brought to bear on social problems – came to dominate debates about social reform in the first half of the century and thus shaped the welfare state settlement of those decades (Perkin 1990: 155–70). The welfare state was a professional state: it depended on professionals both for the expertise needed to formulate policy and to deliver that policy – a dependence illustrated to perfection by the National Health Service. Thus, for the Victorian professional settlement the rise of the interventionist state in the twentieth century was a double-edged sword: it represented a threat, but it also offered opportunities because the state relied so heavily on expertise, and professionals were recognized as key holders of expertise. But this bargain between medicine and the modern interventionist state had, we shall soon see, a Faustian character: at the close of the twentieth century the state turned on the profession with new, ambitious projects of occupational control.

Doctors and the modern regulatory state

The character of the Victorian regulatory state, and of its twentieth-century legacy, was critically linked to the timing of its development. Like so much else in the evolution of British institutions the fact of early industrialism was crucial. The Victorian regulatory state was created in a world where formal democracy existed only as a frightening spectre, and where oligarchies, both local and national, controlled politics; where business was a hegemonic interest, and therefore where the crucial struggles were between different factions of business; and where the state had few of the fiscal and bureaucratic resources that it acquired in the twentieth century. The early decades of the twentieth century saw challenges to the system of club rule: the extension of formal democracy; the rise of the Labour movement, itself a muffled echo of the frightening threats to the established order from the revolutionary socialism that swept across large parts of Europe; the growing scale of state intervention; cultural changes – like the decline of established religion and the changed condition of women – that threatened traditional hierarchies. Embedding Victorian regulatory institutions and practices in the twentieth century helped provide defences against these developments: it privileged the tacit knowledge of insiders over systematic, public knowledge and it insulated regulatory worlds from those of parliamentary and electoral politics. Viewed thus, the persistence of these patterns into the era of democratic politics ceases to be a surprise; persistence was needed to provide protection from democracy. In this way the great Victorian apprehensions about the revolutionary consequences of popular rule were averted.

Institutionally and ideologically the system of self-regulation was at the heart of all this. Its watchwords – informality, flexibility, cooperation – summarized the dominant British regulatory ideology. The club-like structure of so much self-regulation in the professions and in the City was the institutional epitome of this wider system of club government. The scale and reach of the system of self-regulation was the key to insulating interests from democratic control, for easily the most effective form of protection was to organize an activity out of politics altogether, by defining it as belonging to the domain of self-regulation. But this was a strange, historically fragile settlement: oligarchy designed to provide protection against democracy. It was bound to pitch into crisis sooner or later. When the crisis came it afflicted the whole club system. Naturally the medical profession saw its own experience as central; in truth it was merely suffering collateral damage from the destruction of club government.

The origins of the great changes in medicine can be traced back to the 1960s. The long historical consensus about the shape and structure of self-regulation in the profession came to an end, to be succeeded by open political struggle both for control of the regulatory institutions and about the substance of the rules. The most important signs of this were open revolt by sections of the profession against the authority of the General Medical Council in the late 1960s followed by the first extensive public inquiry ever – by the Merrison Committee – in the early 1970s (see Stacey 1992: 29–44 for the revolt). Although Merrison's language faithfully reflected the ideology of club government, intoning the traditional defence of the flexibility of self-regulation, the mere existence of the Committee was a hugely damaging development. The hearings and the report inevitably undermined one of the key requirements of club government: they converted the tacit and the private into the explicit and the public. More damaging still, Merrison produced no stable regulatory settlement. No new consensus capable of returning control of the regulatory institutions to the professional elite has been possible in the intervening years. A symptom of this is that for a generation now we have lived through constant reform of the structure, powers and culture of the General Medical Council.

One reason for this continuing instability is that there have been recurrent scandals about the behaviour of doctors, forcing constant changes in both the content of regulations and the structure of the GMC itself. One of the most striking features of these scandalous cases is the gap they revealed between the conception of professional standards that guided the General Medical Council's own workings and what an increasingly assertive lay public thought were appropriate standards. Thus a number of highly publicized cases of callousness, incompetence and neglect were admitted by all, professionals and non-professionals alike, to be quite unacceptable – but could not be deemed unprofessional given the GMC's narrow conception of professional misconduct. Here was a particularly stark instance of the encounter between the nineteenth-century club system and modern democratic society (see Smith 1989 on these cases). There was consequently increasing legislative intervention in the regulatory affairs of the profession, including intervention to reshape the composition of the regulatory institution itself (Stacey 1992: 51–85).

Behind all this lies the collapse of the compact that doctors successfully negotiated with the state at the foundation of the NHS, a compact memorably summarized in Klein's phrase 'the politics of the double bed': the compact assigned control of the everyday allocation of medical resources to medical professionals, and confined the state to the role of deciding the absolute level of resources to be allocated to the Service (Klein 1990). It thus 'modernized' the nineteenth-century bargain between the state and profession in such a way as to protect the autonomy of the medical club. But after the great economic crisis of the 1970s, and the rise of a state increasingly concerned to squeeze maximum efficiency out of welfare state professionals, the Faustian character of that bargain became increasingly apparent. Doctors found themselves the object of increasingly detailed public intervention in their working practices (see Harrison *et al.* 1990 on the growth of all this). Thus the particular turmoil in the regulatory institutions was compounded by a wider breakdown of the political bargain between the profession and the state. As Salter put it in 2001, in the wake of a spate of crises in medical authority: 'Medical regulation, as much as medical self-regulation, is now centre stage in the politics of the National Health Service and the profession can expect to be subject to the full range of devices at the disposal of this particular theatre' (Salter 2001: 871).

In summary: at the turn of the millennium the regulation of the medical profession is subjected to unprecedented, and growing, public debate, increasing intervention in the daily professional activities of physicians, and increasing oversight by the central state. The key to understanding the forces that shape this changing world lies in recognizing that they are not confined to doctors, or even to the wider health care system. A similar story of growing public contestation, the breakdown of the informalities of club government, and increasing state oversight can be told about a host of other domains in British society: about the financial services, notably the City of London, the great template of British club regulation; about the system of schools inspection; about the regulation of the physical environment; about the regulation of other professions such as accounting and the law.

Part of what we are witnessing in the case of medicine, therefore, is a wider crisis of a characteristic British system of self-regulation. When British arrangements for regulating markets – including professional labour markets – are considered comparatively and historically, the British emerge as highly peculiar. By comparison with arrangements on the continent of Europe there is little tradition of government through public law institutions; the characteristic British regulatory institution was either a private association or, like the General Medical Council, left so much to its own devices that it might as well have been. And Vogel's famous comparative Anglo-American study of regulation established that by comparison with the United States, British regulation hesitated to use the law, open argument and adversarial bargaining (Vogel 1986).

The historical boundaries of the system of self-regulation in Britain were indeed hard to describe: as the case of the GMC exemplified, it was hard to say where the state stopped and civil society began. The traditionally uncodified and unorganized character of British self-regulation lay at the root of the problem. But this descriptive difficulty is itself highly revealing about self-regulation in Britain. It was precisely the fuzzy boundaries – allowing self-regulation to shade off into civil society at one end, and to shade into the world of quasi-government at the other – that created constitutional ambiguities and silences. That gave self-regulation great ideological power, and facilitated one of the most important functions of regulatory ideology: mystification. The shadow-like nature of self-regulation meant that lines of accountability and responsibility were lost in labyrinths. Watchwords like 'flexibility' – signals of the supposed superiority of self-regulation over more 'rigid' modes – could be invoked to legitimize any one of a large number of different institutional arrangements. This kind of mystification was needed because the dominant parts of the self-regulatory system were by the closing decades of the twentieth century operating in an alien historical environment. Creations of a pre-democratic, nineteenth-century world, they now had to function in the very different world of the late twentieth century.

What was it like trying to live in this new world? It was to experience incessant change from a novel, threatening kind of state. Everywhere saw the reconstruction of self-regulatory institutions along more formally organized, more codified, and more state-controlled lines. The history of self-regulation in the last third of the twentieth century exemplifies the age of hyper-innovation. Few important self-regulatory settlements were immune from change, and few of the new settlements 'stuck'. These self-regulatory institutions were confronting a new and ambitious kind of state, and this was what so comprehensively undid them. It is not difficult to see the contingent forces that produced this new state. After the great economic crisis of the mid-1970s the state was struggling, especially in the Thatcher years, to reconstruct an economy capable of withstanding the threat of global economic competition. Since huge areas of the self-regulatory system were themselves entangled with an old economy of cartels and restrictive practices, dismantling these restrictive practices entailed dismantling the institutions of self-regulation. And since other areas – of which health care is the most obvious example – were both large economic sectors and huge consumers of public resources it was natural to turn on them in the attempt to squeeze out more efficiency.

High modernism and the government of medicine

When described in terms of historical contingencies the experience of the government of medicine in Britain seems comparatively straightforward: a mid-nineteenth-century governing settlement finally succumbed to the pressures of the modern world. Yet there are huge puzzles in the outcomes, puzzles which reflect difficulties in making sense of the wider fate of club government. The puzzles may be best expressed by reference to what is perhaps the now dominant paradigm in understanding British government. For shorthand I summarize this as 'post-modernism'. On this account we are witnessing the dissolution of hierarchies: the displacement of Weberian bureaucracy by 'soft bureaucracy' (Courpasson 2000); the displacement of command and control government by 'governance' through networks that span the conventionally distinguished public and private sectors (Rhodes 1997). In summary, we are seeing the rise of a post-modern state: 'abstract, disjointed, increasingly fragmented, not based on stable or coherent coalitions' (Caporaso 1996: 45). These developments reflect forces as diverse as the inherent complexity of modern social organization, and the particular institutional features of the governing system of the European Union which looms ever larger in the British domestic system.

The difficulty in applying a post-modern paradigm to the government of doctors will be immediately apparent. Not only is it hard to reconcile with the bruising institutional encounters with the state in recent decades; it actually seems to be the very reverse of the observed direction of change. The destruction of club government in medicine displaced, precisely, a pattern of government through informal networks with fuzzy boundaries and replaced it with something more hierarchical, codified and state-controlled. This seems to conform to a very different available paradigm: not post-modernism, but high modernism. In Scott's account of high modernism, the informal, historically evolved jumble of civil society is displaced by systems of control and surveillance that are designed to facilitate ambitious projects of social control and economic and physical reconstruction. Scott's own accounts focus on authoritarian high modernism: the kinds of projects associated with some of the totalitarian regimes of the twentieth century, such as Soviet collectivization of agriculture or Mao's Great Leap Forward (Scott 1998). But high modernism as a broader ideology is driven by imperatives that immediately surface in the government of medicine in Britain in recent decades: 'standardization, central control and synoptic legibility to the centre' (Scott 1998: 219).

Why did the government of medicine, and the wider government of the UK, take this high modernist turn? We can dismiss one tempting explanation: that since the system was pre-modern, a passage through modernity is needed before post-modernity can be reached. We can dismiss it because it implies, without evidence, an evolutionary account of the development of the British system of government. A more convincing account takes us back to the historical contingencies of the change. In part what has happened is the consequence of secular social and cultural change. In other words, it is the product of the slow dissolution of the hierarchical cultures and social practices which survived even into the era of formal democracy. By the close of the twentieth century nineteenth-century governing settlements could not survive, even in Britain. But the rapidity of dissolution in the closing decades of the last century, and the radical, wide-ranging character of the institutional changes, is surely traceable to something more contingent: to the great economic crisis of the 1970s and to the emergence first of Thatcherism, and then a new political consensus which was a legacy of Thatcherism. Faced with a crisis of national competitiveness in a world of intense global competition the response has been to use the state to reorganize, and control better, civil society. And the revolution in the government of doctors has been a by-product of that process.

4 Medicine and Government: Partnership Spurned?

Stephen Watkins

The British medical profession became a statutorily closed profession with the Medical Act 1858. A positive view of the origins of this Act is that in 1832 the Provincial Medical and Surgical Association, later to become the British Medical Association, was founded by doctors concerned by quackery and inadequate professional standards and campaigned for over twenty years with seven bills before its success with the Act of 1858 (Muirhead Little 1932). The profession had grown from three occupational groups – physicians, surgeons and apothecaries. Surgeons were craftsmen and apothecaries were tradesmen. Physicians were largely excluded from the Provincial Medical and Surgical Association by refusing to accept members from London. They were of higher status than the other groups but the rich still saw them as a high-grade domestic servant. At this time:

> the average medical practitioner was a man of little culture or general education. The graduates of Oxford and Cambridge and of the Scottish universities were probably as well educated as the members of the learned professions of the church or law, but the rank and file of the profession had received its training through the system of apprenticeship ... At its worst, if the master neglected his duties, or the pupil was idle and cared little to learn, the period of apprenticeship too often represented so much precious time wasted.
>
> (Muirhead Little 1932: 6)

According to this positive view of the Association, the changes to the standing and standards of the profession since these times owe much to the BMA. It addressed the ideals of medicine – improving standards and promoting the health and safety of the people. In the latter half of the nineteenth century it addressed the exploitation of doctors by the friendly societies and the Poor Law institutions and the problems of the Armed Forces Medical Service and the Indian Medical Service. It was actively concerned with public health and some of its views on housing and factory legislation placed it unequivocally on the side of social reform. It campaigned for improved vital statistics, playing its part in the 1836 Act for the Registration of Births, Marriages and Deaths, and held scientific meetings and founded a journal which became one of the major medical journals of the world. Its scientific work made it an increasingly authoritative point of reference on matters of medical science. In 1877 it established a special committee to investigate the use of chloroform. This set a precedent for the appointment of special BMA committees to look at scientific matters and initiated a pro-gramme on the safety of anaesthetics and a campaign against the sale of dubious patent medicines. To protect the public it maintained unrelenting opposition to quackery and fraud in the field of healing and adopted an altruistic ethical code. Through these efforts and those of its creation, the General Medical Council, the BMA was able to improve ethical and educa-tional standards. As a consequence the profession became an ever more effective servant of the sick and rose in status.

Other interpretations of the development of the medical profession are less positive. They question, for example, why such an altruistic drive for improved standards met so much opposition even from a *laissez-faire* Parlia-ment; whether medical education suppressed alternative approaches to healing; why the most educated members of the profession (the physicians) were excluded from participation until the future pattern of the profession had been set; whether the support for social reform was as daring as made out or played up in the official history to show the far-sightedness of the BMA; and whether the scientific work might have been driven by a desire to es-tablish scientific hegemony. However, this chapter is not a history of the professionalization of medicine but an exploration of ideological forces which that process set in motion. And for that purpose the question of what actually happened is less important than how the individuals involved in the process rationalized their behaviour and the assumptions and understandings they passed on to their successors who stabilized and developed their creation.

The ideology of the medical profession

The ideology of the medical profession has been shaped by the manner of its creation and by the myths and rationalizations created around that process (Watkins 1987). Because it was forged in struggle, the 'unity of the profession' has been the driving force of medical politics. Indeed the elaborate politics of medicine is a process of negotiating the terms for unity of the profession. Because it was forged in struggle it sees itself as embattled. Objectively the medical profession is very powerful, certainly more so than any other group in health care. But it feels itself to be powerless, pushed around by self-interested hostile forces (unions, politicians, patients' organizations, social workers, managers, other health professions) intent on clawing back some of the influence the profession has so painfully acquired in its pursuit of the public good. Its resistance verges on the paranoid. For example, the BMA opposed the very limited product liability clauses of the Health and Safety at Work Act 1974 in case they were applied to health care and therefore inhibited clinical freedom. The articles written in the 1970s and 1980s in *World Medicine* (a house journal for the thinking of ordinary doctors) are an instructive source of the thinking of the profession showing a fierce libertarianism, radical in an unfocused and often unrealistic way, yet impatiently dismissive and fearful of all other groups. The editor of *World Medicine* topped the poll in all the elections to the General Medical Council in the late 1970s and the 1980s.

Because the formation of the profession was rooted in the claim that statutory closure would protect the public, medical ethics have been central to the profession's self-image. They embody a powerful idealism and altruism but also (at least until relatively recently) the restrictive practices of the profession. They also express collective understandings of good professional practice which in turn are based on an intellectual approach that there are factually correct answers to any question and they are the answers which the profession believes. Yet members loyally believe that it is a profession of individualists.

This ideology has elements recognizable as both left- and right-wing. The left include the idealistic commitment to health and health care which has led the profession to oppose cuts in health services and to make common cause with social reformers on health matters. The BMA is still the country's foremost public health pressure group and it has made common cause with civil libertarians over refusal to disclose medically confidential information to help criminal investigations. The right-wing elements include a small trader mentality and, although recently moderated, an opposition to NHS democracy and planning and to power sharing with other groups. The profession itself, however, does not see its ideology in political terms. Indeed it sees itself as depoliticized, offering medical advice without regard to the political connotations, a position that paradoxically offers shelter to the more political elements of the profession, such as campaigning public health physicians or the Medical Practitioners' Union.

Depoliticization does not mean that the profession takes up no political position but that its positions are not derived from the general left–right spectrum of debate. If this is probably true the BMA has also developed a careful rationing of support for causes with political connotations. Where a cause is directly related to health and is uncontroversial within the profession the BMA will fight with the gloves off, even to the point of directly opposing a government. Where the relationship to health is more tangential or there is controversy within the profession the BMA will be more muted, often limiting itself to legitimating the campaigns of others through low-key statements. Where the cause falls into this more carefully pursued area, and it is also highly politically charged (of the 'capitalism is bad for your health' variety of public health cause) the BMA will usually limit itself to scientific legitimation, producing the scientific facts and leaving it to others to argue them. Thus, there is nothing naïve or apolitical about the depoliticization of the profession. It is a political weapon, shaped by a sophisticated understanding of politics.

The attitude of organized medicine to the NHS

To understand the attitude of organized medicine to the NHS two different concepts of an NHS must be distinguished: one is medicine free at the time of use, financed out of general taxation, and the other is the mechanism by which society pursues health as a social goal and plans health care to meet need. Organized medicine for almost all of the last century favoured the former but opposed the latter. In part, at least, the support was instrumental, arising from the difficulty of collecting debts from the sick (*BMJ Supplement*, 4 April 1911) – who better than the state? When National Health Insurance was introduced it covered only the working population and only general practice. Nearly twenty years later, 26 April 1930, the *BMJ Supplement* reported 'Proposals for a general medical service for the nation', in which the BMA advocated extending National Health Insurance to everybody and to specialist as well as general practice, i.e. a National Health Service. When the wartime coalition government began to contemplate such a national scheme, the BMA set up a Planning Commission to prepare its own proposals. It subsequently fought very hard, harder than the left, for the inclusion of industrial health services in the NHS, and this battle was lost not because of opposition from doctors or employers but because of opposition from Ernest Bevin who saw the Beveridge report as 'an ambulance service for the nation' and did not want it to get anywhere near hard policy areas like industry (Watkins 1982).

From this account it could be supposed that the BMA was an active advocate of the NHS and played a prominent role in the campaign to create it. What is missing is the fierce opposition, to the very verge of industrial action, which the BMA fought against the details both of National Insurance and the NHS itself. The dispute about National Health Insurance centred on BMA demands for an income limit on benefit and a free choice of doctor by the patient. They eventually lost on the first but won on the second. This dispute can best be understood by referring back to long disputes between doctors and friendly societies in the nineteenth century (Muirhead Little 1932) for when National Health Insurance was introduced the BMA saw it as simply one large friendly society and sought to extract the same terms of service that they had been seeking from the private friendly societies. Although the wisdom of this approach may be questioned, the BMA probably passes the test of defending economic interests rather than opposing principles.

The arguments surrounding the creation of the NHS were more complex. The establishment of the NHS had bipartisan support and the support of the BMA. But controversy centred on two issues – the nationalization of the hospitals, and the role of doctors as salaried employees. These are precisely the issues which separate the two concepts of the NHS – should the state plan health care or merely pay for it? Since the introduction of the NHS, the BMA has defended private practice but opposed cuts and tighter management and planning. It has therefore consistently supported state finance but opposed state control.

A former BMA Secretary, Elston Grey Turner (1982), suggests that the BMA was driven by more political motives. In this view the BMA was concerned at the loss of power of Churchill's Conservatives, the claims and language of Labour after 1945 (represented by 'we are the masters now') and 'so long as the Minister of Health exhibited a high-handed, truculent attitude towards the medical profession the doctors were united against him' (1982: 75). This view overlooks, however, the fact that the BMA attitudes to Bevan were the same as to his Tory predecessor, Willink, and the BMA was preparing for a fight long before 1945. If there was any difference in its attitude to the two ministers it was only because Willink surrendered and Bevan fought. However, more telling may be the way Grey Turner's analysis might have reflected the attitudes in BMA House in the late 1960s and early 1970s when he was Secretary. This was a period when BMA membership fell below half of the profession, the functioning of its machinery was widely criticized and it had many conflicts with government including those in 1975 which shattered the Castle/Owen health ministry (Iliffe and Gordon 1976; Watkins 1987).

The 1989 White Paper

The 1989 White Paper, *Working with Patients*, contained a mix of old and new ideas and organizational change which would allow the NHS several different futures. It provoked considerable hostility within the medical profession and created an unusual unity between the Labour opposition and the profession. A number of the ideas, such as medical audit, prescribing controls, shifting consultant contracts to district level, merger of district health authorities and family practitioner committees and reform of merit awards, had long been on governmental shopping lists but none had felt able to confront the medical profession with them. The majority of informed non-medical opinion, and some medical opinion too, welcomed these changes. However, much more significant were the proposed two main organizational changes: the flow of money through the primary care sector and the centralization of power in the NHS Executive.

The shift in fund flows through fundholding general practitioners and primary care-orientated district health authorities (DHAs) meant increasingly that money reached secondary care through decisions made within primary care. This approach, which at last allowed the dog to wag the tail, meant that individual doctors or practices became the budget holders and therefore the agents of the government in allocating resources. The fundholding GP had a choice from a limited range of services, with the government deciding on the scope of that range and the size of the GP budget itself. If GP budgets were inadequate the GP would be allocating cuts. This was not the usual understanding of the doctor–patient relationship.

This mechanistic system was not decentralization but the transfer of NHS cuts from the hospital service to general practice with GPs as managers. Moreover, DHAs were to be in the hands of government political appointees. Thus, the intention when the time came to negotiate contracts with its provider hospitals was for the DHA as customer to demand results in return for money. Consultants who were disinclined to do what the DHA wanted were to find that tenure was less secure when the contract for their speciality was lost. With capital having to be borrowed and repaid the dynamic of survival rather than the priorities of consultants would demand that equipment was bought only if it helped meet the customer's objectives. If the customer demanded particular approaches and attitudes – patient access to notes, for example, or appointments systems which put a premium on the patient's time instead of the doctor's, or reduced quality of care in order to gain higher quantity – the customer would get its way. And the customer would not be a diverse range of isolated individuals but instead a small group of the government's political appointees, with the only other major customers being other small groups of political appointees of the same government. Thus power in the new NHS was to be redistributed so that small groups of the Minister's appointees acting as dominant customers would ensure that the self-governing hospitals were able to exist only if they did the Minister's will. The freedom of the self-governing hospital was to choose the means to meet this will, not a freedom to set objectives.

Power is rarely centralized without a purpose. What was the purpose of creating such a centrally directed monopsony? Produced by a government of the left, it could be used to overcome the power of the profession and reshape an expanding service. DHAs would have adequate budgets, use market research and community development to assess public wishes, and emphasize quality of care and the explicit construction of service priorities. Their dominant figures might be the managers responsible for community participation and quality assurance. The effect might be an enabling centralization that would break with the traditions of the NHS and the profession, and of the Labour mainstream too. Produced by a centre-right or even centre-left government, the new organization might be used in a more technocratic way. DHAs would be run by reformed hackers sitting in front of large computers trading off outcome indicators against costs. The dominant figures in the DHA would be the Director of Public Health and the Director of Information. This might be called directive centralization and be more in accordance with NHS traditions as well as the centralist habits of post-war consensus politics.

Working for Patients, however, was a White Paper from a government strongly influenced by the far right and so the purpose of its centralization was believed to be the reduction of public spending. In the trade-off between quality and cost, cost would win unless private spending came to the rescue. The DHA would be underfunded and would sacrifice quality to maintain quantity, and the dominant figures in the DHA would be the Director of Finance and the Director of Commissioning. Since the government was committed to privatization as a matter of principle, the expectation was that self-governing hospitals would not remain public corporations for long but would be sold. And the DHAs and fundholding GPs were seen as transitional, to be replaced eventually by commercial insurance companies. The vision was of destructive centralization for it would convert all medical practices into marketable commodities and so would be in constant conflict with medical traditions of meeting need. The ultimate irony of the 1989 White Paper was that it was introduced into a service more tightly centralized and controlled by the Minister accountable to Parliament that at any time in its history. Nye Bevan's idea of a centrally controlled and centrally planned service was at last to come to fruition.

From markets to New Labour: the triple way

These predictions of destructive centralization never came to pass. Perhaps because of the demise of Mrs Thatcher's government, DHAs were not in the end allowed to destabilize hospitals, the hospitals themselves were curtailed in their use of the new freedoms, and fundholders were never placed in the position of managing cuts – indeed they were sufficiently well funded to bring about some improvements. However, both the Major (centre-right) and Blair (centre-left) governments used the powers of commissioners in a directive way as an instrument of planning, including latterly to trade off outcome indicators and vote-related indicators against costs. And what we argued for in 1989 (Watkins and Iliffe 1989) is coming to pass with the 2001 structural reforms, *Shifting the Balance of Power*, which are devolving powers to Primary Care Trusts and scrutinizing them by patients' forums and local authorities. Yet this leftish liberation coexists with the reformed hackers of our centrist scenario and the threats of privatization of our Thatcherite scenario. It is as if the Blair government is seeking to introduce all three scenarios at once. Not so much the Third Way as the Triple Way.

To understand this phenomenon we must understand three developments that would have been difficult to predict in 1989. The first is the way that the idea of community-based primary care organizations as commissioners became 'locality commissioning'. In 1989 locality commissioning was unheard of except in select circles thinking the unthinkable. However, in the run-up to the 1992 election the health spokesperson for Labour, Robin Cook, held a meeting at which he asked for alternatives to Thatcher's internal market. Two coherent alternatives were put forward: locality commissioning and the traditional idea of going back to directly managed services. Until Harriet Harman in 1996, Labour shadow ministers baulked at confronting fundholders who were thought to be a powerful lobby. Since doing what Labour actually wanted to do was not therefore an option, it adopted locality commissioning as part of its 1992 platform by default. Whether locality commissioning would have been implemented had Labour won in 1992 is open to question. It was a shallowly rooted commitment. But between 1992 and 1997 locality commissioning continued its rise to orthodoxy.

This ascent owed much to its adoption by the medical profession. During the 1990s there was much debate about whether to accept or reject fundholding. Those who rejected the idea of practices acting in isolation usually turned to locality commissioning as the alternative. Sometimes, as in Birmingham, they did this through large groups of fundholders acting as a geographical entity. Elsewhere, as in Tower Hamlets or Nottingham, locality groups operated under DHA auspices. In Stockport the DHA became a fund manager for a group of fundholding practices. Whichever legal base they used, this model came to be seen at first by the profession's leaders and later more widely as preferable to both the bureaucracy of DHAs and the anarchy and individualism of individual practice fundholding. As some health authorities also instituted locality commissioning it began to gain its adherents amongst managers as well.

The second development has been the Private Finance Initiative (PFI) and its now sacrosanct status as the mechanism for financing capital investment in the public services. Under the PFI, the state uses the private sector to provide the initial capital and build and then operate a public service facility for a given number of years in return for an agreed revenue stream for using the facility. In its early days under Major this idea was as strongly opposed on the left as it was supported on the right, but mainly for political reasons. Yet during the 1990s it became the sole means of raising private capital for public investment. Before the PFI, private capital schemes had to involve the taking of real risk by the private sector and be tested for value for money against conventional ways of raising capital. Although this has never been formally abandoned, the PFI schemes approved under the Major and Blair governments have been pursued as instruments of policy very largely to reduce the short-term borrowing requirements of government. Thus the risk taken by the private sector has been lowered and the value for money tests made more generous.

The whole notion has been discredited by a substantial critical literature, much denied but as yet not effectively refuted. One critique imagines you taking out a mortgage. You have a choice of two providers, one of whom has served your family for years and offers a straightforward deal by which you borrow the money and pay it back at a very low interest rate – 3 or 4 per cent. The other is a new financial organization called (say) Innovative Financial Instruments. It has a more complex deal: as well as lending you the money it will build the house and paint it for the first thirty years, insure it against the impact of meteorites, and its Managing Director will choose the wallpaper. In return you pay the money back at an interest rate of about 15 per cent. However, this is expressed as a charge and is called 'servicing capital' rather than paying back a loan, so if anybody asks Innovative Financial Instruments if you owe it any money it will say that you don't, thus supposedly improving your credit rating. A second critique questions the claim that the private sector is better at project management and brings in schemes more cheaply than the public sector thus counterbalancing the extra costs of servicing capital. But nobody has explained why the solution to this is not to reform public sector estate management or to buy in project management as in the way the Bechtel consultancy was successfully engaged to finish the con- ventionally publicly financed Jubilee Line of the London Underground.

PFI schemes in the NHS have regularly led to service reductions to fund the servicing of capital and at the 2001 general election the people of Kid- derminster returned an Independent MP on this very issue. The bemused horror with which virtually everybody views the PFI deals that are being signed is matched only by the determination with which the political establishment insists there is no alternative. But there is as a result a degree of privatization in train in the NHS.

The third development in the rise of the 'triple way' has been the way the injection of large sums of money have produced dramatic financial difficul- ties for the NHS, far worse than any they faced when cash starved. The advent of the Labour government was not expected to alter overall levels of NHS funding: after all, financial prudence was the watchword. In 1998, however, the government announced a three-year funding plan adding recurrently £11bn in real terms to NHS spending. This was hyped and made out to be more than double what it really was, which was unfortunate because when the hype was exposed the dramatic nature of the reality – a huge investment that was double what even the British Medical Association had asked for – was overlooked. Yet within two years after this investment the NHS was in deep financial crisis and the government responded with a further investment plan intended to raise health spending to the average European level that in turn led to health authorities proposing to cut non-priority areas and critics to point out that average levels of investment lead only to average levels of service.

These extraordinary turns of events prompt at least a pair of questions. First, why should the injection of large sums of money into the NHS precipitate financial crisis? Although ministers understandably expect that such investment will put the basics right neither they nor their managers and professionals realized how large was the reality gap created by institutionalized lying about the state of the NHS during the Thatcher and Major governments. Ministers also believe that in allocating such high investment they are entitled to set goals and earmark funds for meeting them. However, what is left sets financial challenges to the NHS as tight as any in the past. Further, news of such investment raises expectation of better conditions and better pay for staff, better services for patients, and better funding for the developments that providers and commissioners want to see. These expectations are bound to be unrealizable by a process in which most of the money is earmarked and that which is not is needed to repair past neglect. Moreover, these repairs need more than money and especially skilled staff that it takes time to train.

Second, why should the NHS, once one of the most efficient health care providers, be unable to provide excellent care with average funding? The answer lies in the way the factors that made the NHS so efficient twenty years ago have been eradicated. Then it serviced its capital at Treasury rates; maximized its use of building and equipment by a process of make do and mend; gloried in high staff morale with tremendous drive and innovation and commitment; maintained a gatekeeper system which ensured that the care provided was professionally assessed instead of indulging consumer demands; kept transaction costs low partly through a lean administrative system; and its hospitals would typically be close to the 700-bed optimum size at which diseconomies of scale start to take effect. Moreover the system was controlled by locally sensitive organizations. At the time of writing ministers do not understand either how all this has changed or why their generous investments of money have not solved the problem. They are deeply impatient of what looks to them like money pouring into an open drain. Their response to finding out that they had been misled about NHS resources in the run-up to the general election was an unexpected reorganization that abolished the organizations that had misled them.

Thus it is possible to paint a Doomsday scenario for health care in the next ten years. Money invested will increase but demand will increase even more. Staff morale will plummet in the attempt to cope. The response will be to curb further the measures which once held things in control, such as professional autonomy, and instead substitute measures which make things worse such as bureaucratic control of standards, concepts of individualistic consumer rights and the empowerment of organizations (such as private sector organizations) which have interests in increasing activity. It is against this scenario that we must understand the Triple Way. First, a genuine commitment to community empowerment leads to the left-wing policy of enabling centralization. Second, terror that financial stringencies will cause vote-losing crises creates an overlay of the centrist directive centralization. Third, the need to prop up the PFI leads to the right-wing privatization of destructive centralization. Tying people to horses pointing in different directions and setting them running is sometimes shown in the movies as a method of execution. It is usually shown as working with two horses but presumably works even better with three.

The medical profession and government in the early years of the twenty-first century

Prior to 1989 the BMA had two kinds of conflict with government: preserving its professional power and promoting the adequate funding of health care. It was not surprising that it should oppose the 1989 White Paper as a threat to the NHS and a planned system to control doctors. In short, its idealism and self-interests found common cause, perhaps for the first time. Kenneth Clarke, Minister at the time, claimed that the BMA's opposition to the White Paper was consistent with its previous opposition to other developments in the NHS. He was both right and wrong. The BMA was indeed opposing state control of the NHS much as it had under Lloyd George and Bevan. But this time it was also motivated by the ideal of the NHS that had sustained some of its more honourable past battles, and it was certainly on this issue that it made common cause with allies who would not have supported it if the power of doctors was all that was at stake.

For most of the 1990s those issues lay suppressed as the coalition of opposition centred on its common and most popular theme of distrusting government intentions for the use of its new powers. If the medical profession generally voted Conservative in 1979, the majority voted Labour in 1997. The election of the Labour government was greeted with applause in the BMA Council and by a whole year in which not a single criticism of government emerged from BMA House. Yet by 2001 the majority political approach in the profession had moved further left and was now Liberal Democrat and was treating the Labour government much as it had the Thatcher administration.

Yet the opposition to Labour is not a revisiting of its traditional positions. The medical profession has changed more in the last ten years than in the whole of the rest of the last century. The BMA no longer resists state planning of the NHS but has clear views about how the NHS should be planned – views arising in large measure from the experience of commissioning – and has come to accept rationing even if its sense of disempowerment may yet undermine its position. It is no longer right to say that its ethical system places as much emphasis on restrictive practices as it does on the idealistic commitment to service. The GMC in the last ten years has de-emphasized professional courtesies and taken a more rigorous approach to quality of practice. Before it received its power to strike doctors off for being unfit to practise medicine rather than just for misconduct (a power it asked for long before Parliament responded), it had developed a similar jurisdiction through the concept that it was serious professional misconduct to practise in fields where you know yourself to be incompetent. It applied those principles, together with stringent expectations of medically qualified managers, in its action against those responsible for the Bristol heart surgery disaster. The profession no longer opposes team work or regards as unethical cooperation with complementary practitioners. The BMA and the Royal Colleges now have mechanisms for liaison with patient organizations and no longer oppose democratic control of the NHS.

The profession has made these changes in response to a perception that its loss of power would be restored as a reward for them. It greeted the election of New Labour with a belief that a historic compromise was in the making by which doctors would deliver the revival of the NHS within realistic resources and in a way which met the legitimate expectations of those groups with whom they had been allied in the last decade. But its belief that this was on offer was wrong. Instead power has been centralized through new targeting systems, the medical profession targeted as scapegoat whenever politically convenient and the BMA bypassed as the new government sought alternative sources of medical opinion such as academics and the Royal Colleges.

Relations between the Royal Colleges and the BMA have improved from the days when the Provincial Medical and Surgical Association defined its eligibility for membership to exclude most Royal College members. For a number of years the BMA and the Royal Colleges have coordinated the representation of medicine through a joint body, the Joint Consultants Committee. The mythology of the left ascribes to the Royal Colleges the role of undermining the BMA in its conflict with Bevan but in reality the Colleges carefully avoid political and representative issues. They are not constituted to represent medicine. Their instinct is to press for high professional standards, which they usually interpret in a way that requires the injection of large sums of money into their own specialty. And as New Labour turned to the Colleges as an alternative to the BMA this process of escalating requirements for investment in secondary care steadily became fed into the guidelines of the National Institute of Clinical Excellence and into the National Service Framework which formed the basis of the new targeting system.

This was a serious political mistake. The consequence has been a truculent attitude on the part of GPs to whom the task of sorting out the mess is now to be passed, on the part of consultants who have seen themselves under increasing managerial control in the pursuit of objectives that are unachievable, and on the part of a BMA which gradually abandoned its commitment to resource optimization and return to more traditional attitudes as it saw the compromise spurned.

Realistically only the medical profession can find a way through the problem of resource optimization and it can only do this by changing professional practice, yet this would require the historic compromise that the government wished to distance itself from. Meanwhilst the problems of capacity have led to a review of the boundary between professional groups. With a shortage of consultants the idea is that more of the work will in future be done by doctors we would now regard as in the training grades (although a shortening of training may lead to them being called consultants), that much of the work now done by training grade doctors will be done by nurses and that much of the work now done by nurses will be done by aides who can be trained much more quickly.

The problem is that to realize this ambition the work of the professions must be turned into tasks that others can be trained to do. Doctors, unlike other health professionals, are brought up in a culture of holistic risk management. Eighty per cent of that decision process can be defined in guidelines and managed accordingly (and certainly should be). Twenty per cent – the art of medicine – cannot, yet, although important, probably life-saving, it stands in the way of the grand design for human resource management in the NHS. So the NHS becomes steadily more risk-averse. And as it does, the morale of doctors falls, the standards of care decline (especially for those not envisaged by the protocol) and the burden escalates.

In terms of social policy nothing could be more absurd than to reject an offer of partnership from a primary care-oriented organization committed to resource optimization and promote instead the alternative advice of those committed to the advancement of specialty interests, and then to set out to undermine the medical profession by introducing more risk averse systems. One is left wondering whether this process is being carried out by refugees from Gosplan trying to revive the NHS by the same methods that destroyed the economy of the Soviet Union. But in political terms it may be inevitable – part of the tragedy of New Labour. We live today in a political system where Parliament and civil society are disempowered, political decisions are made according to crude concepts of image and marketing, and those who know what they are talking about are assumed to be a vested interest. There was never any possibility that this environment would deliver to the BMA the partnership that it expected in 1997. Yet probably that spurned partnership was the best hope the government had of success in the NHS. The Triple Way will not be as effective.

Acknowledgement

Parts of this chapter draw on 'The Political Behaviour of Organised Medicine: an Ideology Shaped by Professionalization', prepared with Steve Iliffe and presented by the author in 1989 at the History Workshop. The author also acknowledges the contribution of Sarah Divall, a general practitioner from South London, who acted as discussant to that paper.

5   Medicine and Management: Autonomy and Authority in the National Health Service

Stephen Harrison

To judge by the recent reluctance to accept the proposed new consultant contract, National Health Service (NHS) physicians are clearly unhappy, and it seems to be a common perception that managers and management are something to do with this (R. Smith 2001; Edwards *et al.* 2002; Edwards and Marshall 2003). Logically, conflict (or at least tension) between doctors and managers is to be expected. Concepts of medical professionalism emphasize *clinical autonomy*, the idea that a fully qualified physician should possess *control over diagnosis and treatment*, including what tests and examinations to order, what drugs and procedures to prescribe, to whom to refer, *control over evaluation of care*, including the appropriateness of the care for particular patients, and *control over the nature and volume of medical tasks*, including being left to determine their own movements, priorities, times and workloads (Schulz and Harrison 1986). In stark contrast, concepts of management emphasize 'deciding what should be done and then getting other people to do it' (Stewart 1979: 69).

This logic of conflict will only manifest itself empirically if the two groups pursue different objectives and/or incompatible means of pursuing them (Harrison 1988: 2); this has in fact only occurred in the NHS over about the last two decades. Further, clinical autonomy and managerial authority are not just micro-level phenomena determined locally in the hospital or clinic, but are supported (or not, as the case may be) by meso-level institutions such as governments and regulatory bodies (Harrison and Ahmad 2000). They also operate within macro-level cultural assumptions about the nature of medicine (the 'biomedical model') and management.

This chapter attempts first to contextualize the present situation using the 1960s and 1970s as a historical baseline from which to judge subsequent changes. Here and throughout the chapter, 'contract' signifies not just the formal contract of employment for hospital doctors or contract for services for most general practitioners (GPs), but also the arrangements for professional regulation and the medical–managerial relationship as practised in the clinical workplace. The second section summarizes the main changes that have occurred since about 1982 in the various elements of this contract. The final section reviews some explanations that have been proposed to account for these changes and discusses some of the possible consequences of the contract as it currently stands.

The traditional medical 'contract' with the National Health Service

A 'baseline' of the 1960s and 1970s has been chosen on both theoretical and empirical grounds. It is the period that first gave rise to the critical socio-logical portrayal of medicine as a 'dominant' occupation that had attained its social position largely through its own manoeuvres rather than, as earlier analysts had often assumed, simply having pre-eminent status bestowed upon it as a response to its self-evident social virtues (Freidson 1970; Johnson 1972). The substantial autonomy enjoyed by practitioners was one factor in the period's characterization as the 'golden age of doctoring' (McKinlay and Marceau 2002). And, crucially for any attempt to review medical–managerial relationships in the NHS hospital or clinic, this period is the earliest in which substantial empirical research on the topic was undertaken (e.g. Forsyth 1966).

The medical contract at this time can be characterized in terms of three elements which, taken together, seem to confirm the autonomy and dom-inance of the profession. First, governments retained and strengthened a system of professional self-regulation that had begun in the mid-nineteenth century. State registration arrangements included not only a heavily medi-cally dominated General Medical Council able to approve the content of training and recognize practitioners (Stacey 1992), but considerable authority over the arrangements in respect of other health professions (Harrison 1981). This was accompanied by government commitment to clinical autonomy for doctors that appeared at regular intervals in official government pro-nouncements from the pre-NHS 1944 White Paper through to 1979 when it was stated by the then newly elected Conservative government (whose suc-cessors went on to make some of the radical changes described below) that 'It is doctors ... who provide the care and cure of patients and promote the health of the people. It is the purpose of management to support them' (Department of Health and Social Security and Welsh Office 1979: 1–2; for other examples see Harrison 1988: 24–6).

Second, the arrangements for employing and managing (or rather not managing) doctors reinforced this freedom from subordination to managers. Consultants' contracts of employment were carefully insulated from man-agerial discretion by being held at the regional, rather than hospital level. There were unilateral rights to engage in private practice and to appeal to the Secretary of State against dismissal. GPs were self-employed contractors, somewhat insulated from the remainder of the NHS. Their contracts were held by separate public bodies and specified their duties in only the vaguest terms (Ellis and Chisholm 1993: 12). GPs were able to refer their patients freely to any specialist in any hospital anywhere in the UK, the financial consequences of such decisions falling upon the hospitals. Subject to administrative intervention only in extreme cases, they could prescribe from the NHS pharmacopoeia in whatever quantities they chose. The reality of medical dominance was also reflected in formal management structures. Until 1974 the local statutory bodies which ran the NHS had large numbers of doctors in membership (Ham 1981) and were afterwards dominated by multidisciplinary consensus management teams, half the places on which were occupied by doctors, each effectively with a power of veto (Harrison 1982).

Third, the practice of NHS management until the mid-1980s may be likened to the practice of diplomacy. Rather than conforming to the stereotype of an authoritative individual, pursuing organizational objectives by means of proactively generated change, the manager possessed little influence relative to doctors, was very much focused on responding to the demands of internal organizational actors, and procured only incremental change. A review of the evidence from some 25 empirical studies conducted up to 1983 (Harrison 1988) concluded that doctors at large, rather than managers, were the most influential actors in the NHS. The overall shape of NHS services was largely created interactively as an aggregate of individual clinical decisions, leaving managers and planners weak in the face of any medical opposition. Thus managers were reluctant to question the value of existing patterns of service or to propose major changes in them; both planning and actual change were incremental, with little of the officially intended redistribution of resources from hospitals to community services; there was a general absence of evaluation; and managerial conflict with doctors was generally avoided and managers behaved as if doctors, rather than the public, were the clients of the NHS with managerial agendas dominated by issues raised by 'insider' groups. In summary:

> Managers neither were, nor were supposed to be, influential with respect to doctors ... Managers in general worked to solve problems and to maintain their organizations rather than to secure major change.
>
> (Harrison 1988: 51)

In broad terms, therefore, there was a consonance between organizational formalities, organization culture and empirical practice, the whole held together by what Dunleavy has termed 'ideological corporatism', that is:

the effective integration of different organizations and institutions ... by the acceptance or dominance of an effectively unified view of the world ... The active promotion of changes in ideas rests quite largely with individual professionals ... bargained or negotiated compromises will be relatively rare ... the distinction between formulation and implementation may dissolve altogether ... so that policy is just what professionals in the field do.

(Dunleavy 1981: 8–13; see also Lipsky 1980)

Declining professional autonomy: 1982 to date

The formalities of medical self-regulation and of doctors' employment relationships have changed markedly since the 'golden age' characterized above. Doctors will be subject to compulsory five-yearly revalidation as a condition of retaining their General Medical Council registration, and the latter organization now has a much greater non-medical membership and is to be subject to an additional layer of statutory governance in the form of a Council for the Regulation of Health Care Professionals (Department of Health 1999, 2001c; Salter 2001). As Salter has noted (2001: 873), this implies that 'NHS managers will be seeking to control precisely the same territories of medical regulation as are the institutions of the medical profession'. In other words, the scene is set for conflict between professional autonomy and managerial authority. In fact, such conflict has already occurred, with outcomes that are consistent with declining medical autonomy. Two successive major reorganizations of the NHS were vehemently but unsuccessfully opposed by the British Medical Association (BMA) (Harrison 2001). Thus the Griffiths recommendations (Department of Health and Social Security 1983) led to the introduction from 1984 of something resembling a textbook management model in place of the earlier diplomatic model. Individual chief executives (originally termed 'general managers') were appointed in place of the consensus decision-making teams, a range of performance indicators developed and internal workload-related budgetary systems constructed. The introduction in 1991 of an organizational split between the health care purchasing and providing institutions (Department of Health *et al.* 1989), the misnamed 'internal market', was similarly and equally unsuccessfully resisted by the BMA (Harrison 2001).

Consultants are now employed by the NHS Trusts in which they work and there is an increasing number of both salaried GPs and GPs who have been induced to adopt more specific (Personal Medical Service) contacts. The governing bodies of almost all NHS institutions are modelled on commercial organizations' boards of directors with doctors in a very small minority. Perhaps of greatest symbolic importance, chief executives of NHS service delivery organizations are now legally and organizationally responsible for the quality of clinical services delivered. Despite its anodyne official definition (Department of Health 1998: 33), clinical governance is a mechanism for controlling the health professions, most obviously doctors. Yet, with the exception of each NHS Trust's Medical Director and the Professional Executive Committees of PCTs, very few managers are medically qualified, with the implication that they must rely substantially on enforcing rules and criteria developed outside their own hierarchical control.

Hence in the place of prominent official statements about clinical autonomy there is a strong emphasis on the need to adhere to such rules and criteria, which are increasingly available. In addition to an increasing emphasis on adherence by doctors to clinical guidelines, National Service Frameworks (NSFs) have been developed as official specifications of services for particular patient groups. These developments have been underpinned by an explosion of regulatory agencies of which perhaps the most prominent examples are the National Institute of Clinical Excellence (NICE) and the Commission for Health Audit and Inspection (CHAI). Established in 1999, NICE has two main roles. It undertakes evidence-based appraisals of (mainly, though not exclusively, new) clinical interventions, and may recommend that particular treatments should not normally be employed by the NHS (Department of Health 1998: 15–19). Such appraisals include evidence of *cost-*effectiveness as well as clinical effectiveness. NICE may also give its *imprimatur* to evidence-based clinical guidelines for the management of particular medical conditions written by academic and professional bodies with relevant expertise.

CHAI has in 2004 taken over and expanded the role of the Commission for Health Improvement set up in 1999, particularly its routine inspection of all NHS Trusts (provider organizations) at four-yearly intervals and its specific investigations into allegations of service inadequacy. It is also responsible for publishing comparative performance information about NHS organizations, on the basis of which the latter are publicly awarded performance 'stars'; three-star organizations are regulated with a lighter touch and enjoy various other incentives, whilst no-star organizations are publicly directed to produce a recovery plan. Poor performance in these terms is, as managers are wont to say, career-limiting; although it is managers who are primarily liable to sanctions, their existence provides an obvious imperative for them to seek greater control and surveillance over doctors.

The more recent of these developments have occurred towards the end of twenty years in which, to judge by available empirical evidence, medical autonomy has been steadily, if gradually eroded by management (Harrison and Ahmad 2000). A review of a further 24 empirical studies conducted in the period beginning with the implementation of the Griffiths recommendations (Harrison *et al.* 1992: 54–92) concluded that the new managers remained relatively weak in relation to doctors, though there was a general acceptance of the legitimacy of the former and little desire to return to the old arrangements. Decision-making remained largely reactive, but there was some evidence of quicker decisions, an increase in cost-consciousness in decision-making, and a feeling of reduced frustration on the part of senior managers. The development of information and budgetary systems, and of performance indicators, had begun to evoke a focus on evaluation and 'performance', though in less than systematic fashion. The major influence on managerial agendas was no longer the need to facilitate matters for professionals, but rather to respond directly to central government agendas. Lately this has meant meeting government performance targets for selected aspects of service. Thus this era of general management following Griffiths (Department of Health and Social Security 1983) has led to modest changes in the medical–managerial power balance, but also to significant changes both in perceptions of managerial legitimacy and in government–management relationships.

The impact of the internal market on medical–managerial relationships has not yet been comprehensively reviewed. According to one preliminary review (Harrison and Lim 2003), managers were by the early 1990s more ready than before to take on doctors, resulting in decisions where managerial interventions were decisive, most notably in the pursuit of the government-approved organizational status as NHS Trust against medical opposition. Doctors were in some locations drawn into cooperative networks with managers, though in others this was not the case, and managers were unable to control the acute medical sector or to make other than incremental adjustments to services. Radical organizational change in hospitals, for instance via 'business process re-engineering', proved extremely difficult to secure. Developments in performance management begun in the Griffiths period continued and, despite the rhetoric of markets and competition, central government influence on managerial agendas was further strengthened. Yet, as in the earlier period, there was little indication of any desire to return to the earlier organization arrangements. Published empirical evidence in respect of the period since 1997 is even scarcer and seems to relate wholly to primary care. Whilst managers still perceive GPs as enjoying substantial autonomy (Marshall *et al.* 2002), there are indications that, in primary care at least, initial medical resistance to management and regulation (Harrison and Lim 2000) has given way to a degree of resignation and unenthusiastic compliance (Dowswell *et al.* 2002; Harrison and Dowswell 2002; Mahmood 2003).

Neo-bureaucracy and its consequences

Although its theoretical interpretation remains contentious (Coburn *et al.* 1983; Freidson 1985; McKinlay and Arches 1985; Navarro 1988; Light 1995), there is a general consensus amongst social scientists that the challenges to medical autonomy outlined above are real and that declining medical autonomy is more widely evident across a range of liberal democratic states as well as the UK (Harrison 2003). Taken together, the present NHS approach to the management of medicine appears to represent a new form of bureaucracy characterized by formal, written rules and policies that reduce the autonomy of both frontline professional and managerial labour processes and which have become the subject of surveillance and/or incentives and sanctions aimed at securing compliance with the rules. Although such developments have been interpreted in Weberian terms as a shift from 'substantive' to 'formal' rationality (Ritzer and Walcak 1988; Harrison and McDonald 2003), they cannot precisely be described as Weberian bureaucracy. The rules are enforced less by conventional managerial hierarchies than by regulatory agencies of various types, thus allowing rhetorical claims to be substituting networks for hierarchies (see the claims of the NHS chief executive quoted in Brindle 2002).

It is perhaps such appearances that lend credibility to the New Labour claim that the third way in the NHS is 'neither the old centralized command and control systems of the 1970s' nor 'the divisive internal market system of the 1990s' (Department of Health 1997). Yet such characterizations of the past are empirically false. The earlier discussion has already cited research showing the diplomatic nature of pre-Griffiths management and studies of the internal market suggest that collaboration was more usual than competition (Flynn *et al.* 1996; Flynn and Williams 1997). The bureaucratization of labour processes outlined above clearly suggests greater rather than the lesser degree of control implied in the third way rhetoric. Indeed Midwinter and McGarvey (2001) have argued that the relevant agencies are better considered as engaged in performance management than in regulation, whilst Flynn (2002: 168) has noted that clinical governance in the NHS has many of the characteristics of machine bureaucracy. The control of public services through bureaucratic rules and procedures is not without its attractions, most obviously its capacity to promote fairness, due process and transparency (Du Gay 2000). But it has also potentially perverse consequences, some at the political level, others at a more micro-organizational level.

First, it is clear that medical autonomy has played an important role in depoliticizing, and hence legitimizing, the management of demand for medical care in the NHS. Micro-level clinical decisions that pragmatically accept resource constraints can appear to patients and public as reasonable attempts to provide 'optimal' levels of care (Aaron and Schwartz 1982: 89ff). Guidelines, protocols, casemix measures and other systematizations of medical practice can be seen as an attempt to substitute a form of blackboxing, that is the condensation of a set of political criteria into a set of ostensibly technical or scientific rules, whose perceived legitimacy suppresses contestation (Latour 1987). But it does not follow that such attempts will be successful. A single-minded application of formal rationality might undermine the foundations of social order (Calabresi and Bobbitt 1978). More pragmatically, examples such as Interferon Beta, an apparently cost-ineffective drug for relapsing–remitting multiple sclerosis which continues to be supplied in the NHS as a result of patient demand (Quennell 2003), and the measles–mumps–rubella (MMR) triple vaccine, a cheap and apparently safe preventive measure that is resisted by many parents in the belief that it may cause autism (Heller *et al.* 2001), demonstrate that explicit policies and rules, even if ostensibly based on scientific research, have merely served to fuel political controversy.

Second, public perceptions of the adequacy of state involvement in medical care finance or provision may well rest on a degree of trust being conferred on doctors, the occupation most centrally associated with such services. Part of the durability of medical self-regulation and autonomy lay in the advantages they offered to profession, government and patient. Yet the developments that challenge medical autonomy and self-regulation all imply distrust of doctors in that they seek to substitute confidence in systems (of guidelines, performance indicators and so on) for trust in individuals, hence abandoning the moral content of the client–practitioner relationship (C. Smith 2001). The very creation of such systems may therefore be self-defeating in political terms; they may communicate to citizens that doctors and the care that they provide at public expense are not to be trusted.

Third, a number of writers have pointed to the cognitive impossibility of fully specifying commands, rules and instructions. A famous example is Polanyi's (1967) concept of tacit knowledge, the notion that we can know more than we can tell. A less well-known, but equally compelling example is Dunsire's (1978) demonstration that organizations are towers of Babel in which vertical and horizontal differences in knowledge, language and culture make top-down detailed command-and-control literally unachievable, requiring instead either that organizational superiors give only generalized instructions or check with subordinates that proposed detailed instructions are actually reasonable ones. Such literature implies that collegiality is more appropriate than bureaucracy for dealing with cognitively complex issues in public administration (Majone 1986).

Fourth, a related point is that these challenges to autonomy seem to have been developed in isolation from the daily context in which doctors work. There is always too much work to be completed, so that such street-level bureaucrats must 'invent benign modes of mass processing that more or less permit them to deal with the public fairly, appropriately and successfully' (Lipsky 1980: xii). In simple terms, professional discretion may be a necessary condition for getting the work done without the exposure of resource inadequacies.

Finally, there is a long-established academic and popular literature concerned with the adverse consequences of bureaucracy in terms of alienation, morale and trust. Blau (1955: 185ff) famously showed that 'goal displacement' (in which adherence to the rules becomes an end in itself) was the result of fear of superiors' reactions to rule breaking and of the existence of performance measurements based on rule adherence. Moreover, bureaucracy may be associated with organizational inflexibility (Burns and Stalker 1961) and mutual lack of trust between managers and other actors (Fox 1974b; Scase 2001), with the result that organizations find it difficult to respond to crises (Fukuyama 1995: 225). These ideas have been more recently extended to observations about the redundancy of trust and moral engagement on the part of workers implied by bureaucratic attempts to enforce control and to minimize risk (Davies 1999; C. Smith 2001; O'Neill 2002). It is not obvious that we want doctors to be narrowly rule-following creatures.

All these potential consequences need to be taken seriously by policy-makers and analysts concerned with the future role of medical professionalism in the NHS. In particular, they suggest that the current emphasis on rules and formalities as key elements of performance definition (for organizations or individuals) should be more critically addressed than is generally the case. The golden age of medicine as a profession may be gone (Foster and Wilding 2000; McKinlay and Marceau 2002), but its replacement by bureaucracy does not constitute unalloyed progress.

6 Practitioner Perspectives on Objectives and Outcomes of Clinical Governance: Some Evidence from Wales

Pieter Degeling, John Kennedy, Fergus Macbeth, Barbara Telfer, Sharyn Maxwell and Barbara Coyle

In 1998 the clinical governance initiative in the UK met a mixed response. Some senior health care commentators (Scally and Donaldson 1998) were enthusiastic that clinical governance would prompt 'leadership and commitment from the top' for systematic and consistent efforts to simplify and improve the process of care. Other commentators were less passionate, expressing concern that clinical governance would not realize the claims made for it (Black 1998; Goodman 1998). These commentators worried that clinical governance would falter as the required information base was lacking (Black 1988) and health care practitioners would inevitably respond wearily to clinical governance's 'empty phrases . . . full of the what but short on the how' (Goodman 1998).

Despite anecdotal evidence that health care practitioners were indeed sceptical about its merits (Goodman *et al.* 2001) there was, and is, little systematic evidence about how practitioners perceive clinical governance and respond to it. We simply do not know how health care workers evaluate clinical governance or whether those evaluations vary systematically between occupation groups. We have little evidence about what might influence their perceptions or of what their perceptions imply for the success of clinical governance initiatives. This chapter therefore presents empirical evidence of Welsh health care workers' perceptions of clinical governance initiatives in 2000–01 in order to improve our understanding of health care workers' responses to clinical governance. It concludes with a discussion of how occupation and experience in clinical governance methods appear to have influenced these perceptions.

The analysis in this chapter draws on two sources of data: focus groups in each of five Welsh NHS Trusts and a questionnaire. The focus groups were organized to obtain the views of different hospital occupational groups and staff. The issues canvassed were, first, clinical governance implementation and modernization and, second, people's immediate work experiences and affiliation with their Trust. Each discussion was audio-taped and then transcribed and examined using content analysis to identify patterns in the views expressed and issues raised.

Participants in the focus group discussions were asked to complete a questionnaire (Degeling *et al.* 2002). Table 6.1 specifies the number of completed questionnaires for each occupational grouping; the higher number of responses for medical and nursing clinicians reflected their higher staff numbers in the participating Trusts. The questionnaire comprised both closed- and open-ended questions. Closed-ended questions used Likert scales to elicit respondents' assessments of their knowledge and experience of a range of clinical improvement processes and their evaluations of clinical governance and its projected outcomes. Responses were examined using principal component analysis. Open-ended questions provided an opportunity to express personal views on the objectives of clinical governance and barriers to its implementation. Individual open-ended responses were coded and explored using frequency analysis in the Statistical Package for the Social Sciences (SPSS).

Table 6.1 Completed clinical governance questionnaires by occupational class

Medical clinicians	Medical managers	General managers	Nurse managers	Nurse clinicians	PAMs[1]	Total
49	10	26	14	63	36	198

[1] Professions allied to medicine (or allied health professionals)

Knowledge and experience of processes associated with clinical governance

Respondents were asked to rate their knowledge and experience of clinical effectiveness improvement, clinical audit, quality improvement, case mix, resource utilization review, clinical risk management, clinical pathway development, clinical practice variation analysis and engendering clinical change. Principal component analysis generated three knowledge factors. The first arose from high correlations in self-ratings given for knowledge of the technicalities associated with case mix, resource utilization review, clinical pathway development and implementation, analysis of clinical practice variation and engendering change in clinical practice. As these techniques are used to monitor and plan activities at both the organizational and clinical practice levels, the correlations were interpreted as indicating **knowledge of prospective systems-oriented clinical management**

methods (KNOW1). Table 6.2 reports that only nurse managers and professionals allied to medicine (PAMs) claimed competence in these methods. Medical clinicians, medical managers and nurse clinicians indicated only a moderate to passing knowledge and, somewhat surprisingly, general managers rated themselves (at best) as having only passing knowledge.

Correlations between knowledge of clinical effectiveness, clinical audit and quality improvement were interpreted as indicating **knowledge of retrospective clinical improvement methods** (KNOW2) as clinical audit is essentially a technique for identifying past shortcomings in quality. Once again nurse managers claimed competence in this area and were joined (but to a lesser degree) by general managers and medical clinicians. The self-ratings of PAMs and nurse clinicians indicated passing knowledge and medical managers only minimal knowledge. Correlations between the knowledge ratings recorded for clinical risk management and clinical management were interpreted as **knowledge of patient specific methods** (KNOW3) (this interpretation is consistent with the meanings of these terms as generally understood by clinicians). Medical managers and (to a lesser degree) nurse managers claimed knowledge of these methods whilst medical clinicians, nurse clinicians and PAMs claimed only passing knowledge.

Principal component analysis of respondents' **experience** ratings yielded the same three factors described above. Table 6.3 shows that nurse managers and PAMs reported the most **experience in implementing**

Table 6.2 Reported knowledge of processes and practices associated with clinical governance

Knowledge of:	Medical clinician	Medical manager	General manager	Nurse manager	Nurse clinician	PAMs	Sig.
(KNOW1) Prospective systems-oriented clinical management methods	−.098	−.021	−.215	.522	−.138	.342	.061
(KNOW2) Retrospective clinical improvement methods	.122	−.344	.283	.478	−.199	−.135	.086
(KNOW3) Patient specific methods	.122	.526	−.335	.313	−.101	−.046	.178

Positive scores represent degrees of agreement with the factor statements and negative scores represent degrees of disagreement. Shaded scores indicate stances congruent with a developmental model of clinical governance.

prospective systems-oriented clinical management methods (EXP1) such as pathway development and implementation, case mix, resource utilization review, the analysis of clinical practice variation and engendering change in clinical practice. These systems-oriented processes and practices are central to giving substantive form to clinical governance *within clinical units*. This did not mean, however, that respondents lacked experience in other modes of clinical practice review. As illustrated in Table 6.3, all groups other than general managers and nurse clinicians claimed some **experience in retrospective clinical improvement methods** (EXP2) such as clinical audit, quality improvement and clinical effectiveness review. Finally, medical clinicians and medical managers claimed significantly greater **experience in patient-specific methods** (EXP3) entailed in clinical risk management and clinical management.

Table 6.3 Reported experience in implementing processes and practices associated with clinical governance

Experience of:	Medical clinician	Medical manager	General manager	Nurse manager	Nurse clinician	PAMs	Sig.
(EXP1) Prospective systems-oriented clinical management methods	−.312	−.090	−.129	.648	−.077	.454	**.002**
(EXP2) Retrospective clinical improvement methods	.241	.004	−.280	.619	−.285	.082	**.010**
(EXP3) Patient-specific methods	.320	.356	−.489	−.020	−.056	−.092	**.029**

Positive scores represent degrees of agreement with the factor statements and negative scores represent degrees of disagreement. Shaded scores indicate stances congruent with a developmental model of clinical governance.

Interconnections between respondents' knowledge and experience scores were (as expected) confirmed when, using Pearson's test, we examined their statistical correlation. Table 6.4 shows that the knowledge factors strongly correlated with their experience equivalents. The data also show that this was the case particularly for KNOW1 and EXP1, the factors which referred to the prospective systems-oriented management methods that are central to clinical government implementation within clinical units, i.e. at the level at which clinical work is done.

The implications of these findings became apparent when matching knowledge and experience items were subjected to principal component analysis. Table 6.5 demonstrates that the resulting combined knowledge and

Table 6.4 Correlations between knowledge and experience

		(KNOW1) Prospective systems-oriented clinical management methods	(KNOW2) Retrospective clinical improvement methods	(KNOW3) Patient-specific methods
(EXP1) Prospective systems-oriented clinical management methods	Pearson correlation	.814	−.114	−.004
	Sig. (2-tailed)	.000	.124	.962
(EXP2) Retrospective clinical improvement methods	Pearson correlation	.182	.622	.202
	Sig. (2-tailed)	.130	.000	.006
(EXP3) Patient specific methods	Pearson correlation	.162	−.006	.592
	Sig. (2-tailed)	.028	.934	.000

experience factors discriminated strongly between occupational groups. Only nurse managers and PAMs claimed extensive knowledge and experience of **prospective systems-oriented clinical management methods**. For their part, the knowledge and experience claims of nurse clinicians and medical managers were more moderate and medical clinicians and general management reported minimal knowledge and involvement. On the second factor, **retrospective clinical improvement methods**, nurse managers once again strongly claimed knowledge and experience followed by general managers and medical clinicians whilst medical managers and nurse clinicians reported only limited involvement. Finally, on **patient-specific methods**, only medical managers and (to a slightly lesser extent) medical clinicians claimed extensive knowledge and experience. Their scores in this regard suggested that patient-specific methods are primary in how they

Table 6.5 Factor scores for combined knowledge and experience by occupation

Knowledge and experience of:	Medical clinician	Medical manager	General manager	Nurse manager	Nurse clinician	PAMs	Sig.
Prospective systems-oriented clinical management methods	−.204	−.081	−.218	.576	−.106	.423	**.011**
Retrospective clinical improvement methods	.153	−.271	.158	.680	−.298	−.037	**.017**
Patient-specific methods	.290	.514	−.592	.041	−.043	−.104	**.011**

Positive scores represent degrees of agreement with the factor statements and negative scores represent degrees of disagreement. Shaded scores indicate stances congruent with a developmental model of clinical governance.

conceive of and perform their work. In a similar vein, the scores (if more moderate) of nurse managers, nurse clinicians and PAMs on the factor indicate the justifiable continuing importance of patient-specific methods within clinical settings. Not surprisingly, general managers reported little knowledge and experience in this area.

Respondents' perceptions of the objectives of clinical governance

Occupation-based patterns in respondents' knowledge and experience of **prospective systems-oriented clinical management methods** were also evident in the way that groups construed the primary objectives of clinical governance initiatives in their Trusts. The data in Table 6.6 were derived from a content and frequency analysis of written statements to an open-ended question that invited respondents to nominate up to seven objectives for clinical governance in their Trust. Responses fell into three broad groupings. Those categorized as referring to **political objectives** included claims that clinical governance was 'a diversion from other [important] issues including overall funding of NHS', the latest swing in government policy with which the health system was at that time having to cope or that local management was merely 'complying with government regulations'. Only medical managers as a group could be considered as casting clinical governance initiatives in political terms. However, some focus group participants highlighted how its implementation had, like previous reforms, fallen victim to 'short-term' and 'unthought-out' political agendas. Thus for one medical clinician, 'One of the key barriers I put down to implementing improvements through clinical governance is the changing goal posts of political interference.'

Idealized objectives included statements that nominated desirable end states such as to 'achieve a first class service for patients', 'minimize risks for both patients and staff' and improve efficiency of resource usage'. Table 6.6 shows that the groups tended to construe clinical governance initiatives in terms of the idealized goals that rhetorically are claimed for them especially in relation to 'improved patient outcomes' (the most frequently nominated objective across all occupational groups) and 'clinical risk reduction'. However, these stances may indicate little more than respondents' knowledge of some of the official rhetoric since the idealized depictions of clinical governance objectives revealed nothing about the processes or practices required to realize them and were largely absent from focus group discussions.

Third, **substantive objectives** referred to practical changes in the performance, organization and management of clinical work. These fell into three broad groupings. *Clinical practice-focused* objectives were expressed in

Table 6.6 Perceived objectives of clinical governance by occupation

	Medical clinician	Medical manager	General manager	Nurse manager	Nurse clinician	PAMs
1. Political objectives	10	20	7.7	7.1	4.8	13.9
2. Ideal end state objectives						
– Improve patient care	54	70	65.4	64.3	60.3	66.7
– Clinical risk reduction	48	50	53.8	57.1	36.5	38.9
– Improve resource efficiency	18	70	11.5	28.6	20.6	8.3
– Improve safety for all	8	0	7.7	35.7	12.7	19.4
3. Substantive objectives						
Practice-focused						
– Standardize care	34	20	23.1	21.4	41.3	33.3
– Clinical review	40	30	26.9	42.9	34.9	36.1
– Accountability mechanisms	20	20	26.9	42.9	25.4	13.9
– Provide data and information	2	0	3.8	21.4	9.5	16.7
Process-focused						
– Professional development	20	0	34.6	14.3	20.6	41.7
– Multidisciplinary	8	10	23.1	14.3	11.1	8.3
– Culture change	8	0	7.7	0	0	0
Patient-focused						
– Patient participation	0	0	0	0	4	3

The figures indicate the percentage (%) for each occupational group that stated each objective by free response. Shaded scores reference the top three issues as reported by each occupational group.

statements such as 'to provide a framework on which clinical practice is based', 'promote audit activity as part of day-to-day practice', 'make more concrete the quality agenda', 'ensure compliance with evidence-based guidelines', 'undertake care pathways/variance analysis', and 'set standards of care within the Trust'. *Process-focused* objectives included 'to integrate medical staff', 'facilitate more integrative practice', 'ensure appropriate training and education for a high-quality service' and 'change behaviour and culture to improve quality of care'. *Patient-focused* objectives included 'to ensure user involvement in service provision' and 'patient involvement needs a structured approach'. In contrast with the general familiarity with idealized objectives, no occupation group registers more than a 43 per cent nomination rate for any substantive objective, an indication perhaps of limited understanding of the grounded practices and processes that are likely to be required to realize clinical governance. Equally notable was how rarely patient participation was mentioned as an objective of clinical governance.

The occupational groups varied, however, in their references to *substantive objectives*. Nurse managers were most likely to refer to objectives with a *practice focus* and mention work-based structures whose introduction would significantly affect clinical production processes (e.g. 43 per cent of nurse managers associated clinical governance with strengthened accountability). In contrast, medical managers were the least likely to mention important objectives with a practice, process or patient focus. 'Clinical review' was the only element mentioned by more than 20 per cent of medical managers. Not too distant from this stance were medical clinicians whose nominations only exceeded 20 per cent for care standardization and clinical review. Of particular note here was how rarely 'data and information provision', 'multidisciplinarity, 'culture change' and 'patient participation' were mentioned as objectives of clinical governance.

These findings raise two questions: first, why, despite their lukewarm interest in substantive objectives, did 40 per cent of medical clinicians and 30 per cent of medical managers nominate 'clinical review' as a primary objective of clinical governance and, second, why was a sizeable proportion of medical clinicians (34 per cent) willing to join nurse clinicians (41.3 per cent) and PAMs (33.3 per cent) in nominating 'care standardization' as an objective of clinical governance? Some answers to the first question may lie in the tendency already noted for medical clinicians to rate themselves as having some knowledge and experience of retrospective clinical improvement methods. So the tendency for some medical clinicians to associate clinical governance with clinical review suggests that they see involvement in stand-alone methods such as audit and quality improvement as enough to satisfy the needs of clinical governance. If so, these medical clinicians are unlikely to see reasons or need for accepting a model of clinical governance which relies on the prospective systems-oriented management methods favoured by many nurse managers.

The apparent agreement between medical, nursing and PAM practitioners on the importance of standardization as an objective of clinical governance becomes understandable when we consider how 'clinical practice variation' (the opposite of standardization) affects each occupation. For example, medical clinicians are often the cause of the variation in clinical practice with which nurse clinicians and PAMs have to cope. So, whilst the different groups might agree about the relative importance of standardization to clinical governance they are likely to differ in how they evaluate it. Nurse clinicians and PAMs will see the objective as both necessary and beneficial, whilst medical clinicians will tend to judge it in terms of its threat to their autonomy (clinical freedom). In turn, these medical clinicians will be unlikely to favour a clinical workplace-focused model of clinical governance that potentially restricts this freedom.

These findings become more generally important when we consider the relative indifference of general managers to objectives seeking practice-based changes compared with their emphasis on process-focused objectives such as 'professional development' and 'multidisciplinarity'. They suggest that general managers are reluctant to deal with issues that are traditionally seen as purely clinical. Equally the lack of interest by either general managers or medical managers in the fact that successful clinical governance initiatives might give them important and useful information may reflect their limited understanding of how to translate the rhetoric of clinical governance into concrete arrangements.

Focus group views of clinical governance

These findings broadly reflected the opinions about clinical governance initiatives voiced in the focus groups held in individual NHS Trusts. General managers, for example, talked about clinical governance largely in terms of the formal stand-alone arrangements for issues such as safety, quality, audit, and staff development, through the committees and groups for governance, clinical audit, infection control, risk management and so on. For example, 'we have developed four key themes, clinical excellence, organizational quality, risk management, educational training and those are relevant to the structure' and 'priorities identified from our benchmark audit [were] clinical benchmarking, seamless clinical records, organizational quality, patient user involvement, clinical risk education program, adverse incident reporting, training, resources for training, electronic information resources, skills and knowledge to undertake peer review'.

Missing from these accounts was any sense of how the concerns of each committee related to those pursued by others. How, for example, for 'total hip replacements' by an orthopaedic unit are efforts on 'evidence-based medicine', 'clinical audit', 'quality improvement', 'risk management' and 'infection control' pulled together so that patients, clinicians, funders and managers actually benefit? Judged in this light, general managers' responses to the range of objectives in Table 6.6 imply that they do not see the chance for broader integration through clinical governance. The relatively low scores for general managers and medical managers on the *substantive objectives* suggest that most of them saw clinical governance purely in terms of goals claimed for it (e.g. patient outcomes), rather than in terms of the practical structures and processes that need to be set up in clinical units to achieve those goals.

The focus groups did express some wider views and hinted at the potential for clinical governance. For example, one medical manager gave an extended account of how work was being reorganized in his clinical setting:

> We have a really well developed pre-admission clinic assessment system that is multi-disciplinary ... so the discharge planning process begins weeks before they come into hospital. The interface with the social services also has started at home on the first visit and any interfaces with rehabilitation ... We have a pathway for total hip replacements and fractured neck of femurs at one site ... (Also) for clinical governance reasons, epidurals are no longer something that can be used on the wards and can only be used in a high-dependency unit environment.

Similarly, a general manager demonstrated a view grounded in the clinical workplace:

> I'd like to see a multi-disciplinary team pathway approach to care because ... that seems to be the only way that the patient is going to be able to see their way through and know whether they got a good service or not ... for me that is what Clinical Governance is all about, whether they've got a good and safe treatment.

The focus groups also highlighted the benefits of grounding discussion about clinical governance within its implications for organizing clinical work for specified patient populations. One PAM said she saw clinical governance as 'a framework in which we all work in order to improve standards of patient care ... it should be part of everyday practice ... it shouldn't be something that is an add-on'. And a nurse clinician described how 'we work as a team ... developing structures ... auditing minimum standards ... I feel much more empowered to be able to have a voice within that team'. Characteristically, a nurse manager presented an even broader perspective:

> My vision would be with clinical guidelines, NSF, national guidelines. [We would be] wasting our time drawing up care pathways in local trusts when every other trust is doing the same thing ... we ought to have a national steering group for care pathways and development ... As a person who may receive care I'd like to see my surgical operation follow written guidelines [and] see audit undertaken on those [and] know there was a heavy evidence base ... If there's a care pathway that could incorporate those guidelines, from that multi-disciplinary point of view, the option for getting the variances recorded is far greater.

However, whilst such views were held by some respondents (especially nurse managers), they were notably absent in both the strategy being pursued in individual Trusts and how respondents understood and related to clinical governance.

Respondents' views of the likely clinical outcomes of clinical governance

Some effects of the generalized absence of a model of clinical governance grounded in the clinical workplace were apparent in respondents' views of its clinical and organizational outcomes. Responses were again analysed using principal component analysis. The resulting factors from the clinical dimension items, together with the associated stance of each occupation, are set out in Table 6.7.

The first factor, **improved clinical practice** (CLIN1), referred to correlations between respondents' views of the impact of clinical governance on the use of ineffective treatments, improved clinical outcomes and unexplained variation in clinical practice. With the possible exception of PAMs, none thought that this would be an outcome of clinical governance. The second factor, **improved patient satisfaction and efficiency** (CLIN2), arose from correlations in the way respondents rated the impact of clinical governance on patient complaints, patient satisfaction and efficiency. Here occupational groups differed significantly, with nurse managers strongly agreeing but medical managers strongly disagreeing that clinical governance will improve patient satisfaction and efficiency. Finally, **risk reduction** (CLIN3) described respondents' assessments of the likely impact of clinical

Table 6.7 Projected clinical outcomes by occupational groups

	Medical clinician	Medical manager	General manager	Nurse manager	Nurse clinician	PAMs	Sig.
(CLIN1) Improved clinical practice	−.088	−.389	−.089	−.156	.056	.249	.458
(CLIN2) Improved patient satisfaction and efficiency	−.269	−.612	.223	.495	.183	−.133	**.014**
(CLIN3) Risk reduction	.003	.097	.315	.129	.062	−.369	.150

Positive scores represent degrees of agreement with the factor statements and negative scores represent degrees of disagreement. Shaded scores indicate stances that are congruent with a developmental model of clinical governance.

governance on critical incidents, adverse events and hospital-acquired infection rates and was interpreted as referring to respondents' assessments of the extent to which clinical governance would lead to reductions in risk. Weak positive assessments of this outcome were given by most occupational groups. Importantly, respondents' confidence of this outcome in no way matched the high priority accorded to 'risk reduction' in the earlier discussion on goals.

Respondents' assessments of the organizational outcomes of clinical governance revealed three further factors. The first, **improved workplace-based clinical accountability** (ORG1), reflects high correlations in the way respondents rated the likelihood of clinical governance increasing the willingness of clinicians to 'balance clinical accountability with transparent accountability' and 'adopt methods which extend their ability to bring their clinical work within the ambit of process control'. Table 6.8 shows a shared equivocation among occupational groups toward this outcome. Similarly there was no statistical significance between the groups (although nurse managers were more assertive) relating to **strengthening team-based financial realism** (ORG2) as reflected in recognition of 'all clinical decisions are also resource decisions' and 'the interdisciplinary and hence team-based nature of service provision'. However, there were significant differences between the group assessments of **improved workplace-based integration** (ORG3) based on correlations of 'closer working relations between managers/clinicians' and 'closer working relations between doctors, nurse and professions associated with medicine located in individual clinical units'.

Table 6.8 Projected organizational outcomes by occupational groups

	Medical clinician	Medical manager	General manager	Nurse manager	Nurse clinician	PAMs	Sig.
(ORG1) Improved workplace-based clinical accountability	.095	−.210	−.047	.185	−.194	.239	.378
(ORG2) Strengthened team-based financial realism	−.221	.274	.233	.533	−.031	−.076	.163
(ORG3) Improved workplace-based integration	−.219	.089	.560	.341	−.039	−.140	**.032**

Positive scores represent degrees of agreement with the factor statements and negative scores represent degrees of disagreement. Shaded scores indicate stances congruent with a developmental model of clinical governance.

These outcomes of clinical governance were rated highly by general and nurse managers but denied by medical clinicians and PAMs.

The patterns in the profiles of individual occupations across clinical and organizational outcomes were also interesting. Tables 6.7 and 6.8 suggest that nurse managers had the most considered understanding of the linkages between desired end-states such as 'improved patient outcomes' and what might be termed 'substantive clinical workplace-based change'. Significant here were the similarities between nurse manager statements about the goals of clinical governance and its projected outcomes. Added to their inclination to associate clinical governance with substantive workplace-based changes (Table 6.6), nurse managers emerged as the most positive about the prospects of change at both clinical and organizational levels.

Respondents' perceptions and evaluations of clinical governance as policy

In light of these findings we now examine respondent evaluations of clinical governance as a policy. Respondents were asked to rate six statements that clinical governance is 'a fad', 'a good idea whose potential cannot be realized', 'unjustified management intrusion into clinical domains', 'multidisciplinary approach to systematizing, monitoring and improving care', 'external discipline and surveillance' and 'enabling clinicians to bring quality and outcome issues into their negotiations with health policy authorities'. In making their assessments respondents were asked to use a five-point scale from 'strongly agree' to 'strongly disagree'.

As represented in Table 6.9, principal component analysis generated three factors. The first, **management intrusion** (EVAL1), arose from high correlations in the evaluations of clinical governance as 'a fad whose time will pass', 'a mechanism for promoting further unjustified intrusions by management into clinical domains' and as 'providing structures which by using external discipline and surveillance will engender a culture of blame within clinical settings'. Medical managers and clinicians agreed with this but general and nurse managers strongly disagreed. The second factor, **strategy to empower clinicians in clinical systemization and resource negotiations** (EVAL2), was based on correlations between evaluations of clinical governance as 'providing structures through which unit-based multi-disciplinary clinical teams can systematize, monitor and improve care' and as 'providing a structure which will enable clinicians to bring clinical quality and outcome issues into their negotiations with health authorities'. Although there were no statistically significant differences between groups, nurse managers strongly agreed that clinical governance was such a strategy whereas general managers, medical managers and PAMs disagreed (albeit weakly). However, medical clinicians and managers as well as general managers saw clinical governance as 'a good idea whose potential cannot be realized because the staff time and other resources required for its development and implementation remain unavailable'. In other words they believed it was an **unrealizable strategy** (EVAL3), whilst nurse managers strongly felt that the strategy was realizable. This positive stance of nurse managers, compared to that of medical clinicians and medical managers, is an important finding which we will return to.

Table 6.9 Perceptions and evaluations of clinical governance

Clinical governance as:	Medical clinician	Medical manager	General manager	Nurse manager	Nurse clinician	PAMs	Sig.
(EVAL1) Management intrusion	.513	.586	−.609	−.545	.080	−.372	**.000**
(EVAL2) Strategy to empower clinicians in clinical systematization and resource negotiations	.054	−.179	−.238	.765	.052	−.184	.070
(EVAL3) Unrealizable strategy	.265	.212	.220	−.738	−.086	−.171	**.026**

Positive scores represent degrees of agreement with the factor statements and negative scores represent degrees of disagreement. Shaded scores indicate stances congruent with a developmental model of clinical governance.

Discussion

This chapter has explored three themes: practitioners' knowledge and experience of processes associated with clinical governance, their perceptions of the primary objectives and the expected outcomes of clinical governance, and their evaluations of clinical governance as policy. The analysis has found:

1   a disjunction between what occupational groups *said* were the primary objectives of clinical governance and the outcomes they *expected* it to produce in their Trusts;
2   an important effect of occupational background on people's ideas and evaluations of clinical governance and their knowledge and

experience of processes associated with a workplace-focused model of clinical governance.

Evidence for the first finding derives from a comparison of how occupations assessed the importance of risk reduction as an objective of clinical governance as against the likelihood of its attainment. For all occupations, risk reduction was the second most frequently nominated objective (Table 6.6). Its perceived importance for all occupations, however, does not seem to guarantee its realization because, whilst general managers and nurse managers exhibited some (if low) confidence about the potential value of risk reduction (CLIN3, Table 6.7), the assessments of medical clinicians, medical managers, nurse clinicians and PAMs swung between ambivalence and pessimism. Similarly, whereas all occupations nominated 'improved patient care' as the primary objective of clinical governance (Table 6.6), they lacked agreement about what this might encompass. With the possible exception of PAMs, respondent groups were equivocal about the capacity of existing clinical governance strategies to improve clinical practice (CLIN1, Table 6.7).

That nurse managers have a positive view of a workplace-based model of clinical governance, compared with the sceptical position of medical managers and general managers, provides evidence for the second finding that the respondents' occupational backgrounds influenced their assessment of clinical governance. Possible explanations for these occupation-based differences are found in how respondents self-rated their knowledge and experience of the various processes associated with clinical governance. Viewed as a composite, the three knowledge and experience factors, set out in Table 6.5, can be seen as referring to three very different views of clinical work and of what is required for its organization and management. Equally, patterns in the way that an occupation rated each of the factors can be interpreted as indicating the extent to which specific constructions of clinical work were embedded in its 'on the ground practice'.

What is involved here becomes apparent when we consider the higher levels of knowledge and experience reported by medical clinicians and medical managers for *patient-specific methods* as compared with their self-assessments (of their knowledge and experience) of *prospective systems-oriented clinical management methods*. Considered together, these results suggest that medical clinicians and managers were continuing to adhere to a model of care construed primarily in patient-specific terms. Nurse clinicians also tended to such a view when they rated themselves as low in both knowledge and experience of each method reported in Table 6.5. Perhaps nurses felt that they have very limited capacity to influence the ways in which clinical work is organized and could be improved. By allowing the doctors to retain ultimate control in this area, they might be avoiding the need to increase their personal involvement in and responsibility for the organization of clinical care.

On a broader front, in apparently accepting their subordination to doctors, nurse clinicians supported the medical clinicians' claimed right to self-define and self-validate their work.

Medical clinicians, however, did rate themselves as having some knowledge and experience in *retrospective clinical improvement methods* such as clinical audit, quality improvement and clinical effectiveness review. Yet, whilst results such as these point to the positive impact of past efforts at reform, they also presage problems that will need to be addressed. Central here is the belief, expressed by some medical clinicians in focus group discussions, that their involvement in stand-alone approaches to clinical audit, quality improvement and patient-centred clinical risk management is all they need do for clinical governance. As noted earlier in this chapter, stand-alone and profession-specific exercises in clinical audit, clinical effectiveness and quality improvement are much less likely to bring about the degree of change in clinical practice that is needed for good clinical governance focused on the clinical workplace.

All these findings provide grounds for interpreting medical clinicians as indifferent to the expected impacts of clinical governance (Tables 6.7 and 6.8) and seeing it as a management intrusion which is not likely to meet with success (Table 6.9). Similarly, nurse clinicians' continuing support for a model of care whose terms are defined largely by doctors is seen in their equivocal view of the organizational and clinical outcomes of clinical governance (Tables 6.7 and 6.8) as well as their overall evaluation of the method (Table 6.9). In contrast, PAMs had both extensive knowledge and experience in the prospective systems-oriented clinical management methods (Table 6.5). What may be involved in this isolation, in part, is illustrated in their equivocal assessment of both the organizational impact of clinical governance (Table 6.8) and the capacity of its methods to empower clinicians in clinical systemization and resource negotiation (Table 6.9). Taken together, these findings suggest that PAMs have difficulty in engaging other professional groups (apart from nurse managers) in the multidisciplinary processes that are inherent in prospective methods.

Nurse managers exhibit the most positive stance on each of the dimensions assessed in this study. They claimed extensive knowledge and experience of prospective systems-oriented clinical management methods and also rated highly their involvement in retrospective clinical improvement systems and claimed some continuing involvement in patient-specific methods (Table 6.5). Their assessments of both the clinical and organizational outcomes were positive (Tables 6.7 and 6.8) and they were the only group whose evaluations of clinical governance were positive (Table 6.9). They strongly supported the view that clinical governance was a realizable strategy for empowering clinicians in both work systemization and in resource negotiations with management. Equally (and again in contrast with the views of medical clinicians and medical managers), nurse managers strongly rejected the view that clinical governance was a faddish, unjustified management intrusion into the clinical domain which would do little more than engender a culture of blame. All told, nurse managers appear best placed to take the lead on clinical governance implementation.

By contrast, the dismissive attitudes of both medical managers and general managers point to worrying structural shortcomings which are likely to prevent good systems for clinical governance being put in place. Medical managers had the least well formed understanding of clinical governance. They were preoccupied with clinical risk, yet lacked knowledge and experience in methods such as clinical pathway development and clinical practice variation analysis that might help them prospectively to reduce the risk inherent in clinical practice. They were strongly inclined to see the policy agenda of clinical governance as a fad-driven, unjustified management intrusion into clinical domains whose pursuit would engender a culture of blame and did not think that it would produce structures which would empower clinicians to adopt multidisciplinary approaches in both systematizing and improving care and in bringing quality issues into their negotiations with management. In short, they appeared to believe that clinical governance would ultimately fail.

Whilst general managers registered some knowledge of *retrospective clinical improvement methods* such as clinical audit, quality improvement and clinical effectiveness review, they claimed little knowledge of *prospective methods* such as pathway development and implementation, case mix and resource utilization review. At the same time, general managers seem to be saying that clinical governance:

- is *not* a fad-driven management intrusion into clinical domains that imposes top-down discipline and surveillance;
- will *not* provide structures which will empower multidisciplinary clinical teams both to improve care and to bring issues of quality and outcomes into their negotiations with health policy authorities;
- *is* a good idea;
- *but* its potential cannot be realized because the resources required for its development and implementation are not available.

A plausible explanation for these results is the failure to pursue a model of clinical governance that is grounded in the clinical workplace. The primary attributes of such a model are found in the methods that are inherent in clinical pathway development and implementation, resource utilization review, the analysis of clinical practice variation and engendering change in clinical practice. Importantly, applying these methods to specific conditions (e.g. asthma) and/or procedures (e.g. total hip replacement) will both ground and integrate efforts to improve clinical effectiveness, safety, quality and efficiency. In so doing they will provide vehicles for enacting the practice and cultural changes that are being called for under the rubric of clinical governance.

Acknowledgement

The research reported in this chapter was part of a project funded by the Welsh Office of Research and Development and carried out in six Welsh health Trusts. We are grateful to the staff in these Trusts for participating in the study and in particular to the local coordinators who distributed and collected the necessary documents and set up focus groups. For a summary of the whole project see Degeling *et al.* (2002).

PART 2
EVIDENCE, SCIENCE AND MEDICINE

7 Evidence-Based: What Constitutes Valid Evidence?

David Byrne

This chapter is concerned with the fourth of the five characteristics of 'clinical governance' identified by the editors of this book: 'the new policy is intimately related to the application of science through the medium of "evidence-based medicine"' (Harrison and Gray 2000: 1). Its objective is to demystify our understanding of 'evidence bases'. This will not be done by following the intellectual fashion of post-modernism in which all knowledge is relative and ultimately a matter of individual interpretation. Rather what is being asserted is a rather hard-nosed and objectivist realism which challenges the understanding of evidence bases in which as Harrison puts it:

> The pinnacle of the hierarchy is occupied by the RCT [randomized control trial] ... Other research methods are ranked lower in the hierarchy, with other types of *controlled* study second to the RCT and uncontrolled methods a poor third. In practice advocates of RCTs tend to regard uncontrolled methods as suitable only for hypothesis building with a view to an eventual controlled study.
>
> (1998: 20, original emphasis)

Far from the RCT representing any sort of gold standard, any consideration of the reality of complex open systems *and* of the problems associated with inferring from frequentist probabilistic statements – the basis of conventional statistical reasoning – to individual cases, should make us recognize that the RCT is a procedure which can only be used in limited and special, although certainly non-trivial, contexts and cannot stand as an ideal against which other forms of evidence generation should be assessed. Evidence cannot be ranked according to the degree to which the procedure which generated it corresponded to experimental protocols.

There are two interrelated issues here. The first derives from the frequentist probabilistic nature of evidence generated by RCTs. The second is a consequence of the reality of complex causation in so many health processes. Experimental designs are inherently probabilistic. This means that any account of reality generated by them is one of what happens in the long run over a very large number of events. Even where RCTs are appropriately employed, and they do have their uses, they offer no guidance to any clinician or other therapist in relation to the individual case with which they are dealing at any point in time. They are of value to those concerned with public health, with the herd health of populations, but not to the practitioner confronted by a single patient. This is a fundamental problem for those concerned with encouraging practitioners to act on evidence. Practitioners, absolutely correctly, worry 'that the importance of holistic treatment tailored to individual patients is being neglected in favour of common approaches drawn from inappropriately aggregated data' (Davies and Nutley 2000: 55).

RCTs at least have a clear theory of causation built into their design. They all work on the basis that there is a single cause for the condition which the intervention under test is addressed to (the doctrine of specific aetiology) and that the intervention blocks the causal relationship between that cause and the effect in terms of outcome. The causal model is:

$$A \Rightarrow B$$

The 'treatment' works if it breaks this link. Thus in antibiotic therapy the causal account is that the micro-organisms' toxins cause the disease and the antibiotic as magic bullet kills the micro-organisms and eliminates the disease. Although there have been therapeutic interventions in which no generative mechanism is understood in detail – in other words say a drug is tested for effect without an account of its actual physiological operation – there is still a mono-causal theory of the form described above. Randomized control trials, however pragmatic, have a theory of causal form built into the statistical design.

When we move from single interventions into complex policy interventions, even this minimal version of causal reasoning is abandoned. Davies and Nutley remark that:

> The pragmatism embodied in the dominant methodology means that rigorous intervention trials have been used to assess whole packages of care ... When this is done, often few attempts are made to 'unbundle' the package in pursuit of full understanding of the mechanism(s) of action. It is not that such understanding is deemed unimportant – better understanding can lead to improved design of future interventions. It is just now widely accepted that even apparently clear understandings have to be tested in real world settings; and, more importantly, even when understanding is imperfect 'best-guess' interventions (or packages of interventions) can still be tested empirically.
>
> (1999: 11)

The word 'tested' is the clue to one of two fundamental errors made when this kind of approach is adopted in an effort to deal with the implications of complex causation. What we have in this passage is a notion of theory as separate from practice. Theories are understood as established prior to intervention and are subject to test through intervention – the essence of the hypothetico-deductive method. Part of the purpose of this chapter is to argue instead for a 'grounded theory' approach to the generation of evidence in which ideas emerge in the process of investigation.

The second error is even more important, so important that it renders any findings from 'merely empirical' investigations of complex interventions essentially useless. If we have more than one 'cause' in play, or in a better language if we are dealing with complex generative mechanisms, then we have the possibility, indeed probability, of what conventional statisticians understand as interaction but is better understood as complex and contingent cause. If this is the case then no findings from any context are necessarily transferable to any other context. Any empirically established relationship holds only for the context – in both space and time – in which it was established. We have no basis whatsoever for thinking that 'what worked' there and then will work in any other here and now.

That this point is vital has been made very clearly by Pawson and Tilley in their discussion of *Realistic Evaluation* (1997). I have modified their terminology slightly to suggest the following general account of complex cause:

Generative causal system & context ⇒ Set of possible outcomes

If we lack an understanding of how the generative causal system works and of the context in which any outcome(s) have been observed, then we are truly up the creek without a paddle when it comes to making evidence-based decisions. Note the use of the ampersand instead of a plus sign in the above expression. This indicates not simply an additive relationship between generative causal system and context but an interactive one.

A web-search for 'evidence-based practice' yielded numerous 'centres', almost all of which asserted a mission statement of some kind. That of McMaster University Canada's Evidence Based Practice Center is typical. It argued for: 'the integration of individual clinical expertise and best available external clinical evidence from systematic research'. Brearley puts it in essentially the same terms in a recent article describing evidence-based practice as: 'the conscientious, explicit and judicious use of robust evidence in making decisions about the care of individual patients' (2001: 7). There is nothing whatsoever to quarrel with this as a general principle but we really do have to realize that in dealing with the individual case there is no connection which can be established between probabilistic evidence derived from techniques based on a frequentist understanding of probability and causal processes at the level of the case. Moreover, in complex open systems the whole logic of control – the central principle of any experimentation (bench as much as statistical) – is entirely inappropriate because we are dealing with interactions and hence with emergent outcomes.

Let me sum the argument of this chapter assertively.

1   Reality in general, and especially that domain of reality where biological and social systems intersect, is composed of open systems with emergent properties. In plain English the whole is greater than the sum of its parts.

2   This means that we can never simply assume that causal relationships established through a process of control – whether physical or statistical – hold in any circumstances other than those of the controlled context – which is of necessity an abstraction from reality rather than a representation of reality. If we want to generalize from the experimental context we have to establish the ontological validity for so doing. That is we have to show that the real situation is simple and mono-causal.

3   Even in the limited set of contexts where we can establish that interaction and hence emergence is not an issue for us, evidence derived from randomized controlled trials based on a frequentist theory of probability can only be applied to large runs of cases and never to outcomes in individual cases. It is valid for public health purposes but not, taken alone, for the treatment of any given case.

Let us address the last of these points first because it leads us into a consideration of case-based methods and away from the mechanistic language of variables which was given to us by Newton but which obscures rather than clarifies the problems we have to contend with. If we first knock statistical inference on the head then we can deal in fairly short order with 'Dracula risen from the grave' – the assertion by those like Oakley (2000) and McIntyre and Pettigrew (2000) who argue for the extension of the RCT into the evaluation of social interventions and policy programmes.

The necessity for single case probabilities

Probability is a scientific construct and there is more than one way of constructing it. Desrosières observed:

> The complex connection between prescriptive and descriptive points of view is particularly marked in the history of probability calculus, with the recurrent opposition between *subjective* and *objective* prob-

ability; or, according to a different terminology, between *epistemic* and *frequentist* probability ... In the epistemic perspective, probability is a degree of belief. The uncertainty the future holds, or the incompleteness of our knowledge of the universe, leads to wagers on the future and the universe, and probabilities provide a reasonable person with rules of behaviour when information if lacking. But in the frequentist view, diversity and risk are part of nature itself, and not simply the result of incomplete knowledge. They are external to mankind and part of the essence of things. It falls to science to describe the frequencies observed.

(1998: 7, original emphasis)

The epistemic view has become codified in Baysian statistical methods which work on an iterative basis in which a specified *a priori* probability is refined through testing to generate an *a posteriori* probability which provides a better ground for specific action. Desrosières considers that the Baysian approach forms part of the science of clues as opposed to the Galilean sciences. The Galilean sciences are concerned with the establishment of general laws and engage with masses of information in order to infer such laws from that mass – from a description of general reality. The sciences of clues are concerned to establish local and specific chains of causation in order to explain particular events. We might consider that the sciences of clues, although they may well be quantitative, are essentially ideographic. They are concerned with the particular and are not part of the nomothetic programme directed at establishing general laws.

This is essentially the point made by Tannenbaum (1994) when she commented on the difference between the traditional foundation of scientific medicine in bench-based physiological and biochemical science in which chains of causation are established in individual cases and the probabilistic reasoning which underpins epidemiological understanding of causal connections. It is exactly what led Znaniecki (1934) to propose a strategy of analytic induction. Znaniecki distinguished the practices of sciences who worked with many cases, either on the basis of a statistical experiment or through surveys from those of 'bench' scientists who worked instead with a single or small number of cases which were studied very intensively. Induction based on many cases was, in Znaniecki's terms, 'enumerative induction' and at best could yield probabilistic accounts of the nature of reality. In contrast the intensive analysis (that word again) of the single case could yield a deterministic account of reality. Analytic induction is analogous, not to the statistical experiment involving randomized control, but to the actually physically controlled bench experiment. This distinction is rather important because analytic induction sought to establish laws by the demonstration of what amounted to constant conjunction and in statistical experimentation that cannot be done.

However, Znaniecki did not propose controlled experimentation as the mode of social analytical induction. Rather he suggested intensive qualitative study. Moreover, although analytic induction uses the idea of hypothesis, it is very different from the hypothetico-deductive method. In hypothetico-deductive reasoning a hypothesis is formulated and tested against data, usually not through direct testing but indirectly by testing a null hypothesis which denies the associations asserted in the working hypothesis. Testing is through measurement and statistical calculation. Analytic induction is much more iterative and works by a process of case-based constant comparison in which hypotheses are continually reformulated in order to develop an adequate overall account of the social processes being considered. We will return to the potential of this kind of strategy in the last part of this chapter.

An example is in order. It is valid to say on the basis of an RCT that the chances of a vaccine causing damage if administered to a large population are such that 0.005 per cent of those receiving it will be harmed – one in two thousand. There is no way in which that can be translated as saying that the individual immunized case has a one in two thousand chance of being harmed. That specific immunization is a unique and statistically independent event. Probabilistic explanations hold at the level of populations but never for cases. This is not an argument against probabilistic explanation at the population level. If immunization against measles damages one child in two thousand but five children in a thousand – a ten times higher rate – are damaged by measles, then there is good population case for immunization and an unanswerable case for massive support and compensation for the damaged children. Blalock (1982) put this with characteristic clarity:

> the mathematician finds it necessary to think in terms of *a priori* probabilities that cannot actually be obtained empirically and that are not dependent upon any particular sample data ... we shall use the term probability not to refer to single events ... but to a large number of events, to what happens in the long run.
>
> (1982: 115–16)

This point is very poorly understood in many conventional texts. The characteristic of a population is presented as a probability in the individual case. It is not that and can't be that. This is bad enough. Experiments are often a deal worse but before we turn to them, let us note the re-emergence of a novel late idea of Karl Popper's – that of the single case probability. Williams (1999) and Ulanowicz (1996) have noted Karl Popper's late attention to 'single case probability'. Both draw on the complexity frame of reference in elaborating how thinking about probability in the singular might help us to establish what determines outcomes for particular cases. Popper, characteristically, had seized on the key problem of frequentist probability – its inability to inform us about what might happen with any individual case. His proposed alternative was to understand probability, not in terms of aggregate proportions but rather through thinking about propensities for individual cases. The problem was the same as that which Znaniecki addressed when he formulated analytic induction. Popper thought that we might establish propensities through repeated experiments but a case-based method which uses an approach of 'constant comparison' would allow us to deal with complex causation in a way which experiments do not. There is such an approach available – Qualitative Comparative Analysis – and we will consider it below.

Let me sum up this part of the chapter. RCTs do not deal with the particularity of cases. They do not generate descriptions of law-like regularities which can serve as the basis for generalization from one instance to another instance. They are, to use a condemnatory phrase of early modern medicine, merely empirical. This does not devalue probabilistic evidence in informing interventions directed at large numbers of cases, provided the interventions do deal with simple causal systems with no interaction/complex generation present, but it does mean that there is no easy logical connection between RCT evidence and action in relation to any given actual case.

Understanding open systems: not so much the difficulty of control as the inevitability of emergence

When I read Oakley's book and similar arguments for the appropriateness of RCTs as a way of informing policy formation in social interventions, I was immediately reminded of arguments current thirty years ago about the form of evaluation which was appropriate in social action programmes. These were described rather well by Marris and Rein (1967) who defined the problem as being one of the incommensurability for ethical and political reasons of *the* scientific method and the actual practices of action research in community contexts. The difficulty was understood in terms of evaluative research ever being able to function in a way which maintained the controls necessary for a proper experimental approach. Sherwood, the researcher associated with Action for Boston Community Development, put it like this: 'Once the impact model is formulated the researcher must continue to remain within the environment, like a snarling watchdog, ready to oppose any alteration to the programme and procedures that would render his evaluation efforts useless' (quoted in Marris and Rein 1967: 201).

This sort of understanding, repeated after thirty years in the work of Oakley, sees the only problem with the RCT or approximation thereto in social programmes as being the difficulties of maintaining the control necessary for the applications of *the* scientific method. It was daft enough then – it is plain delirious now. Any understanding of emergence and open systems, of the whole complexity frame of reference, indicates that the problem is not one of the difficulties of control but that in complex open systems we cannot 'isolate out' single factors and generalize as to the potential impact of those factors. At the simplest and most basic level if there is any trace of interactive effects then there is no basis for generalizing from the experimental situation. Hayles is good on this:

> Abstraction is of course an essential component in all theorizing, for no theory can account for the infinite multiplicity of our interactions with the real. But when we make moves that erase the world's multiplicity, we risk losing sight of the variegated leaves, fractal branchings, and particular bark textures that make up the forest.
>
> (1999: 12)

Hayles takes apart the logics of both experimentation – the old 'Platonic Backhand' as she puts it – and simulation, the new 'Platonic Forehand'. The former works by abstracting from the complexity of the world, the latter by constructing emergent complexity from simple rules. She concludes that 'When they work together, they lay the groundwork for a new variation on an ancient game in which disembodied information becomes the ultimate Platonic Form' (1999: 3). The forehand of simulation is not, and I note this with some interest, generally part of the evidence base of health practice as I understand it. This is worth thinking about.

I have reached a point of impatience with non-complex understandings of social processes, which includes all intersections between the social and the biological natural (see Khalil 1996 for a development of this point), and am simply going to say 'complexity' and treat that word as the stake, raggy wooden pole in Geordie with which we dispose of RCTs in social contexts (for an elaboration see Byrne 1998, 2002; Cilliers 1998). Let us turn to how we might get some interesting evidence for our practice because there is a procedure which uses the kind of data we have and can certainly be considered at least as a powerful exploratory tool in developing evidence-based practice at all levels.

Qualitative Comparative Analysis: looking at cases and seeing what happened

Boolean logic works in large part through the use of the 'if' statement which can be used to specify on the basis of the satisfaction of multiple conditions – in essence through the creation of polythetic Aristotelian categories (those where a case has to fulfil more than one criterion for membership) as a pre-dicate for action in an algorithm. 'If' statements act in large part by distin-guishing kinds. This sort of Boolean approach is the basis of 'Qualitative Comparative Analysis' (QCA) (Ragin 1987), also referred to as 'Qualitative Configuration Analysis' (Huber and Garcia 1991). Fielding and Lee describe this as 'a simple, compact, if somewhat restricted, way of analysing patterns of causation in a small to moderate number of cases' (1998: 157). The procedure is based on careful examination of cases and the categorization of aspects of the case but this is not a variable-centred analysis. Rather the cases are what matters and the description of them does not abstract variables from them but rather describes them in terms of what I have called 'variate traces' (Byrne 2002). Fielding and Lee put it like this:

> Unlike the data matrix in quantitative research, where the analytic focus is on variables displayed in the *columns* of the table, it is the *rows* which are important here. What is being examined for each row is the *configuration* of causes associated with the presence or absence of an outcome for the case.
>
> (1998: 158, original emphasis)

The method works in a stepwise fashion in which elements are eliminated at each stage through comparison of cases so as to identify the most parsi-monious instance of causation. Ragin (1994: 12) considers that this approach follows an experimental logic of reduction equating stepwise elimination with direct physical control. However, the approach explicitly allows for multiple 'prime implicants' – that is, the most parsimonious representation of cause may include more than one cause. This is essentially different from the re-ductionist mono-causal model which underpins the controlled experiment. QCA can deal with complex causation even if the Newtonian imagery remains so powerful that this is understood usually just in terms of factors in inter-action. Moreover, practitioners of QCA recognize that a particular outcome might result from different combinations of conditions and that single factors might combine with different other factors to produce different outcomes. There is more to this than just a recognition of complex cause. The systems being examined in QCA are at least implicitly understood as complex systems with all that is implied by that. This means that significant changes in them are changes of kind, not of degree, and that the origins of those changes are likely to lie in combinations of control parameters.

The significance of changes of kind is important. A lot of the literature on evidence-based medicine and health care talks about significant changes being incremental changes of degree but this derives exactly from confusing aggregate data with what happens at the micro-level. Five-year survival rates after treatment for cancer may change incrementally but the patients themselves are either alive or dead – a really definite matter of categorical rather than incremental condition. This matters at all levels in terms of the objects towards which intervention is directed. We may change aggregate figures incrementally, although even here significant changes – e.g. health transformations – are often non-linear, but cases, whether patients or urban social systems, change qualitatively.[1]

Hicks (1994) notes that QCA seems to work in the same way as 'neo-analytic induction', a description of analytic induction as practised when comparisons are made not only with cases with positive outcomes but those with negative outcomes, comparisons are made on a multiple case basis rather than successive pairwise comparisons of single cases, and there is an acceptance of the limited and local character of theoretical description. Again this is essentially compatible with a complex realist account.

QCA requires input in the form of dichotomous variables – binary attributes in which a condition is absent or present. This is the same requirement as that of cluster analysis procedures when working with nominal-level data. Essentially in QCA, elements are either present (1) or absent (0) for cases and the cases are compared on the resulting pattern presented as a 'truth table'. This takes the form of a description of the kinds of ways in which a given outcome can be achieved. QCA, like numerical taxonomy procedures and with neural net approaches used as classificatory devices, deals with cases rather than variables. Both have a categorical conception of change – phase shift in complexity speak. This is what matters for the real cases with which policy is concerned.

Case-centred approaches have the potential for resolving both of the problems which apply to the use of evidence derived from RCTs. They cope with the problem of inferring from the aggregate to the individual by sorting out different paths of causation for different sorts of cases. This can be illustrated by reference to the immunization example. If immunization damages only small numbers of children the appropriate policy response is not to suspend immunization but rather to examine case-based data in order to establish the causal preconditions of immunization damage. Then children can be assessed in relation to their individual liability for damage – a propensity approach. Those children who demonstrate propensity can be excluded from the programme. If the numbers with the propensity to be damaged by immunization are so large as to compromise herd immunity, then the programme should not be implemented in any event unless there is a catastrophic potential from the epidemic. This logic of interpretation applies to any intervention directed at 'single cause' systems. Of course the whole idea of 'contra-indication' in treatment is a recognition of the necessity for this sort of approach. The point is that case-based comparative methods make the establishment of individual propensities central to any therapeutic programme. This has far more potential than simplistic genetic determinism where the genome is the basis of all propensities, although genetic typing *might* be *part* of the case-based data set required for the establishment of individual propensities with genotype considered as a component of the individual generative system in interaction with environment and life history.

The other advantage of case-based comparative methods is that since they can generate information about complex causation, they enable us to define in a useful way all the terms in my modified version of Pawson and Tilley's expression:

$$\text{Generative system \& context} \Rightarrow \text{Outcome set}$$

This means that we can establish knowledge which can be generalized beyond specific context because we can explore the character of relatively permanent generative systems in interaction with different sorts of contexts and make suggestions as to which of a possible range of outcomes might be brought into being. In other words, we do have a basis on which we can generalize beyond the specific situation in which a complex intervention set has been applied. We can say that this approach might work with cases like that one, and that another approach might work with cases of a different kind.

Dyer (2001) has applied numerical taxonomy techniques in the time ordered classification of cases passing through a 'custody diversion' process in the northeast of England. Her cases were people directed to a mental health-based programme as an alternative to processing through the criminal justice system. In simple terms she was able to classify them as they arrived in the programme in terms of 'inputs' – what they were at that point – then classify them at different stages of processing through the system according to the interventions the system made in relation to them, and finally to classify their current status at an end point. Note that this was possible because the data relating to the cases was stored in a relational electronic data base. The data base was created for administrative convenience but it modelled the real social processing system which it was created to serve.

Dyer was able to establish in detail how different sorts of people responded to different sorts of intervention. Her data was all quantitative categorical and her techniques involved mapping movement of cases among clusters at the different time points. Since clustering works by comparison this was a highly systematized version of neo-analytic induction.

The case-centred approach has another major advantage. Davies and Nutley note that one of the major shortcomings of merely empirical evidence is that it offers no information on comparative costs: 'Effectiveness may be quite context dependent, and costs will certainly vary between different settings. There assessing the value of evidence, and making decisions on implementation, requires thorough consideration of local circumstances' (1999: 11).

Case comparisons can include enumeration and assessment of costs in different contexts. Indeed, data bases often incorporate this information for routine accountancy purposes. There is nothing particularly original about this in form. It is much like cost accountancy in industrial production. However, the ability to relate outcomes to cost structures does absolutely depend on having a clear idea of the causal processes in operation and about the way different components combine to generate different emergent processes.

Concluding remarks

There is a good science studies PhD (or several) to be written about the RCT and evidence-based health practice. Why is it so attractive? Of course we could talk about the power of the discourses of frequentist statistics and that is not wrong, but we might begin with the beams in our own eyes first. Professor Sinclair from York University Social Work Department made a very interesting point at a recent Durham seminar when talking about evaluation. One of the great attractions of the RCT is that it enables us to do something – to create variation in the world – to be little gods, and then to see what difference we have made. The strategies of case-centred study proposed here are essentially retrodictive – they say what has happened and why. The only forward reaching strategy which allows us to engage with complex systems is action-research, but then we are moving from research to praxis and realizing that perhaps either or both of the following dicta might apply:

> The only way to understand the world is to change it.
>
> (Mao Zedong)

> The philosophers have described the world, the point however is to change it.
>
> (Karl Marx)

Note

1   Non-linear changes in aggregated time ordered data series are an indication that categorical change is going on, or at least one level which matters for the outcomes measured in the data series.

8 Limits of Governance: Interrogating the Tacit Dimensions of Clinical Practice

Andy Bilson and Sue White

The clinical governance framework is a central plank of New Labour's modernization agenda. As other chapters in this book have described, clinical governance is an umbrella term encompassing a range of audit, risk management and quality assurance activities which are now built into the day-to-day business in health care provider agencies. Managers and practitioners in services are given joint responsibility for the quality of services and the development of best practice based on sound evidence. Clinical governance is normative and prescriptive and requires clinicians to self-regulate and to assess their own performance against guidelines and protocols produced and disseminated by the National Institute for Clinical Excellence and it also renders them accountable for failure to do so.

In this chapter we consider the limitations of the current approach to governance with a particular focus on its ability to deal with the hurly burly of everyday practice in health settings. We conclude that the current approach is unable properly to interrogate these practices and hence is limited in its ability to promote what we shall call compassionate action. We go on to suggest how a different methodology can be used which works with the strengths of clinicians and their teams to promote a more responsive, ethical practice.

Scientific bureaucratic governance

We discuss below how, in making their judgements, professionals make use of a number of different kinds of reasoning, all of which are important in understanding the processes of clinical decision-making. However, these different ways of knowing are not equally acknowledged and represented in policy developments and practice guidance. Indeed, as Harrison has noted and as has been discussed elsewhere in this book, one particular dominant form of rationality underpins contemporary policy in the form of New

Labour's modernization programme. This form of rationality Harrison terms the 'scientific–bureaucratic' model, which he defines as follows:

> Scientific–bureaucratic [rationality] centres on the assumption that valid and reliable knowledge is mainly to be obtained from the accumulation of research conducted by experts according to strict scientific criteria ... It further assumes that working clinicians are likely to be both too busy and insufficiently skilled to interpret and apply such knowledge for themselves, and therefore holds that professional practice should be influenced through the systematic aggregation by academic experts of research findings on a particular topic, and the distillation of such findings into protocols and guidelines which may then be communicated to practitioners with the expectation that practice will be improved ... The logic, though not always the overt form, of guidelines is essentially algorithmic...
>
> (Harrison 1999b: 3)

So, this model is 'scientific' in the sense that it promises a secure knowledge base which can provide rational foundations for clinical decisions. It is bureaucratic in the sense that this knowledge is codified and manualized through the use of protocols, guidelines and computer models adherence to which may be monitored by managers or through internal and external audit.

This internal auditing activity has been augmented by the establishment in 1999 of two new bodies, the National Institute for Clinical Excellence (NICE) and the Commission for Health Improvement (CHI) – since 2004 the Commission for Health Audit and Inspection (CHAI). The former has the role of undertaking 20–30 appraisals of new interventions each year, which are intended to inform a range of clinical guidelines or protocols that clinicians are expected to follow (unless they can make a very good case against so doing). CHAI, like its predecessor (CHI), is a body quasi-independent from government and one of its functions will be to monitor the compliance of services with the guidelines issued by NICE.

Thus, clinical governance in its current incarnation relies on a view of professional practice as wholly rational–technical and linear. The guidelines and protocols depict the processes of diagnosis and treatment as consecutive. The clinician makes a decision about 'what's wrong' and then consults the protocol to find out 'what works'. This does not fit with the realities of professional decision-making. We can illustrate this with an example (Extract 1) taken from White's ethnography of paediatric services (White 2002; White and Stancombe 2003). Here a paediatrician and registrar are discussing a case in an outpatient clinic. The child has been referred because she has problems with wetting and frequency and urgency of micturation.

Extract 1

This and other extracts used in the paper are transcribed word for word. As we wish to preserve the ambiguities and complexities of ordinary conversation, no attempt has been made to tidy up the talk to assist readability. Square brackets indicate passages of overlapping talk.

Consultant:	... Right let's just see what this was ... This is a child who came to see Dr Anderson ... urgency of micturition, very, very nervous, erm father was the carer, parents were split up mother with new partner, two younger sisters. No warning when wees. I think there was like an underlying message that parents were split up and father was the carer and I think she was just a bit worried that there were alternative psychosocial agendas, you know what I mean, which were not explicit.
Registrar:	Right
Consultant:	Right, she was seen at Bristol when she was about 4 with a cyst to do with her kidneys and it was inflamed, whether they meant cystitis [rather] than a cyst –
Registrar:	[Yeah]
Consultant:	– I don't, I don't know, urgency, few days of accidents erm. Didn't know really whether she's had urinary tract infections or I didn't know whether or not she just had an unstable bladder so I did, because there was such a lot of anxiety about it and the letter was an urgency, I did both. I gave her antibiotic prophylaxis and oxybutinin [drug to relax the bladder wall and reduce urgency]. I thought well I'll start with the, the lot –
Registrar:	and work backwards –
Consultant:	and work backwards (laughs). So, erm, no accidents on treatment ultrasound showed a small ... erm continue treatment for 6 months, see her for review, hopefully stop the trimethoprim [antibiotic] and see at intervals, if she continues to stay dry, wean her off the oxybutinin, suggested that she double micturition, standing up and sitting down OK, so...
Registrar:	mmm

The paediatrician is considering a range of aetiologies for this problem including a suggestion that it may be psychosocial and the implicit proposition that it may be due to the parents splitting up and father being the main carer. This is an allusion to the possibility of sexual abuse, which is not considered further in this particular section of talk. We can see in the consultant's third turn that in this case the treatment(s) preceded a decision about aetiology, which could be ascertained retrospectively. This is explicitly referred to by the registrar as 'working backwards'. The clinician clearly felt the need to account for the backwards reasoning and refers to the degree of anxiety and urgency about the case. These kinds of messy contingencies, which are part of the everyday practice of clinical judgement, are excluded from the rational– technical approaches prescribed in policy, which devalue individual judge- ments, are mistrustful of practice wisdom and pay scant regard to the kinds of reasoning used in everyday clinical practice, which we have seen in the ex- tract above.

Tacit dimensions of clinical practice

The concept of 'tacit knowledge' was developed by Polanyi (1967) to refer to knowledge held by human agents which is taken for granted and hence is difficult to articulate explicitly. He is referring to the capacity of human actors to develop routinized and habitual ways of doing and being, whether this is as a mother, a child, a banker, a lawyer, a nurse, a social worker or a doctor. The very familiarity of the task or judgement at hand and the need for off-the- shelf remedies renders the reasoning processes involved invisible and indeed largely unconscious. Thus, practitioners do not tend to reflect on those as- pects of their practice they consider most admirable and supportable using the conventional reasoning of the time. These aspects are thus unavailable for debate and are unlikely to be cited as a rationale for decision-making simply because they are habitual and treated as 'the only right and proper way to think', for a given occupation, at a given historical moment.

Thus, tacit knowledge has the potential to make clinicians very confident about their competence, but what serves as competence is socially and cul- turally mediated. Presuppositions and preferred formulations come camou- flaged against the familiar thickets of the clinicians' culturally available repertoires. As Green notes:

> Common sense is a powerful rhetoric because it creates a sense of shared values between speaker and audience, which is difficult to resist without explicitly rejecting these values. It is also a device which constitutes expert knowledge as redundant, simply because what is said is self-evident and known by everybody.
>
> (2000: 470)

Thus, culturally shared notions of practice can be a powerful force of stasis as they will be used as a filter in the interpretation of 'evidence' and 'facts'. They are also relatively invisible and hence are rarely debated: that is, they render social systems and cultures relatively immune to change.

With this in mind, we advocate that closer attention is paid to the emotional, social and cultural contexts in which professional judgements take place. Clinical decision-making is not the outcome of individual minds; like any other domain, it is subject to social influences. As Atkinson notes:

> In many organizational settings ... decision-making itself is a collective organizational activity ... 'decisions' may be subject to debate, negotiation and revision, based on talk within and between groups or teams of practitioners ... The silent inner dialogue of single-handed decision-making, therefore is by no means the whole story.
>
> (1995: 52)

For example, the 'facts' of a case rarely speak for themselves; to assess its relevance and its validity, even relatively 'hard' information derived from X-rays or laboratory tests requires interpretation and negotiation. The 'facts' of a case are frequently approximations and equivocations, requiring the exercise of qualitative judgement. For example, in White's study of paediatrics, an eight-month-old baby, Joanne, was presented by her mother at Accident and Emergency, with an injury to her right leg. The paediatrician examining the child and her X-rays on admission was of the opinion that the leg was fractured. Moreover, unconvinced by the mother's account of the circumstances of the injury, he had raised concerns that the child may have sustained a non-accidental injury. Second opinions were sought from orthopaedic consultants and radiologists including experts from a regional children's hospital. Despite considering precisely the same X-rays, the different clinicians could reach agreement neither about the nature and extent of the injury, nor indeed about whether it was a fracture at all.

Yet, the paediatrician and other professionals involved in the case still had to act. Their responsibility did not end with diagnosis. They also had to think about 'who did it?', 'in what circumstances?' and 'will it happen again?' They had to rely on more interactive methods, such as their assessment of the plausibility of the mother's story, how she responded to the child and vice versa, and what they could find out about the family history. These processes depend to a large extent on various kinds of (substantially moral) reasoning which are culturally laden and rely substantially on historically situated ideas about what constitutes a competent, common-sense formulation.

The following data (Extract 2) provides a further example of the interaction of a range of rationalities in clinician-talk and judgement-making. For example, it illustrates how the paediatrician's formal, domain-specific knowledge of 'chronic idiopathic constipation of childhood' interacts with moral judgement in her discussions with a registrar prior to commencing an outpatient clinic. The extract shows how detailed analysis of talk can help to make visible the tacit dimensions of practice. This is a point we develop further in due course.

Extract 2

Square brackets indicate passages of overlapping talk.

Consultant:	Mark Smith – you've not had the pleasure, of this mother. Mother is under our psychiatrists, she is a oh fictitious illness gives the wrong impression. She's got a [neurotic] state really, somatization.
Registrar:	[Right] right
Consultant:	[Somatization], really *severe* somatization disorder
Registrar:	[Right] yeah
Consultant:	You, you may have met her [... as soon as you meet her, she'll go on] –
Registrar:	[I think I probably, what's he got?]
Consultant:	He's constipated, severely constipated –
Registrar:	Yes, it's all, yes
Consultant:	She looks ill and as soon as you meet her she looks ill and she'll come out with all of her complaints. He has severe constipation actually required a when they first brought him in to extract the masses of faeces, but recently he's relapsed and the problem seemed to be that mum had relapsed as well so everything went down and he had to come in for an enema –
Registrar:	That's right, that's right. That's how I know him, I didn't [see him]
Consultant:	[No well] and mum couldn't er, it had to be done here 'cos mum can't cope at home, she can't cope. He was much better but he was on sort of 30 mls of Picolax a day. His bowel is just sort of –
Registrar:	Huge
Consultant:	Huge because of the rocks that had to be removed, erm ... I suppose I'd better try and see him just because I've felt his belly before and I'll know whether the rocks are there or not (rustling of case notes).

Despite the presence of a physical complaint, constipation, this case is told largely through complex and morally laden characterization of the mother. The character work in the telling is heard by experienced clinicians as part of the diagnosis and clear attributions of cause and effect are made: 'but recently he's relapsed and the problem seemed to be that mum had relapsed as well so everything went ... down'. The bowel is referred to as 'huge', the hardened faeces described as 'rocks' which are professional descriptions and metaphors which function to transmit an interpretation of the severity of the problem. Explicit reference is made to the paediatrician having 'felt his belly before'. This marks her professional judgement as a personal phenomenon – embodied know-how – which cannot straightforwardly be taken over by her registrar.

These more tacit dimensions of practice have received some attention in the literature on clinical judgement. For example, in contrast, to the rational–technical models, Donald Schon stresses the importance of experience and seasoned professional intuition. He sees uncertainty as inevitable in professional practice. He accepts that some problems can be solved by the application of the artefacts of science, in the form of research-based theory and technique. This is the 'high hard ground' of practice (Schon 1988: 67), but the problems that can be addressed on this firm terrain are the most straightforward, such as 'is this a case of tonsilitis?' For Schon, the most important professional questions arise in the 'swampy lowlands' (Schon 1988: 67), and here practitioners must draw on something within themselves, some form of artistry, craft or intuition. The competent clinician is depicted as a spontaneous and skilful *actor*, who just 'knows' how to act. This actor becomes aware of using particular knowledge and skills only at certain times.

However, whilst Schon's work acknowledges the complexity and messiness of clinical practice, it does not provide any methodologies through which clinicians may be helped to render these important aspects of their practice visible and reportable. We have already shown how analysis of professional talk can be useful in this regard and we provide some further ideas below particularly relating to how the local cultures that sustain and produce tacit knowledge can be addressed.

Culture as a sustaining medium for routinized action

We have noted that policy initiatives talk about changing organizational cultures in particular kinds of ways, as Liam Donaldson, the Chief Medical Officer, notes:

> Above all ... clinical governance is about the culture of NHS organizations. A culture where openness and participation are

encouraged, where education and research are properly valued, where people learn from failures and blame is the exception rather than the rule, and where good practice and new approaches are freely shared and willingly received.

(Department of Health 2002)

Yet the concept of culture is itself taken for granted and its capacity to shape what can be thought, said or done is ignored. Culture is seen not as a source of habit or routine, but as a medium relatively easily changed. Yet, research into teams in social care (e.g. Pithouse 1987; Hall 1997; White 1998), medicine (e.g. Bloor 1976) and nursing (e.g. Latimer 2000) show how cultures are locally accomplished and reproduced and can sustain the tacit practices of occupations, organizations and teams and indeed may be used to resist the sort of approaches to policy and practice change usually associated with rational approaches to governance.

The sort of organizational culture that Liam Donaldson suggests in his quotation above that is open to and can identify and learn from its mistakes is rare. In fact a key problem in cases where practice is framed in a strong local culture that supports the problem behaviour is recognizing that there is a problem at all. This is because these cultures and the practice that is supported by them are based on tacitly held assumptions that are difficult to challenge as they are taken for granted as truths. As Armstrong (1982) says of a rational approach to changing assumptions:

> The rational approach is rational only for the change agent. For the changee, change seems *irrational*. Should we change important beliefs each time someone thrusts disconfirming evidence on us? It is not surprising that 'people are resistant to change'. The rational approach implies that the target of the change is irrational.
>
> (Armstrong 1982: 463; emphasis in original)

For example, Paul Thagard's (2000) case study of the development and acceptance of the theory that peptic ulcers are primarily caused by a bacterium, *Helicobacter pylori*, illustrates how a complex range of activities, processes and events affects the production and acceptance of new ideas. The hypothesis, generated during the mid-1980s, that gastric ulcers were the result of bacterial infection was initially considered preposterous. The established belief at the time was that peptic ulcers were caused by excess acidity which eventually eroded the stomach wall and caused lesions. Due to this established belief, which was treated by both clinicians and scientists as the only right and proper way to think, the new hypothesis was slow to gain acceptance. This was in spite of the rigour with which experiments were conducted by Warren, the pathologist who first noticed the spiral bacteria in a biopsy specimen, and Marshall, the gastroenterologist with whom he collaborated. It was not until the mid-1990s that the idea gained widespread acceptance. This depended, as Thagard notes, on a number of factors:

> The development of the bacterial theory of ulcers depended on the physical use of instruments such as microscopes and endoscopes and on the devising of experiments to test the association of *H. pylori* and gastric problems. It also had important social dimensions, including the collaborative work of Marshall, Warren and their associates; the processes of communication by which the new concepts and hypotheses spread; and the processes of negotiation by which new consensus began to form.
>
> (2000: 39)

Thus, until Warren and Marshall's discovery about the role of *H. pylori* had been argued and negotiated in an interactional context, it remained contested and fragile. Its entry into practice was initially blocked by the constraints imposed on thinking by the popularized 'excess acidity' explanation which operated as a culturally available resource through which clinicians 'just knew' how to treat peptic ulcers.

A further example of how the rational–bureaucratic approach to governance fails because it is unable to challenge strong team cultures can be seen in social work practice regarding contact between parents and their children in care (Bilson and Barker 1994, 1995, 1998). This area of child care has a well-developed research base that stresses the importance of regular contact for the well-being of children. Following the 1989 Children Act, which was built on a raft of research into good practice, massive attempts were made to govern this area through new legislation, extensive training programmes, regulations and rules, publishing research reviews and good practice guides. Research undertaken by one of the authors into 1068 children (approximately 2 per cent of the total number in care in England) in five local authorities following this range of activity aimed at governing practice found that levels of contact varied widely within and between local authorities. It was found that variations between teams could not be explained by the factors usually linked to differing levels of contact (e.g. age of child, reason for becoming looked after, time in care etc.). For example, in one local authority half the teams had levels of contact ranging between 32 per cent and 38 per cent of children seeing their parents at least once a month whilst the other teams ranged from 69 per cent to 71 per cent. Evidence that team culture played a part in these differences can be seen in feedback from the teams received after the results of the research had been reported back. Comments from the teams with low parental contact and social work activity to promote it included statements to the effect that the issue in some cases was not so much encouraging contact in long-term placements but helping children accept the reality of parents' poor commitment. In contrast, teams with high levels of contact made comments such as how they put a lot of effort in at the beginning of a placement to gain parental cooperation and build up a pattern of contact and that they deliberately allocated time to work with looked after children, frequently doing activities with them outside the placement.

Thus we may conclude this section by noting that the main problem with the clinical governance agenda as currently operationalized is that human agents easily develop routinized patterns of thought, action and interaction in relation to their activities. These aspects are supported by local cultures and tend to be relatively invisible to those within the culture and thus are also extremely durable. They are vitally important in understanding reasoning and action, as Varela notes below:

> ... my main point is that most of our mental and active life is of the immediate coping variety, which is transparent, stable, and grounded in our personal histories. Because it is so immediate, not only do we not see it, we do not see that we do not see it, and this is why so few people have paid any intention to it ... Yet the question remains: how can this distinction between coping behaviours and abstract judgement, between situatedness and morality, be applied to the study of ethics and the notion of ethical experience?
>
> (1992: 19)

Varela's point is that it is important both to have an analytic approach to ordinary activity – a way of making the familiar and taken-for-granted strange – and an emotional and ethical engagement with the moral nature of inter-actions with others. This is particularly relevant to the clinical domain. There is no doubt that this tacit dimension of practice is often very difficult to extract and articulate. However, precisely because it is social, it cannot be located entirely inside the clinician's head. It must in some way, at some times, be visible, available and reportable – how else do we account for the induction of novices into established ways of working? Therefore, if we are to develop the capacity of clinicians to evaluate whether they want to make changes to tacit aspects of their practice, we need techniques to help them make what is familiar strange.

Principles for more reflexive governance

Our approach, then, stresses the need to address the emotions and engage participants in reflecting on their assumptions by making the familiar strange. So how does our approach differ from the scientific–bureaucratic model? First, there is a different approach to data collection. In particular we want to stress the importance of studying inter-professional talk in everyday settings. This is because cultures must necessarily 'speak themselves' and this making and remaking of occupational or team cultures takes place most visibly in talk between professionals, as we saw in the data extracts earlier in the chapter. Thus, as Anspach notes:

> Although much has been written concerning how doctors talk *to* patients, very little has been written about how doctors talk *about* patients ... This analytic focus on the medical interview occurs even though the way in which physicians talk about patients is a poten- tially valuable source of information about medical culture. Rarely do doctors reveal their assumptions about patients when they are talking to them.
>
> (1988: 358)

Another key difference in terms of data collection and analysis is that artefacts such as written records, statistical data, transcripts of talk are read not in order to evaluate or prescribe practice but for what they can tell us about the tacit presuppositions which order professional activity. For ex- ample, it is recognized that files represent 'a potential resource for vindicating practice' (Pithouse 1987: 34). However, it is the very way in which profes- sionals attempt to vindicate their practice, which gives important informa- tion about their view of the official definitions within which they operate. Thus the aim is not to find more about the reality of the lives of patients, or to evaluate the adequacy of recording against some normative template, but to consider what presuppositions or world views informed the clinical decisions being made.

The third and crucial difference relates to the use made of findings. In the scientific–bureaucratic model 'evidence' is used to prescribe practice in a top- down manner. Our approach starts from the idea that any actions that need to follow data collection should come from clinicians and managers them- selves and should be realized through reflection on their own understandings of what is good practice. To achieve this is not simple and the following practical principles (based on Bilson 1997 and Bilson and Ross 1999) will form the basis for a more reflexive approach to governance.

News of difference

Bateson defines information as *news of difference that makes a difference* (Bateson and Bateson 1988: 78). This stresses the fact that information is relational and not absolute and also that what makes a difference is 'news'. In health services the attention of those who provide services is often focused on the individual. In this situation a source of difference can be found in data drawn from research or information systems about patterns of services. This approach recognizes that such data do not provide truths with which to bludgeon into submission those who see things differently. Rather it can be interpreted in many ways and is itself a social construction. Its usefulness is as a source of news of difference and when presenting it in this way our experience is that there is little resistance from professionals because alternative viewpoints are accepted as valid and treated with respect and curiosity; and the limited nature of any findings is stressed.

Reflexive conversations

Reflexivity is a process of continually critically reviewing one's premises (Lawson 1984; Taylor and White 2000). A reflexive conversation thus seeks to focus attention on the tacit assumptions that shape practice. Atkinson and Heath suggest that a reflexive approach to research needs to encourage the consumers of research 'to be more open to the research process' (Atkinson and Heath 1987: 15), stressing the need not only to give direct access to the research 'data' but also to demonstrate how the researchers constructed their results from them and the premises they use. We would go further and argue that data can be given back to clinicians to help them to interrogate their own practices and generate new understandings. For example, transcripts of mundane clinical talk such as those used above can create distance and strangeness from everyday practices so that clinicians can consider whether there were alternative readings of cases and reflect on the range of warrants and rationalities they use.

Emotion

Putnam and Mumby see emotion as 'the process through which members constitute their work environment through negotiating a shared reality' (1993: 36). Tacit knowledge is thus framed within an emotional context which we can see illustrated in the examples above. By recognizing the central role of emotion in human reasoning (Damasio 1994), clinicians can be helped to debate some of the historically and culturally situated beliefs that shape their understandings. This is important if we are to foster an ethical practice.

Ethics

Our view of ethics stresses the role of emotions and particularly empathy for the humanity of others as the basis for ethical action. The approach here stresses the need to promote cooperation, mutual respect and justice and not to rationalize away feelings of empathy for others. This has implications for the process of governance, which should properly promote these values. These guidelines are therefore intended to be used in a way that opposes coercion and promotes mutual respect and cooperation.

One approach based on these principles was used in the case of the research into contact with parents mentioned above (Bilson and Barker 1994, 1995, 1998). The research was presented in a series of seminars in a way that addressed the emotions of participants through using case studies that showed the emotional significance of contact with parents and family. This approach helped to promote an acceptance of the difficulties the families faced. The seminars went on to reflect on the patterns of practice and the tacit understandings that underpinned them. This reflection allowed practitioners and managers to examine the tacit understandings that led to the different practices found in the study and to think about new approaches. A further follow-up study showed significantly higher levels of contact in all teams. Interestingly, in a neighbouring local authority the research was not presented back other than through providing a report and here no improvement was found in the follow-up study. In short we would assert that these principles can be used in a reflexive approach to governance as a means to encourage what Varela (1992) has called an attitude of compassionate concern.

Conclusion

> How can an attitude of ... compassionate concern be fostered and embodied in our culture? It obviously cannot be created merely through norms and rationalistic injunctions. It must be developed and embodied through disciplines that facilitate the letting-go of ... habits and enable compassion to become spontaneous and self-sustaining. It is not that there is no need for normative rules ... clearly such rules are a necessity in any society. It is that unless such rules are informed by the wisdom that enables them to be dissolved in the demands of responsivity to the particularity and immediacy of lived situations, the rules will become sterile, scholastic hindrances to compassionate action rather than conduits for its manifestation.
>
> (Varela 1992: 73–4)

It is easy for our arguments to be misread as a critique of all rationalistic forms of governance. That is not our intention. As Varela notes above, we are fully cognisant of the need for normative rules. However, we have argued that all aspects of practice, including the normative rules themselves, need to be open to revision in the face of the contingencies and ethical dilemmas of practice. We have proposed an alternative and complementary approach to the research process and its products, designed to make the familiar strange. Cultures have the capacity to sustain forms of professional reasoning which function as situated forms of common sense. These forms of reasoning have the tendency to shut down debate. Our intention has been to outline ways in which forms of popular wisdom may be dissolved if clinicians so choose on the basis of an ethical engagement with their work. We hope that the concepts and methods we have illustrated can help to provide clinicians themselves with a means to examine what they take for granted, so that they can let go of their habits if they so wish. We have sought to re-embody clinical judgement, challenge the sterility of rule-bound behaviour and give the responsibility for compassionate and creative action back to practitioners themselves.

Acknowledgements

White's research was supported by the ESRC grant number R000222892.

9 Telemedicine and Clinical Governance: Controlling Technology, Containing Knowledge

Maggie Mort, Carl May, Tracy Finch and Frances Mair

> The new information and communication technologies offer a major vehicle for modernization ... Few, if any, parts of our society will be able to opt out of the new information age. The Government is encouraging managerial and professional leaders throughout the public sector to embrace new technology in the drive to improve the quality, efficiency and convenience of services ... Opportunities in the field of telemedicine will be seized to remove distance from healthcare.
>
> (NHS Executive 1998)

> The challenge for the NHS is to harness the information revolution and use it to benefit patients.
>
> (Blair 1998)

In the publication of *Information for Health* (National Health Service Executive 1998) and the *NHS Plan* (Department of Health 2000a), the British government outlined a view of new technology as a major problem solver in the provision of health care and located technological change at the centre of a broad modernization agenda. Indeed, the current association of new technology with modernization resonates with Harold Wilson's claim that the 'white heat of technology' fired the expansion of his government's policy agenda. Contemporary health policy is no less optimistic about the potential for change, and is equally explicit about the need for a technocratic agenda. We find this agenda located firmly at the centre of policy and practice around ICTs (information and communication technologies). The development and implementation of telemedicine provides us with a point of departure for exploring this technological imperative and for developing an understanding of how it is moderated in practice around the codification and production of professional knowledge.

Telemedicine has vocal champions who make ambitious claims for its potential. In its potential impact on the NHS it has been likened to the discovery of antibiotics (McLaren 2001). Whatever the claims made by telemedicine's champions, as a field of policy and practice it is defined by struggles and contests between medicine and nursing, clinicians and managers, humans and machines and between public and privately funded health care services. But underpinning these are more subtle tensions: between forms of tacit and explicit knowledge, algorithmic and experiential learning and aggregated and contextual approaches to the formation of evidence. This chapter is about ways in which the field of telemedicine is a locus for these struggles and how they are oriented around problems of governance. The chapter draws on fieldwork since 1997 that has explored the development and implementation of a series of telemedicine projects and services. Our focus has been on the relationships between new technology and health. The work is multidisciplinary; however, the perspective offered here draws on insights from the field of science and technology studies within sociology.

Enrolling believers, agnostics and others

Telemedicine and telehealthcare are being promoted in the NHS through a series of policy documents and statements about the benefits of 'new technology' for patients. They are also being promoted by research and development funding under a variety of different programmes and initiatives. Importantly, the nature and form of the practices of promotion vary according to how close actors are to the sites of knowledge production about telemedicine. The authors of policy documents take a broad brush to telemedicine, eliding its problems; whilst clinical researchers give more ambivalent and fragmentary accounts. In our work, we find that the policy community discourse around telemedicine employs the most positive and unproblematic perspective, whilst the accounts of practitioners reflect ambivalence and uncertainty. There is an intermediate level of discourse too: technologists and systems developers' talk is stretched between the policy and practitioner communities, reflecting their membership of both.

In science and technology studies, the term enrolment is used to mean the definition and distribution of roles within a world of entities generated by an actor-network, in this case telemedicine and telehealthcare. The term is a useful one to apply to the emerging eHealth community because it encompasses the range of believers, sceptics and agnostics – those who are loyal, ambivalent or even outsiders. That is, *all* who have a position in the field are connected irrespective of the nature of their commitment to this new model of practice (Callon *et al.* 1986; Law 1989; Singleton and Michael 1993). For example, at the 2001 Telemedicine Symposium of the British Association of

Dermatologists speakers ranged from loyalist to ambivalent and in coffee breaks we heard informally from those we would class as 'resigned', i.e. clinicians with reservations but who believed that telemedicine was *inevitable* within their specialty. Also in this shifting field of health technology we find there are multiple enrolment processes taking place: some elements within eHealth are already asserting the 'death' of telemedicine and its integration into a broader field of global electronic health (Mea 2001). Indeed Gorm Kirsch, keynote videophone speaker at a recent eHealth conference, reflected this wider perspective when he told the participants: 'Healthcare is the world's largest industry, accounting for some three trillion US dollars annually ... yet this vast and essential industry is plagued by gross inefficiencies, inequities and quality variations. Many of these are directly attributable to poor information flow' (Kirsch 2001).

Defining telemedicine

We offer a simple definition of telemedicine for the purposes of this chapter: 'doing medicine at a distance' and 'employing technical artefacts to mobilize representations and information about patients'. This means the use of either *synchronous* systems that are analogous to business video-conferencing equipment; or *asynchronous* systems that store clinical data for subsequent transmission and review. However, the *definition* of telemedicine has itself become part of the debate about effectiveness. For example, Benger has observed (2001) that 'telemedicine is anything that doesn't work', implying that where telemedical applications have been absorbed into practice, they are seen as normal components of medical work, whereas if after a period of engagement they remain impractical, unworkable or obdurate, they stay in the distinct field of research.

The concept of distance in medicine is complex and changing. Distance has been introduced in the form of telephone, facsimile and post into medical practice without arousing controversy. Such technologies can be used conservatively or radically depending on the clinical context. Sending samples to pathology labs for testing is asynchronous, since representations of the patients on slides are transferred to enable decisions. Store and forward telemedicine mediates remote diagnosis electronically, dispensing with the need for on-site experts by the use of a new kind of *machine*. A conservative use of this technology would, for example, be an email referral to a consultant with attached images to aid in triage. Radical use may concern the remote diagnosis by image, where patient and expert do not meet.

Knowledge, evidence and workability

At the level of practice we therefore find that whatever the mode and technology being applied it is the situated, contextual and personal form of *knowledge* being mobilized that is at issue. Crucially, *knowledge* here is not about whether the machine works or not (sometimes it does, sometimes it does not) but is about the production of reliable *evidence* that meets particular externally defined normative standards. In this context, evidence about the machine is construed within R&D as being like evidence about a drug or treatment. This is the locus of the problem for clinician proponents of telemedicine. The duality of radical or conservative applications of, for example, store and forward adds to the evaluative confusion and also mirrors what we discuss below as the strong and weak programmes in telemedicine.

Of course it matters whether the machine works or not, but workability is negotiated in practice and this presents another problem for evaluators of telemedicine. The labour involved in making the machine work often remains invisible. At the level of detailed observation it is recognized that it is the complex interplay of explicit and tacit knowledge that makes technologies work (Roberts 2000). We will argue that this interplay is subtle and not amenable to the explicit evaluative tools which are held to be valid for judgements about effectiveness. Here we are concerned with what counts as reliable evidence and also whose knowledge counts in judgements about effectiveness, against a policy background which elides and conflates complexities within an unproblematic information for health agenda.

Weak and strong programmes in telemedicine?

Borrowing a concept developed within the sociology of scientific knowledge, we view the policy pronouncements and initiatives within the modernization agenda to represent what we take to be a weak programme, i.e. a view of telemedicine as a vehicle or tool for the delivery of services. Examples of this can be found in the conflation of information (neutral and beneficial) and telemedicine in the discourse, both unproblematically mobilized by information and computer technology. In this weak programme the content of medicine within telemedicine is not under consideration; rather it is the speeding-up, performance-enhancing and efficiency-strengthening role of access to information which is privileged. In contrast, the Research and Development mode exemplified by Health Technology Assessment programmes represents strong programmes, i.e. telemedicine as a development in medical science which should be tested and evaluated according to scientific norms which produce evidence from rationalist philosophy. (For a discussion of the strong (and weak) programme in the sociological analysis of science see Bloor (1976) and Woolgar (1988) and in health policy see Ashmore *et al.* (1989) and Bartley (1990)).

Whilst operating in distinct political and epistemological frameworks, both weak and strong programme members can be said to be proponents of the telemedicine movement. The policy makers are proponents because they align the adoption of healthcare-at-a-distance with reducing waiting lists/ times and more broadly with the discourse around modernization. The clinical R&D community participants are largely proponents because they spend time and resources trying to test these new technologies against notions of equivalence, convergence and replicability in clinical science. In this way telemedicine becomes reified, cohered around communities of practice which enable clinicians to mobilize projects to build specialized expertise and sectional interests and enable developers and manufacturers to design, trial and sell.

Our work indicates that the dynamic nature of telemedicine often fails to lend itself to rationalist gold standard RCT research where a high degree of stasis and control is required over data collection (May and Ellis 2001). In this way the strong programme contains important weaknesses. Such, however, is the normative, technologically determinist framing of telemedicine by policy makers and industry, that some researchers from the strong programme may describe themselves as Luddites whilst making presentations which report the often poor or ambiguous data deriving from telemedical trials or pilot projects. In addition, some clinicians who favour the strong programme view appear to be particularly tolerant of less scientifically rigorous studies which nevertheless support either further research projects or implementation of telemedicine. This latter group, in experiencing what seems to be an uncomfortable journey between science and technology, begins to align telemedicine with beliefs about the neutrality of technological change, and such actors can be found sharing conference platforms with weak programme policy makers. Indeed, the overwhelmingly positive, optimistic policy statements about telemedicine (weak programme) coupled with the often ambivalent reports of clinical trials (strong programme) are beginning to lead some actors from the telehealthcare industry (such as Greenaway 2001) to propose the abandonment of R&D and trials in favour of roll-out.

Actors who perceive telemedicine to be primarily about *medicine* appear most likely to express ambivalence about large-scale implementation, whilst those who perceive it to be about *technology*, defined as a tool for delivery, a vehicle for health care, are most likely to become advocates for roll-out. We are reminded here of the 'certainty trough' described in MacKenzie's (1990) account of the development of missile technologies in the US: where programme loyalists displayed low levels of uncertainty, whilst engineers themselves expressed heightened awareness of contingency and complexity. In this context our certainty trough would look like this:

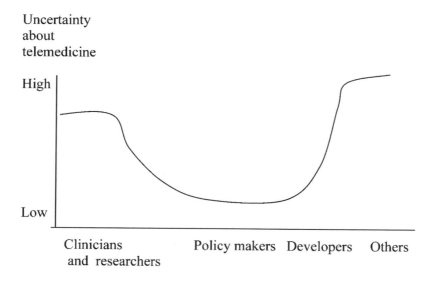

Figure 9.1 Expressions of uncertainty by actors in telemedicine
Source: MacKenzie 1990

There are of course others who are marginalized by both the strong and weak programmes in telemedicine but whom we find to be included, co-opted or coerced in some way into the programme. Most notable here are patients whose participation in the programmes exists largely as respondents to the ubiquitous Patient Satisfaction Questionnaires which accompany the major-ity of telemedicine projects and the health services researchers, co-opted to deliver these non-clinical components of the work that focus on users' views. Also on the outside are those obdurate actors who perceive a rather sinister agenda of depersonalizing, deskilling and dumbing down of health care. Linked with these are those critics of telemedicine who highlight problems involving fragmentation of the patient, of skills (Mort *et al.* 2003) and of medicine itself.

Somewhere in between the loyalists and the others a more pragmatic, contextualized approach exists, often linked explicitly with constructions of rurality, in which the goal is improved access to health care from a position of spatial deprivation, e.g. telemedicine in developing countries and for remote communities. Ironically, telemedicine projects are most often to be found focused on (sub)urban spaces, where there is a ready supply of patients, yet much is made in the telemedicine literature of the promise of remote consultations for addressing health inequalities in rural areas.

Occlusion of practice

The growing failure of traditional rationalist research to prove the efficacy of telemedicine and telehealthcare, and the current push for roll-out within the modernization agenda are in danger of underestimating the serious concerns of clinicians and patients about quality (Mowatt *et al.* 1997). At the level of practice this research failure is also in danger of ignoring the dynamism of local innovation and possibilities for interpretive flexibility which we find taking place on the ground. Such creative practices, we argue, remain invisible to large multi-centre trials, or evaluations based on notions of convergence or replicability, or questionnaires, that is invisible to the dominant knowledge-producing instruments adopted for telemedicine. How these telemedicine technologies get used in day-to-day practice is either not recorded or becomes tidied away for the journal article or conference presentation. In the example given below we find this enacted in the difference between the nursing and medical approach to practice. In nurse-led schemes, the nurses are required to engage with, manipulate, even subvert systems in order to make them work. Developers often see and work with this ground-level creativity and dynamism, but they are not members of the constituency of knowledge producers (at telehealth conferences they often remain in the demonstration halls with their trade stands). This interpretive flexibility can also remain invisible to doctors whose work is assumed to be 'further down the line'. This division of labour within the development and practice of telemedicine projects contributes, we believe, to underestimation of complexity and to the ultimate poor quality of evaluations.

In contrast, a minority of developers are beginning to reject large-scale technological fixes, preferring to develop technologies from contextualized, situated knowledge, prompted by the increasing number of 'failed' projects. This approach recognizes that technologies which are marketed 'off the shelf' or transferred unproblematically around very different settings are the most likely to fail because these ignore the tacit, situated knowledge which ultimately makes systems work in practice.

By drawing on empirical data from a longitudinal study and using some other fieldwork material we aim to show how these perspectives appear and are enacted through contact with the *materials* of mobility, i.e. the telemedicine systems themselves and the complex interactions which can be observed. These interactions, both human-to-human, and human-to-machine-to-human, may furnish us with ideas for a theoretical framework for the adoption of telemedicine systems. However, the purpose here is to elucidate the struggles to produce and maintain evidence and to control expertise, in a moving context where technology and power are deeply enmeshed.

The struggle to produce evidence

The following extracts are taken from an interview with a senior clinician who is leading a large trial of a telemedical intervention. It shows a catalogue of difficulties involved in shaping, holding down and containing the study in order to produce evidence. The italicized emphases are ours and entries in square brackets indicate where we have had to anonymize the data.

Clinician: . . . far simpler than the project we're actually doing, which *is suicidally complicated*. The original intention of this project was to do a three-way trial of telemedicine for new adult cases . . . The clinical outcome was intended to be judged on the basis that all patients, whatever the modality, would be seen face-to-face by a second consultant. One of the weaknesses I think of the study is that *we were never able to ensure that that could be done immediately*, so they're booked in as fast as we can put them in, but it's still a few weeks . . . a significant weakness, but the logic of it is that *there aren't any [consultants]*. It's all very well saying 'buy them in' but there aren't any to buy . . . and the clinical question made it very challenging as well because what we were saying was, we were not just saying we want to look at a certain difference, we're actually looking at *the test of equivalence*, the question we're saying is that in effect the clinician has to be persuaded that [the system] is useful, it should *be no less effective than that for the patients, so it's going to be the same*. We're not bothered whether it's better, we think it's highly unlikely that it'll be better, but *the issue is the stability*, and is for those who decide they can manage it that way that it's got to be *no less effective*. So that actually puts very *challenging sample sizes*, it makes the sample sizes for the full trial [high number] patients. We're at [much lower number] at the moment in total so I think *we're highly unlikely to get anywhere near it*. We did intend an interim analysis when we'd got to say [a higher number] in each of the store-and-forward and the control group with a view to saying is it already obvious that store-and-forward is inferior in which case we don't proceed with the other patients in effect. At the moment it's quite likely that that's all we'll be able to do because although we've got eight [sites] who refer 60 or 70 patients a month *they're only recruiting a small proportion of the patients they refer* ... it raises a very big issue of whether the studies, including ours, are in *any way representative of what would happen in real life* anyway. The clinical effectiveness is based on *agreement on management between the two consultants*, and we've still got to do a certain amount of work on the early cases to actually make that operational ... description of clinical dermatology but they all accept that it's the management that matters and not the diagnosis.

Question: *So management would be more important than diagnosis?*

Clinician: We're collecting data on both. And we've *got to decide what do we call agreement on either*, and we still haven't gone into that, we're going to do that with the ... data, actually look and say *what do we think constitutes, actually we'll probably end up using more than one level*. And we've also asked them to commit themselves to a *scale of certainty* about the diagnosis, just a ... 1 to 5, 'absolutely certain' to 'haven't the faintest idea really but wrote that down' ... sort of ... *you can't say it's terribly meaningful but it gives you some idea* of how each individual is responding ... the only [consultant] who's been using the store-and-forward so far ... has said that he finds quite a lot of them unacceptable. There is a facility for him to say 'the [images] are no good, take some more', but *he's tended not to use that*, he's tended to just transfer the management I think. So we're actually *considering replacing the cameras* ... It was a challenge to get it on to one side of A4 ... we've actually got in effect basically four different sorts of conditions, which are [names] or, there's an interesting group who've got no signs at the time they're seen and they, intermittent type things, so we've got scope for that ... a different section of the form for each. So it's *structured but it's very limited, because we're trying to keep it on one side (of paper)*. It's not rocket science, believe me. But *if you've got a 3 or 4 page questionnaire, GPs aren't going to use it.*

The respondent here outlines a series of problems about generating reliable knowledge common to many telemedicine projects. The problems he refers to include: complexity of study design; movability in both time and technology; judgements about equivalence; recruitment biases; artificiality of the trial; uncertainty in diagnosis; persuading reluctant actors; and pragmatism in data collection. Few of these problematic features would, we suggest, survive into the scientific journal articles which will eventually appear, because they are all issues which become surmounted using tacit rather than explicit skills. The skills involved will thus remain invisible. But, crucially, the position that this respondent adopts is also ambiguous: he moves between strong and weak programme positions, and between loyalist and ambivalent perspectives. In doing so, he represents a key problem for those producing knowledge on the ground. It is not clear whether he is aggressively testing a medical technology, a treatment, or a new means of service organization and delivery. He moves between different points on the compass of health services research, uncertain about whether he is working to *extend* or *contain* the field of telehealthcare.

Controlling data

The problems described above are echoed by many other respondents who have discussed the evaluation of telemedicine. For these researchers, undertaking the project becomes an exercise in controlling the trial: controlling data flow, controlling participants (in this case referring clinicians), controlling time, controlling technology, and controlling agreement about what is normatively 'good' diagnosis and management. The first respondent's comment that 'the issue is stability' seems to crystallize the problem.

Many telemedicine projects face problems in building and maintaining a research team. Such teams are often multidisciplinary and each research project may bring different perspectives about types and methods of data collection to the study. The following extract describes a struggle about the legitimacy of different kinds of data which took place in research project meetings, namely the marginalization of patient views:

> Researcher: It's very interesting that in any meetings we've had it's [the component of the study] been sidelined – the qualitative aspect and patient satisfaction ... the main outcomes very much have been the clinical equivalence between a control and a store-and-forward consultation, and the economics, and they see that as primary ... it's been buried, it's not an important outcome really and I think it's a shame.

Again, patient satisfaction is described very much as added onto the central framework of the controlled trial and is constructed quantitatively to align with the perceived scientific norms of the research mode:

> Researcher: The proposal was accepted on the basis that we did a questionnaire. ... it was given to me that that was what we

> had to do ... there had been some studies that had shown the reliability and validity of [factor X], so that's why we decided on that ... now I just feel embarrassed with it because I just feel it's not reflecting anything ... I just feel it will give a very broad area but I think it will just come back out with what every other telemedicine questionnaire has, 90 per cent are going to be satisfied with it and that's it.

Patients are not asked about the *content* of telemedicine or its outcomes, but about their experience of the service, of the mode of delivery or mode of diagnosis, typically if they minded 'having their photograph taken' and whether they prefer 'telemedicine' or face-to-face consultation (they usually prefer the latter; Mair and Whitten 2000). Patients are asked about the technology or the tele-clinics but not the *medicine*:

> Researcher: I don't think there's any real difference; obviously there is different experience, but general experience there is just that compared with the control group who are just receiving the traditional care, and them going up to the [hospital] and receiving two consultations rather than just the one, so they're getting two opinions, which I think is quite nice for them, if the diagnoses match; if it's not they're feeling a bit peeved because they don't know which one to believe.

These different perspectives are often reinforced by divisions of labour which can in themselves create uncertainties and misunderstandings. One of the most frequent of these divisions of research labour is between medicine and nursing and is discussed more fully in the examples below.

Containing technology

In another project digital images of the (partial) patient were taken by a specialist nurse in outreach clinics in primary care. The images were to be accompanied by an online pro-forma on which the nurse was to record the patient's history. This combined 'information' was stored and read later by the consultants who were to make a diagnosis and management plan in the absence of the patient.

> Nurse 1: I do put acne under 'rashes', simply because it does fall in to the question you're asking, but I've used it a few times and, like you say, you just make it up as you go along and sometimes you feel afterwards – that's something they're

looking into for me – after the patient's gone once you've got all the information you log off then, you go on to your next patient, sometimes you think 'I forgot to ask them that', or 'I asked them that but I've not documented it' and you can't go back in, so you can't add information.

The online datasheet was constructed to be the *explicit* version of the medical consultation and so contained pre-set questions with tick boxes. The nurse here is talking about putting what she considers to be one condition under the box officially designated for another condition. It became obvious in practice that the preconstructed tick boxes did not relate to the 'live' issues as they arose. Another problem was that the pro-forma 'locked up' and couldn't be accessed once the consultation ended. There was a very small space in which nurses could write in free text to record their situated impressions or extra details which the patient wanted to convey. But this space was at first hard to locate and its status has remained ambiguous within the pro-forma as a whole. Significantly, after the first round of clinics, this 'free text box' was expanded and its use became more significant:

Nurse 2:   The referral note there is free text, so I can write whatever I want. Whether or not they decide to read it at the end or skim through it or read it, I feel I can put everything I feel is necessary down. So if the questions on the history don't fit, if there's something in there I think it doesn't fit in there; they may have already been referred to the department ten years ago and had treatment, there's nowhere to put that, but I can put it in the free text.

Question: *Why would you use that free text?*

Nurse 1:   For any information, like for example (I'm trying to think of someone I've seen today) ... a chap who was concerned about [name of symptom]. There was nowhere in the set text for me to put down that he's worked abroad, he was in the navy, he was concerned because his dad has got [name of disease], had two [previous episodes]. So it's things like that, additional information, which I've not been able to put anywhere else. And the patient's point of view. I put down he was really concerned about this and I also gave him, because he was going on holiday, some ... advice.

What emerged in this project was that the nurses were using an inflexible telemedicine system but adapting it to reflect the needs of a face-to-face encounter with the patient, by making use of free text and by, for example, shifting the identity of particular symptoms. In the advice giving, they also stepped out of the mechanistic role created for them by the project design, in order to accommodate the needs of the patient. This *interpretive flexibility* has since disappeared in the official evaluation of the project as it has emerged in publications and conference presentations:

> Dermatologist: I personally think that the nurse was in a frustrating position. Really I think her role there is obsolete. We need to get the information transferred by the doctor himself, [images made] by the doctor or the practice nurse but it has to be done in the practice and then the information has to be sent over. A skilled nurse is probably better off looking at nurse-run clinics.

A space existed on the pro-forma for 'Nurse Opinion' and in spite of the fact that there was reportedly a high concordance between the nurse diagnosis and the consultant diagnosis, this data is ambiguous and so far remains un-analysed.

> Nurse 3: So we've had to wait for some figures, so some of this is best guestimates, the nursing thing we reckon about 80 per cent of nursing opinion was right ... It might be a bit higher than that ... And that's why we haven't got those figures, because it looks to me like they audited and they picked out how many they'd seen and I asked if they'd got the nursing fig-ures whilst they were doing it, because I'd already asked if they'd pick out the information for me, and they said they'd not done that yet and I've just got the feeling it might possibly have been forgotten.

Another example of interpretive flexibility during the running time of this project occurred during a waiting list crisis. To improve the throughput of patients, the nurse manager arranged for the telemedicine equipment to be used in the hospital using some extra nurse-led sessions. Whilst this could not be counted as part of the project, because of the original research design, it was an example of flexibility at the level of practice that has also remained invisible to the evaluation of the telemedicine system as a whole:

> Nurse 3: That was because of waiting lists. Even though the project had been running for some time and we'd looked at a number of waiting list initiatives in order to reduce the numbers of patients, we were actually under a lot of pressure from the hit squads that were going to come in and look at areas that weren't getting their waiting lists down, and we

were one of them. So in desperation, it does seem a bit silly I have to say – and I think it was my idea actually – in that if I freed up the nurses for some additional sessions, 'how about running them here?', so the patient, although they're coming in to the centre they'll still get seen and they're off the waiting list basically because that's classed as their first appointment, and then at least if there's a problem with anything they're on site and they could always get the dermatologist to have a quick look at them. So that's what we did.

Question: *Those clinics weren't part of the project, so they're not counted in the 600 or anything?*

Nurse 3: No, those were taken out. We didn't book many of those actually, just a few, just to try and get the numbers down a bit more.

The problem of interpretive flexibility is an important one. In this section we have seen that it is not simply the definition and construction of reliable knowledge that is at issue, but also how activities are defined as meriting the status of knowledge production. Local innovations have no place in trial methodologies: indeed, they undermine the very notion of a trial, with its strict construction of acceptable practices. But the whole business of *development* runs through the trials with which we are concerned, whilst the trial protocols 'fix' the system in place and define the activities that are to be undertaken; they also permit us to identify the practices that make up these local innovations.

In these last three extracts we see creative practice, stretching of boundaries and interpretive flexibility, all of which helped to make the telemedicine system work, but all of which will not 'count' at the end of the day in an evaluation of effectiveness. We argue that this partly reflects what the first respondent (from a different project) described as the need for stability.

Concluding remarks

Discussion of telemedicine and clinical governance is suffused with contradiction and paradox. Each telemedicine project to some extent constructs what is medicine and what is technology within its local context, yet must produce evidence seen to be legitimate within the wider framework demands of evidence-based medicine and clinical governance. Meeting the demands of evidence-based medicine requires robust programme researchers to engage in extensive 'heterogeneous engineering' (i.e. the management and control of disparate elements and their shaping into a network; Law 1989). Paradoxically, weak programme proponents seem less concerned about evidence than about modernization and roll-out of unproblematic 'new tools'. If the demands of clinical governance (a domain requiring forms of evidence which we have already seen to be problematic) place too high a burden upon telemedicine and telehealthcare then we may see roll-out taking place using other criteria. Such criteria may include where there is failure to recruit consultant specialists, meeting waiting list/time pressures, in constructing 'partnership' with private sector providers and more broadly in configuring the future patient, responsible and skilled in self-management (Kendall 2001).

In practice telemedicine is dynamic in the sense that it is changing and moving and being interpreted all the time. What is needed is stability, control, containment, if anything is to be assessed, measured, evaluated for the EBM agenda. What is needed for roll-out is a homogeneity in practice which our fieldwork indicates is unworkable. We argue that meeting both these sets of demands has the effect of silencing and rendering invisible practices and features of trials and projects which get in the way of such measurement or roll-out. This in turn has the effect of reinforcing existing hierarchies and power relations, e.g. between forms of knowledge generation, between nursing and medicine, between health services and patients.

Acknowledgement

We are grateful to Nikki Shaw for her contribution to our work.

10 Affect, Anecdote and Diverse Debates: User Challenges to Scientific Rationality

Marian Barnes

Both the theory and practice of user involvement and public participation are becoming more sophisticated. Contemporary public policy in the UK prioritizes the direct involvement of citizens, both individually and collectively, as a means of: achieving better public services; increasing the legitimacy of decision-making; revitalizing democracy; creating responsible citizens; and resolving major policy problems (Barnes and Prior 2000). Such a range of purposes or aspirations implies a wide range of practices. But *how* to do public participation is still a challenge for many public officials trained to assume that their task was to act as the expert. Whilst the health service came rather later to such practices than some other parts of the public sector, since the early 1990s there has been an explosion of initiatives to engage with service users, citizens and communities within diverse arenas across the NHS. It is now official policy to involve users and the public throughout the health system in relation to a range of processes and practices, including research and development, clinical governance, community development for health, and shared decision-making within clinical encounters (Barnes 1999; Department of Health 2000a; Hanley *et al.* 2000). What is less clear is that such initiatives have led to a real challenge to professional decision-making.

Theories of deliberative democracy are increasingly utilized to distinguish the democratic potential of participatory models of decision-making from traditional models of representative democracy. However, deliberative democracy also has its critics and there is considerable evidence that the practice does not (and critics would say cannot) live up to the potential claimed for it. In this chapter I want to consider three factors which are insufficiently theorized in the context of deliberation, applying this in particular to a health services and health policy context:

1 affect – the role of emotion within the process of debate;
2 anecdote – the nature and role of story telling;
3 diverse debates – the potential for deliberative spaces to engage with cultural difference.

Deliberative democracy

Proponents of deliberative democracy point to the lack of attention given to deliberation in standard theories of democracy and highlight the necessity for a conception and practice of democracy which includes discussion of moral disagreement (Gutmann and Thompson 1996). Dryzek (1994) argues that liberal notions of democracy are associated with voting, strategy, private interests, bargaining, exchange, spectacle and limited involvement. In contrast, participatory modes of democracy emphasize politics that are discursive, educational, oriented to truly public interest and 'needful of active citizenship' (1994: 13). Fishkin (1991) suggests that the closer a democracy gets to the ideal of deliberation at every level within the political process the more complete it is.

Deliberative democracy aims to develop the capacity of citizens to take part in public debate by providing opportunities to engage in critical reflection. It can generate a stronger democracy with citizens empowered in relation to both politicians *and* bureau-professionals. Many of the critical issues of public policy require access to knowledge which has traditionally been restricted to particular scientific or knowledge communities. The practice of deliberative democracy is intended to open such knowledge to lay scrutiny, as well as to open up political arenas to more direct processes of citizen involvement. Thus citizens' juries and related deliberative practices have been held in relation to issues such as: genetic technology (Dunkerley and Glasner 1998); waste disposal (Petts 1997, 2001); the future of agriculture and the food system (Wakeford 1999); as well as a range of policy issues facing local government and the NHS (LGMB 1996; Coote and Lenaghan 1997; McIver 1997; Barnes 1999b). Such practices are based in a belief that the issues such problems raise are not solely technical. They are political and ethical: concerned as much with what sort of society we want to create as with decisions about the most efficient way of dealing with particular problems. The issues raised within clinical governance clearly fall within this arena.

The design of deliberative processes is often intended to enable lay people to access and debate technical information rather than enabling technical experts and politicians to access lay or experiential knowledge. Thus citizens' juries are based around the presentation of 'expert evidence' by witnesses who are then questioned by citizen jurors. The jurors subsequently debate amongst themselves their response to the evidence they have heard, before coming up with a consensus view and recommendations for action. Renn *et al.* (1993) base their conceptual model for participatory decision-making on the need to integrate three types of knowledge: 'knowledge based on common sense and personal experience; knowledge based on technical expertise, and knowledge derived from social interests and advocacy' (1993: 190).

In order to achieve this integrative potential, deliberative democracy theorists have emphasized a process of rational debate amongst equals (e.g. Fishkin 1991). Rationality in decision-making is regarded as being the overarching achievement of the Enlightenment. Its priority as a basis on which administrative systems should be built was accompanied by an objectivist basis for scientific method which continues to define the way in which evidence is judged (albeit under increasing challenge from within academia as well as from the user perspectives which are the subject of this chapter, e.g. Harrison (1998) and this book). The theoretical underpinning of deliberative democracy derives from Habermas's work on communicative rationality (1984). Habermas was interested not only in how the state could improve the legitimacy of its decision-making, but also in how the dominance of scientific rationality in the organization of society could be challenged. Communicative rationality was considered to have such a potential through the development of practices enabling different ways of knowing to communicate with each other and thus enhance the potential for cooperation between people. Such practices require free and equal participation in the public sphere in a discourse about socio-political or practical issues. Such participation in turn demands communicative competence. Webler (1995) has defined four elements to communicative competence: '*cognitive competence* – the ability of an individual to master the rules of formal logic; *speech competence* – mastery of linguistic rules; *pragmatic competence* – mastery of pragmatic rules; and *role competence* – mastery of rules for interaction' (1995: 44).

Thompson and Hoggett (2001) have argued that it is not possible to understand the process of deliberative democracy solely in terms of rational debate between free and equal citizens. They suggest it is equally important to address the issue of group emotions within deliberative forums such as citizens' juries. This is an important counterbalance to the overemphasis on the rationality of deliberative processes. But here I want to develop a rather different analysis of the significance of emotion in the process of dialogue in the particular context of health services and health policy. This concerns the emotions which participants might bring to the process of deliberation, rather than those generated by the process itself.

Affect

In an evaluation of a citizens' jury held in Belfast to consider the future patterns of health and social service in Northern Ireland (Barnes 1999b), one of the 'expert witnesses', a health service manager, expressed some disappointment that she was unable to gauge the real feelings of jurors about the topic being discussed. She compared this with the experience of public meetings in which there is often considerable heat and anger in the discussion, but it is clear that the views being expressed are intensely felt and derive from particular experiences which have motivated people to attend the meeting. She suggested that the jurors were putting questions to her because that was what they were there to do, rather than because this was something they really wanted to know about.

Observations of the jury in action suggested that, by and large, the deliberative process was successful in enabling complex issues to be explored and the jurors were largely satisfied that the process had enabled differences of view to be expressed. On those topics on which jurors did deliberate in some depth, different views were expressed, different perspectives offered and initial ideas were clarified and distinguished as a result. There was evidence of increased understanding as well as increased knowledge and this had caused some people to reflect on pre-existing views and to draw different conclusions. However, it is not clear how any fundamental difference or conflict between jurors might have been addressed. Interviews with jurors conducted for the evaluation suggested that the contributions of two jurors had provoked some feelings of antagonism, but there was little overt expression of this during the conduct of the jury. The imperative to reach a resolution within a specified time period may have caused jurors to emphasize consensus rather than difference, but one juror also implied that the fear of conflict within Northern Ireland is so great that people may have been very wary of opening up any possibility of difference along religious lines.

There are two points which arise from this. First, it is possible that fear of conflict may have closed down avenues for exploration within the jury as Thompson and Hoggett (2001) have suggested. But the other point goes to the heart of deliberative processes such as citizens' juries in which there is a deliberate attempt not only to bring together a cross-section of the population to engage in debate, but also to deliberately exclude people who might have any 'special interest' from the deliberative process. In this respect, proponents of citizens' juries have claimed their superiority over public meetings, precisely because the intensely felt views of those who tend to go to such meetings can get in the way of rational debate (e.g. Crosby 1996). What is the implication of excluding from citizens' juries precisely those people who have a real (personal) interest in the topic under discussion?

If we consider other spaces within which deliberation takes place in order to inform health policy-making and service delivery, it becomes clear that it is neither possible nor helpful to exclude emotionality from the process of debate. In considering what types of knowledge participatory decision-making requires Renn *et al.* (1993) distinguish common sense and personal experience from social interests and advocacy. In their model 'social interests and advocacy' are drawn on in order to identify the full range of concerns and objectives which need to be considered within the decision-making processes.

This is the first stage of the process. The second stage is to subject to scrutiny the concerns and evaluative criteria derived from stage 1, with the objective of reconciling 'conflicts about factual evidence and [reaching] an expert consensus via direct confrontation among a heterogeneous, preferably representative, sample of experts in the field' (1993: 191). The third and final stage is the evaluation of the various options resulting from the first two stages by one or more randomly selected groups of citizens. In this model the three types of knowledge are given priority in three different stages. It is a process designed to ensure that the 'special interests' that form the starting point for the whole process are subject to two different types of scrutiny which will filter out the inherent bias within them.

But this filtering process can serve to remove from the process exactly those types of knowledge which can only come from those who have a 'special interest'. The experience of living with illness and of receiving services is an experience which contains many emotional components. It is precisely these emotional, affective experiences which can only be brought to the process of deliberation by those who have experienced them. The authenticity of such experiences derives from having a special interest in them. The motivation of many of those who take part in processes of consultation around service design and delivery is precisely so that their experiences can inform future developments from which others may benefit. But many health professionals find emotionality very difficult to deal with and consider that it is not something that has a legitimate place within dialogic processes.

One example of this comes from an excellent study of consumer participation in policy-making in relation to community mental health services in Ontario, Canada (Church 1996). In this instance, official members of a committee experienced considerable discomfort when consumers or survivors of mental health services expressed pain and anger during the process of discussion. Whilst the committee had set up a series of meetings with the express purpose of inviting survivors to speak about their lives, the actual experience of this was sometimes something official members were unable to handle:

> My [the researcher's] strongest memory here is of a young woman who told the subcommittee a painful story of her life both in and outside of hospital. In the awkward silence which followed she began to cry. 'It's no good for you to send committees', she lamented. 'Unless you actually *do* something, the next time you come back I'll be dead.'
>
> (1996: 33)

The invitation to survivors to speak offered an opportunity for them to express the real issues for them in their lives. Since these did not necessarily fit within the framework determined by the committee, some members tried to reject these 'horror stories' as beyond their remit. Another way in which members of the committee tried to deal with the unaccustomed emotionality of the proceedings was by constructing the behaviour of survivors as 'bad manners':

> Members lived a palpable tension between the emotional turbulence of participants' experiences and a code of professional etiquette which implicitly defines emotionality as irrational. This was the ground for much of the contestation between professionals/bureau-crats and consumers/survivors. Could survivor stories, issues and style of presentation be deemed 'rational' and thereby become more broadly discussible as part of the institutional agenda? The battle over this question is present in my transcript material as a major debate over 'manners'.
>
> (1996: 39)

There was evidence of a similar inability to take on board the emotional impact of the experience of receiving services in a study of a mental health services user council in which I was involved. In this instance the anger of service users about what they saw as an infringement of human rights in the way in which they were treated was constructed as 'ignorance' by a senior psychiatrist in the hospital concerned. His suggestion was that users needed to become better informed about the role and responsibilities of psychiatry before they could make legitimate claims about the nature of their experiences of it (Barnes and Wistow 1994).

A rather different perspective on the issue of affect within deliberative forums comes from studies which have sought to explore the impact of involvement in them on participants. One issue which emerges from such studies is the importance of the personal impact of participation, almost regardless of any evidence of objective outcomes from their involvement. This has been evident in studies of, for example, older people's involvement in user panels (Barnes and Bennett 1998), of carers' involvement (Barnes and Wistow 1993) and of mental health service users' involvement (Barnes and Shardlow 1997). Whilst personal benefits can be mitigated by a failure to observe any real change, the immediate experience of having experiences valued, of sharing experiences and learning from each other, and of developing skills and confidence, suggests that deliberative processes should be designed in order to maximize such intrinsic benefits to participants. Whilst it is important to distinguish 'therapy' from 'empowerment' in terms of the objectives of such processes, neither the process nor its outcomes can be understood solely in terms of rationality or instrumentality.

Anecdote

When people who use services have the opportunity to engage in dialogue with health professionals, they tell their own, their families' or friends' stories. They recount their histories of illness and its impact on their lives; they tell others what happened to them when they were being assessed, or waiting to be discharged from hospital, or about their day-to-day encounters with the home help or distinct nurse. As we have seen above, sometimes those stories can be painful to tell and to hear. When service users tell those stories amongst others who have similar experiences – because they all use the same service, they are all older people making frequent use of the same type of service, all people who have been given a psychiatric diagnosis, or all people who play a role in supporting friends or family members who are ill or disabled – they compare experiences, look for similarities which confirm what happened to them and receive some comfort from the fact that they are not alone.

In some circumstances exchanging experiences can lead to the development of a collective story which encompasses key aspects of those experiences. In the older people's user panels referred to above, the telling of stories about difficult experiences of hospital discharge led to a distillation in the form of what good practice would look like (Barnes and Cormie 1995). For the benefit of service providers this was expressed as a series of indicators, but one can imagine how this could also have been told as a contrasting story to the one which panel members recounted from their own experiences. In other contexts the collective story has been told through drama or other explicit forms of story telling. For example, a research project exploring the experiences of mental health service users as victims of crime was reported through the medium of a play and a video recording. Whilst the precise events in the play were made up in that they were not a depiction of actual experiences of any of the people who took part in the research, the play communicated the nature of the experiences which the research had uncovered, and what they meant to the people concerned.

Even when people are telling an individual, personal story this is not simply a process of recounting what happened. Through recounting, story tellers are engaged in an active process of making sense of the experience. They are engaged in a process of reflection and interpretation for themselves, as well as a purposeful performance directed at the hearer – they want to achieve an impact. As in the case of the young woman in Ontario (quoted above) they are looking for a response to what they have offered. Narratives are not simply a description of events that have taken place; they are created within a particular context and for a particular purpose.

> Narratives mean to be provocative. They request a different response
> from the audience than denotative prose. Narrative offers meaning
> through evocation, image, the mystery of the unsaid. It persuades by
> seducing the listener into the world it portrays, unfolding events in a
> suspense-laden time in which one wonders what will happen next.
>
> (Mattingly 1998: 8)

If the nature and purpose of narratives are not recognized by the listener,
however, the value of stories may be dismissed. One response to the older
people's panels was that they were simply producing what were dismissed as
anecdotes. Those of us working with the project used to speculate amongst
ourselves: 'how many anecdotes make a fact?', because we were being asked:
'how many people said that?' There appeared to be some implicit break point
at which service providers considered an experience had been recounted
sufficiently frequently to be believable. But this misses the point of narratives,
which are a process through which people are making sense of events that
have happened to them, rather than a means of trying to determine how
prevalent a particular experience may be.

The value of narrative has been recognized within some types of clinical
practice, in work with children with fluid backgrounds to recreate their life
experiences, as well as a means of conducting interpretative research (e.g.
Booth and Booth 1994; Etherington 2000; Middleton and Hewitt 2000). Story
telling is being used as a means by which service users seek to enable others to
understand their lives and experiences (e.g. Barker *et al.* 1999; Leibrich 1999).
It is also necessary for the theory and practice of deliberation to be able to
accommodate narrative as well as rational argument if different types of
knowledge are genuinely to be included within the process of debate.

Conclusion: diverse debates

People whose motivation to take part in such discussions is to contribute their
experiential knowledge, based in experiences which include strong emotional
aspects, may find means other than rational, disinterested debate more effective in communicating their messages. Critics of deliberative democracy
have argued that it ignores both the cultural and social differences of those
the practice seeks to engage (e.g. Young 1990). The concept of 'communicative competence' is a normative one with the potential to exclude those
considered incapable of achieving such competence – Webler (1995) suggests
this may include people with mental illness as well as those unable to use
language – and those whose norms of communication may be different from
the dominant culture. It is significant that many of these critiques have come
from feminist writers and from new social movement theorists. Young (2000)

has developed her critique of the prioritization of 'argument' within deliberation by emphasizing the important not only of narrative, but also of rhetoric and greeting as styles of communication necessary to a deliberative democracy which is inclusive rather than exclusive.

Within mainstream political science literature much of the debate about how to ensure that different groups have a voice in decision-making is expressed in terms of representation or presence (e.g. Phillips 1995; Rao 2000). This is also the case in debates within health services about practical user or public involvement initiatives and was evident within most of the examples of public participation in local government and health service contexts studied by Barnes *et al.* (2003). The significance of representation in legitimating public participation forums was evident in the discourse of citizen participants as well as that of public officials. This led to considerable attention being given to who was taking part in the forums and how they were recruited. But much less attention was given to the way in which a process of deliberation could be designed to ensure that a diverse group of participants could bring to the table issues *they* wanted to talk about and could discuss those issues in a way which was genuinely inclusive.

In this chapter I have drawn from a range of theoretical literatures and from examples of some very different types of practice in order to argue the need for a theory and practice of user participation in health policy-making capable of including diverse voices and experiences. I have suggested that mainstream ideas and practices of deliberative democracy cannot sufficiently accommodate the reality of emotional experience and the role this needs to play in developing policy and practice. I have also argued that story telling should be regarded as not only legitimate, but essential to the development of understanding as well as knowledge through processes of exchange between officials and service users. What are the practical implications of such a position?

I have suggested that dialogue between officials and the public is often weighted in terms of imparting official knowledge to the public and providing opportunity for that to be questioned, debated and possibly challenged. This can be an emotionally charged experience for professionals who are used to occupying positions of authority. For example, some of the witnesses I interviewed in an evaluation of citizens' juries described themselves as being 'unsure or 'frightened' and one as 'terrified' at the prospect of such questioning. But one of the implications of my current argument is that there needs to be at least equal space for the process to be reversed. The example from Ontario of a policy-making committee inviting users/survivors of mental health services to come to speak to them is an example of an attempt to do this, but one which created many problems for both groups. As the committee's work progressed, involving ongoing collaboration between officials and survivors, tensions remained and were reinforced by the fact that the game was played by professional rules (Church 1996). The experience of the older people's panels also cited earlier indicates the importance of officials coming to meet users on their territory and learning to play by their rules (Cormie 1999). The dynamics of engagement are entirely different when a health or social service manager comes out of his or her office to meet with a group of older people who are familiar with each other, and have spent time together working out what they want to say, than if one or two older people attend a meeting of officers to represent the views of the group.

In the Ontario example, the failure to accord legitimacy to survivors' stories and the emotional content of them led to continuing conflict. As long as user participation in decision-making processes takes place within the context of rules determined within professional and bureaucratic institutional procedures, the value of emotional experience communicated through story telling will be marginalized.

Beyond the importance of officials stepping outside their territory to engage with users there needs to be the opportunity for more creativity in the way in which ideas and experiences can be explored. Deliberative forums need to be spaces in which interactive theatre is accepted as having the same legitimacy as the debating chamber as a means of enabling user experiences to be included within discussion of health and health service policy and practice. Forums that are solely task-based or problem-solving can close down the opportunities for developing understanding and valuing diverse experiences and styles.

There can be benefits for health professionals as well as for users in enabling users to contribute in ways which might be more immediately open to them. The use of drama and other more literary or visual forms of communication may make it easier for them to recognize and acknowledge the relevance of the emotional experiences being presented, as well as to recognize their own response to it. The distinction between 'user' and 'health professional' is an arbitrary one – there will be times when health professionals are also users. 'Healers' as well as 'sufferers' have acknowledged the benefits of being able to describe what they do using a narrative structure rather than framing this within a biomedical discourse (e.g. Sacks 1995). Our notions of dialogue need to be expanded if the challenge to scientific rationality from service users is to result in more creative ways of working, rather than to provide another site for conflict.

PART 3
REALIZING CLINICAL GOVERNANCE

11 What Counts is What Works: Postgraduate Medical Education and Clinical Governance

Nancy Redfern and Jane Stewart

If clinical governance is to be integrated into clinical practice and provide a system for developing and monitoring quality of care, policy-makers and managers need to understand the culture in which the medical profession is educated, trained and practises and how this shapes its thinking about managerially driven policy. With such an understanding, health policy-makers and managers (including doctors) could implement strategies that are sympathetic to the very powerful values of the profession and facilitate clinicians' engagement with clinical governance. This chapter outlines the factors that shape a doctor's practice and discusses what doctors, managers and medical training can do to embed clinical governance.

The work of today's doctor

Medical knowledge represents a huge mass of continually changing information which is accessible to both clinicians and patients. Despite advances in technology and a vast evidence base available, there remains considerable uncertainty in clinical practice. The human body is both amazingly robust and distressingly fragile and presents enormous ranges of normality and disorder. Patients describe their symptoms in different ways and seek advice at different stages of illness. There is variability in the effect a treatment may have on an individual as well as the complications that may arise. The expectation is that all doctors keep their practice up to date so that they deliver high-quality evidence-based treatment, and all advances in medical knowledge and technology are related appropriately to the management of individual patients.

Patient expectations from medicine also vary: some want their doctors to take responsibility for the choice of treatment and others want to influence their own care. Ensuring that doctors meet individual patient and carer needs for information and that all patients are given an appropriate level of involvement in decisions about their own management adds another variable to patient care (as illustrated in Box 11.1).

Box 11.1 Dealing with complexity

After two uneventful births, a mother experienced a very unpleasant forceps delivery of a big baby whose head was not in the right position to descend through the pelvis. For her fourth baby, she told her consultant decisively that she wished to be delivered in the midwifery-led unit away from the high-tech environment she found so traumatic. Although the guidelines did not recommend this, he felt he should respect the mother's wish as the fourth baby was smaller so less likely to be a difficult delivery. In labour, she was cared for by a kind, but relatively inexperienced midwife. Unfortunately, matters did not go according to plan, and she was transferred to the local hospital in great pain in the late stages of labour, again for a forceps delivery. The baby had to be admitted to the special care unit.

The consultant had concerns that the midwifery-led unit was not the best place for this patient to give birth yet he had no strong clinical evidence to support the need for her to attend the larger unit. In following the patient's wishes the obstetrician was not following clinical guidelines for such cases but felt that they did not take into account the need to respond to individual patients. He knew the senior midwives on the unit and was confident that they would be able to spot early on if there were any problems with mother or baby. He had no knowledge of the recent decision to offer posts in the unit to recently qualified midwives. Perhaps he should have been less accommodating to the mother's wishes, particularly now she was expressing concerns about the care she received, and was planning to pursue these.

The midwife looking after the lady was unhappy, having felt out of her depth when things had started to go wrong. Senior staff were busy with other labouring women and she didn't feel they had listened and responded to her questions. She did not feel empowered to phone the main hospital for advice from an obstetrician. At the 'untoward incident' review meeting, the hospital manager expressed his concern to the obstetrician that he had not followed the guidelines relating to the selection of only low-risk women for delivering in the midwife-led unit.

Where previously decisions made by doctors may have been unquestioned they are now more likely to be challenged. Patients may have specific expectations of what treatment they will receive and how long these processes will take. Discontent may start as soon as something contrary happens or any explanation is perceived as unsatisfactory. In 2002 the General Medical Council received 3943 complaints against individual doctors (GMC personal communication). On 13 December 2001, the BBC news reported an almost 11 per cent rise in complaints about treatment in hospital (to about 96,000) and 12 per cent about treatment in primary care (44,000). Such increases may reflect a client group that is more informed than in previous decades and has more specific expectations from their care and doctors. Patients are also increasingly litigious and now able to pursue claims against NHS Trusts under 'no win, no fee' arrangements with lawyers that reduce substantially the need to consider the costs of action.

Box 11.2   Making judgements in professional training

Doctors in training in ear, nose and throat surgery have to learn to pass instruments into the pharynx, oesophagus (gullet) and upper airway. The doctor must learn to find small abnormalities but the view is restricted and only the person handling the instrument gets a good view. Significant damage can be done if they are used roughly, but a certain amount of pressure is required to manoeuvre instruments into place. Using manikins for practical teaching is of limited value as the amount of pressure required to pass an instrument down a plastic dummy is very different to that used in life. Most of the learning therefore takes place in the operating theatre, with a senior doctor supervising the trainee. He or she must develop the trainee's skills and confidence whilst ensuring the patient receives the highest level of care.

A consultant and trainee have set the learning points for their theatre session together. Halfway through the list the trainee experiences difficulties with a procedure. Identifying the relevant learning points and helping the trainee to change technique is time-consuming especially in a busy operating list. Given the potential for damage to tissues or for abnormalities, including cancerous changes, to be missed by the doctor in training, the senior doctor could take over the procedure rather than continue to advise and supervise a trainee who is having difficulty. But this is a good learning experience for this trainee, so despite the apparent disquiet of the theatre nurses, the trainee is allowed to continue. At the end of the session the trainee has achieved the learning objectives that they set together but the nurses and support staff are not happy as the list has taken longer to complete, people have had to stay late and there is no time for a debriefing session with the trainee.

The difficulty for the consultant is when to intervene so the patient receives high-quality treatment, pathology is not missed but the trainee has the opportunity to learn from the senior and the list finishes on time.

We suggest that today's doctors are now more likely to feel threatened and may sometimes act more defensively with patients than in previous generations. For some this change in relationship significantly adds to the complexity of clinical work. Moreover, professional responsibility dictates that in order that mistakes can be averted or learned from, a doctor must recognize that an event did not go well, notice what happened and review ways in which a similar situation might be handled differently next time. But openness in the discussion of problems, identifying relevant learning points and ensuring commitment to appropriate change can be challenging and difficult to achieve within the time constraints of everyday practice and in a culture of litigation and blame. Critical reflection and self-challenge does need to be managed otherwise the reflective process can descend into a morass of self-doubt or retribution from others. The GMC stipulates that 'You must protect patients from risk of harm posed by another doctor's or other health care professional's conduct, performance or health' (GMC 2001: 10). Recognizing that oneself or a colleague is in difficulty is often less the problem than dealing with it in such a way that allows for meaningful professional development. Even when problems are recognized and acknowledged it can be hard to identify exactly what difficulties affected the doctor's practice and the educational interventions that best support the practitioner's learning, and to provide these to a definable standard within a busy practice context.

Professional and governmental initiatives have driven more critical and reflective practice with transparent systems and processes for monitoring the delivery of care and its quality. All doctors are now required to undergo regular annual appraisal, have annual personal development plans and compile a portfolio of evidence to inform the appraisal discussion, the summary of which is part of the evidence provided for revalidation (from 2004) and is available to the management team and Trust. For revalidation a doctor needs to have evidence to show he or she provides good medical care, keeps up to date, has good relations with colleagues and patients, provides teaching and training to a high standard, behaves with probity and has no health issues which affect his or her ability to practise. Although these initiatives have been regarded as valuable, the time-consuming collection of evidence can easily become an adjunct to an already busy job. Added to this, the validity of what currently constitutes 'evidence' of competence to practise does not always stand up to scrutiny. Being present at a scientific meeting is equated with 'maintaining their level of knowledge' and gains the doctor validation credits. Learning outcomes are rarely set or assessed and it is questionable as to how embedded this information becomes into a practitioner's everyday practice. For clinicians the imperative becomes jumping through hoops rather than an engagement with a process of professional development.

The NHS continues to introduce major changes such as the reforms to SHO training and shorter, competency-based Specialist Registrar training, clinical governance, performance league tables, National Service Frameworks, National Institute for Clinical Excellence (NICE) guidance as well as structures of care such as Primary Care Trusts, the National Patient Safety Agency, the National Clinical Assessment Authority (NCAA) and the Commission for Health Audit and Inspection (the 2004 successor to the Commission for Health Improvement). With purchasers and patients, the NHS also continues to expect more work from doctors. The managerial responsibilities of consultants and general practitioners continue to grow and doctors are increasingly accountable for them in formal systems and processes such as documenting trainees' progress and recording changes made as a result of critical incident reviews or audit. Moreover, a consultant appointment now no longer guarantees stability of employment. Trusts merge, departments are moved, mechanisms of funding change, and there are major changes in the contractual arrangements for doctors in primary care.

Box 11.3   Some challenges facing today's doctor

Individual patient care

Relating an evolving evidence base appropriately to individual patients

Unpredictable nature of emergency work

Appropriate involvement of individual patients in decision-making

Managing an increasingly litigious client group

Maintaining professional competence

Keeping up to date

Finding sufficient opportunity to reflect

Prioritizing time for one's own professional development

Ensuring self-challenge as a 'professional' – monitoring one's own practice and critically analysing and addressing one's own strengths and weaknesses

Managing the relative inexperience of trainees

Undertaking revalidation

Identifying and collecting evidence of competent practice

Living within a high-pressure culture and strained relationships

The work environment

Increased workload and pressure for results

Increasing responsibility and more formal accountability

Requirement to fulfil targets set by outside bodies (e.g. NSF, CHAI, NHS Executive)

Isolation

Frequent change

Uncertainty about future employment

Establishing and maintaining a quality of life outside work

(Drawn from Redfern *et al.* 2000)

Uncertainty and change on this level is the cause of immense stress and pressure for some individuals, contributes to disillusion amongst the workforce and inhibits greater efficiency and quality. The NHS, purchasers and patients continue to expect more work from doctors, whilst Royal Colleges and Postgraduate Deans expect clinicians to place a greater emphasis on high-quality training and assessment. Consultants and general practitioners' managerial responsibilities continue to grow and doctors are increasingly accountable for systems and processes such as documenting trainees' progress and recording changes made as a result of critical incident reviews or audit.

Pressure of work inhibits doctors seeking out colleagues for casual conversation, and split site working, early starts and lunchtime commitments lead to increasing isolation. Hospitals no longer have a doctors' mess or senior staff dining room where doctors could meet colleagues informally. Doctors also have increasing concerns about the quality of their lives outside work. Hardly surprisingly, more doctors than ever seek part-time practice and early retirement. Indeed, the number of doctors working in the NHS is so far below requirements that the 'Improving Working Lives' group from the Department of Health offers 'retainer, returner packages', in the hope of attracting back into practice some of those who have left the profession or retired early (Department of Health 2001a).

Box 11.3 summarizes the challenges inherent in today's clinical practice. Although these refer only to doctors, the challenges face all health service professions, each having to manage professional and institutional demands within an arduous political climate. But each profession will have characteristics that make particular demands more acutely felt and difficult to meet. To understand what these are in medicine and how these relate to clinical governance it is helpful to review the culture in which doctors train and work.

The culture of medical education

To become a medical student, a person must be bright, with innate ability, and to succeed, the student requires considerable personal drive, motivation and stamina. Medical students enter university knowing how to succeed academically and, importantly, how to pass exams. The ability to pass exams or other assessments remains important throughout a doctor's career and may engender a somewhat functional approach to knowledge and learning; the aim sometimes being to pass the exam rather than to engage intellectually with the subject material. Coming from the academic elite, a student may have no experience of how to respond to feedback on poor performance, or accept and learn from it. Fear of failure can become a significant personal driver.

The student learns specialized language and theories, with written work dominating assessments and, in traditional medical schools, subject experts or specialists as teachers. The traditional medical school encouraged doctors to adopt independent, isolated and competitive approaches to learning, producing incisive, confident decision-makers, whose currency is fact-based knowledge. Changes to curricula such as problem-based approaches encourage collaborative enquiry and provide opportunities to develop the skills to set, monitor and achieve common goals within teams. It is not known, however, whether these formative approaches to medical education influence the practices and values of the profession or the graduate when in practice. Over the five undergraduate years, the medical student's time is spent increasingly in clinical practice observing and executing tasks under the direction of a doctor. Here, students learn about the practicalities of clinical medicine and the ways doctors work. They are socialized by their interaction and observations of seniors and, to a lesser extent, other health care professionals. In contrast to the intellectual atmosphere of medical school where knowledge is demonstrated by exposition, what is valued in clinical practice is experience, diligence, reliability, safety, effectiveness and responsibility. Here knowledge is demonstrated by action, as practitioners must do the job and focus on what needs to be done, thus taking responsibility for the patient's care (Eraut 1996). The student learns that practice involves pragmatic decisions where first-hand experience is more valuable than abstract principles and knowledge is derived from the practitioner's experience and validated by personal judgement.

As a consequence of living in these two cultures, the medical student adopts two sets of values, those of the academic world of medicine and those of the practice world of medicine, that continue to support education after graduation. These academic and practice discourses may be manifested in 'talk' of current 'best evidence' (the academic values) and 'action' informed by experience from personal knowledge (the practice values), perhaps akin to Sinclair's front and back stage discourses (Sinclair 1997). Although postgraduate training develops doctors' respect for research as it applies to biomedical science, it often provides limited insight into alternative epistemologies. This may explain the suspicions some have about implementing educational and organizational initiatives based on qualitative research or anecdote that can be quickly challenged and dismissed when compared to the rigour of randomized controlled trials. Although most doctors are aware that a realist paradigm comes short of describing the ways in which they work and practise, change supported by research within a relativistic paradigm is easily refuted on evidential grounds.

Undergraduate and postgraduate medical education, however, are beginning to embrace alternative approaches to research, question the nature of knowledge and apply different philosophical stances to learning and clinical practice. But these ideas remain alien to many. Doctors enter independent practice as consultants or general practitioners often without an understanding of the methods likely to be relevant and appropriate in reviewing the patient journey, educating junior clinicians and developing new ways of working, all important in the delivery of effective clinical governance (Fraser and Greenhalgh 2001). Doctors may recognize that their epistemological stance to research, to education and to practice is not always appropriate, viable or sustainable but without alternatives they will rely on what is familiar.

To function effectively in a constantly changing environment, in which paradox and uncertainty are inherent features of the system, doctors require insight into how to understand, work and research complex systems. To facilitate their contribution to clinical governance, doctors need to question, learn from and understand their own and others' behaviour in teams, how individuals and groups apply factual, personal and organizational knowledge in different situations and what would make each group member more able to contribute to knowledge and decision-making. Managers learn this as part of their training. Doctors, although expected to act in this way, have at least until recently received little if any formal management training. Indeed, the NHS provides little in the way of induction and few opportunities to develop and review organizational aims and culture. This is an area in which managers could make a contribution to the education of doctors in training.

Until ten years ago, most UK undergraduate and postgraduate medical teaching relied on an instructivist model, with the teacher as 'sage on the stage' presenting facts and assessment based on reproduction of these facts. But to be able to develop organizational knowledge, students need to feel comfortable exploring and challenging alternative perspectives in an informed manner, and recognizing and working on their individual learning needs. Teachers then become 'guide on the side', using methods such as small group, problem-based learning, simulations, feedback, reflection and appraisal. Although the recent increase of 'doctors as educators' programmes has skilled up consultants and GPs to use teaching methods other than lectures, there are still many doctors who remain unfamiliar and uncomfortable with these approaches. Students learn which consultants comfortably explore uncertainty, and which prefer to present a rational picture of practice.

The culture of medical training

It is useful to think of doctors in training as working within communities of practice. Here they learn to interpret, analyse and act 'appropriately' and 'safely' whilst constructing identities and roles within that community (Lave and Wenger 1995). Mizrahi (1985) suggests that the dominant socializing influence on junior doctors in this community is not the deliberative world of academic faculty but practising colleagues only marginally more experienced than themselves. This results in solidarity and camaraderie between junior staff but may mean that these doctors' allegiance is first to the patients and secondly to their 'communities' rather than the organization and its objectives and processes.

The junior doctor passes through several grades of seniority during training. These grades describe both the stages of doctors' training and also how patient management is organized. Each doctor is responsible for the patients under the care of his or her team but can hand over responsibility to a more senior doctor. Through this hierarchy, responsibility moves upwards and decisions move downwards. Each doctor is ultimately accountable to the consultant but in practice is accountable to the consultant's representative on the ward, a more senior doctor. Even when juniors are competent to take care of the patient they keep seniors informed of the patient's status. Thus more senior members of the profession guide, monitor and instruct junior members of the team. Senior doctors must provide trainees with appropriate educational opportunities and a supportive training environment, whilst ensuring that standards of practice are maintained.

Box 11.4 Teaching whilst maintaining a safe service

A trainee doctor does not pick up the subtle clues that a quick intervention is needed in the care of a patient to avert clinical adversity. When, at last, the junior recognizes that something is 'not right', the clinical problem has escalated into a life-threatening emergency. The trainee knows, in theory, what to look for and can describe how to manage emergency situations; what presents the challenge is his or her lack of ability to see the problem coming. Exactly what the trainee's difficulties are in observation of the patient's condition or diagnostic reasoning skills, and which educational interventions would best help him or her overcome this problem, are all hard to define and manage. The middle grade doctor who sees the junior doctor's problem does not have the educational knowledge and experience to provide the appropriate help yet has to decide whether to tell the consultant about the difficulties the more junior colleague is having, with potential consequences for references, or keep it hidden, potentially preventing the trainee and the patient receiving help.

The culture within that 'firm' of doctors will have a major influence on the action taken. If the consultant is seen as a kind and respectful person, who will help the trainee, an open exchange is probable. There still remains the challenge of how to 'teach' the trainee something that is a sixth sense for nearly all doctors, developed from repeated experience of similar clinical episodes. If the consultant is seen as either likely to put negative pressure on the trainee or unlikely to take any action, the trainees will probably close ranks and try to manage the situation themselves.

These arrangements allow the doctor to work safely whilst also learning from seniors and provide an excellent opportunity for experiential learning, balanced feedback and reflection. However, they rely on middle grade and senior trainers having the necessary time and skill and junior doctors being aware of their limitations, calling for help and being amenable to negative feedback from their 'bosses'. These conditions are sometimes not met. This may explain why significant proportions of errors in patient management are made by more junior doctors, said to be due to inexperience, high stress or lack of good supervision (Firth-Cozens and Payne 1999).

Training thus takes place whilst also delivering a service. Both can be safely accomplished if the senior is acknowledged as the ultimate arbiter within a hierarchical process of decision-making. As a consequence junior doctors are deferential to their seniors who carry ultimate responsibility for patient care as well as the junior's training and career progression. This creates an important power dynamic within a group of doctors and, unsurprisingly, challenges from junior-to-senior are rare. Although doctors work in teams, the consultant has overall responsibility and the team comprises the consultant's representatives rather than partners in care.

Although immersed in practice the doctor will continue to sit exams until passing the final membership or fellowship examination of the Royal College or Faculty of an intended specialty. Pass rates for postgraduate medical examinations are low (sometimes only 30–50 per cent) and competition is sometimes high. This can reinforce fears of personal failure, drives to succeed, insular approaches to resolving difficulties and even provoke an inability to manage the workload. This ways of responding are not consistent with the behaviours needed to review clinical team problems, risk management issues and treatment failures as required for effective practice as well as by the formal demands of clinical governance. Indeed, they may contribute to what is often seen as a medical culture of tribalism in which responses to criticism are deference from trainees and aloofness from senior potentates (Department of Health 2001b). Perhaps because of the individualistic nature of their training, present groups of senior doctors set, maintain and review their standards of practice as individuals. The maintenance of professional competence relies on their own internal belief in the correctness of these standards, their duty of care to each patient and their knowledge of what their peers would do in similar circumstances.

These core professional values can result in conflicts for doctors working within organizations. As Edwards *et al.* (2002: 836) point out, doctors are:

> trained to deal with individuals, not organizations, to take personal responsibility rather than to delegate and to do their best for each patient rather than make trade-offs in a resource constrained environment ... Training and professional values based on an individualistic orientation, and towards management of disease, does not prepare doctors to function effectively as members of large, complex organizations.

We suggest, however, that doctors can function effectively as managers and policy-makers by adopting not the values of the academic or the clinical context but those adopted by the organization and espoused in its strategies and policies, including clinical governance. Implementation of such policies is furthered by the involvement of clinical stakeholders. However, having clinicians engaged in the development of a policy does not always ensure changes at a practice level. As Eraut explains (of teachers) 'Though talk or writing may influence the perception or conceptualization of action, it does not itself constitute that action' (1996: 31). Therefore, the design and implementation of policy, even that constructed by clinicians, must be mindful that clinical action and policy call upon different knowledge and skills and represent different ways of thinking about practice.

Box 11.5 A good policy is not always used

A registrar was changing a patient's pacemaker. As he was about to insert the one he had been given by the technician, he realized that it was more complex and expensive than this patient required. He selected a more appropriate model. In discussions with the technical staff afterwards he suggested they might jointly design a form indicating exactly which pacemaker is required. This could be completed by the technical staff or the doctor, prior to the procedure. In fact such a form already existed but it had fallen out of use because the hospital had been involved in a research project looking at the function of the two pacemakers and during this time the manufacturer had provided both at similar prices. Now that this study was completed, the price differential had been reinstated. One consultant preferred the more expensive model and wanted all 'her' patients to receive it. A debate about cost pressures at a departmental meeting resulted in some acrimony with this consultant believing that 'management funding issues should not be allowed to compromise the care of her patients'.

　　Logic suggested using the most appropriate and least expensive pacemaker. In practice, the wishes of an influential consultant led to different action.

Doctors do work in teams but often find members of the team deferential to them and consequently feel accountable as individuals, feeling personal responsibility and blame for patient outcomes in a way that team members from other professions (managers, nurses, midwives or allied health professions) do not. Managers approach their roles and responsibilities in relation to accountability, guidelines, targets and finance in different ways. The tension between doctors and managers may result from the different underlying beliefs of two disciplines (Edwards and Marshall 2003).

Developing effective clinical governance in an organization

The previous sections described the cultures in which doctors are currently educated and trained and, by implication, some of the challenges facing those developing and delivering clinical governance. There has emerged a shortfall between the ideal required for developing and delivering effective clinical governance and with this ideal being incongruent with some of the core values of the profession. One should not underestimate, therefore, the significant shift that clinical governance represents in the move away from a working environment and culture that demands individualism and stoicism to one which shares responsibility and provides the appropriate levels of stimulation, support and challenge (Egan 1993).

Figure 11.1 draws on the work of R. Harrison (1995) and helps conceptualize the balance needed between support and challenge in an organization and the potential consequences for its employees of these being set appropriately and inappropriately. Harrison's model suggests that with neither support nor challenge (low support and low challenge) work is dull with insufficient stimulation and, consequently, people may not achieve their full potential. There is a lack of commitment to the job and the organization. If the environment is supportive but relatively unchallenging (high support but low challenge) individuals who are self-motivated and enthusiastic do well, generating their own goals and creating their own agendas. However, because individuals are working to their own outcomes, the organization lacks a common purpose and direction and important issues can remain unresolved, because confrontation is avoided. Within this culture common or shared goals can be difficult to achieve, especially if they involve compromise and change (Department of Health 2001a).

Faced with challenge and inadequate support (high challenge and low support) individuals may attempt to exercise as much control over their environment as possible, perhaps because when change is imposed on them by others it makes little sense from their perspective. As a consequence, individuals are less receptive to change, and do not feel empowered to think innovatively (Pedler *et al.* 1995). There is a tendency to place blame on circumstances or on others rather than to be open in discussions about difficulties, and to become defensive about the management of problems in which they may have had a part to play. In contrast, a high challenge, high support environment allows those involved in delivering and using a service to work toward collective goals. Individual contributions from all members are recognized and valued, there is openness, creativity, innovation and identification with collective effort, leading to quality improvement. Difficult issues are resolved by discussion, and people are encouraged to report problems and to expect help from others in the organization until the matter is resolved.

A health care organization's culture influences the way it goes about developing its clinical governance arrangements, delivering and monitoring the quality of care it provides. The structures it sets up, and the style in which people are managed, shape the way in which individuals engage in the pro-

High support and low challenge	High support and high challenge
Opportunities only when the individual is capable of generating his/her own goals Individuals communicate frequently People feel valued, and help each other Confrontation may be avoided and thus important issues remain unresolved Common goals difficult to achieve	Opportunities generated by individuals and the organization Difficult issues resolved by discussion Openness Individual contributions recognized and valued Corporacy Creativity Innovation Quality improvement
Low support and low challenge	**Low support and high challenge**
No growth in organization No growth of individual Boredom Low stimulation Lack of commitment/involvement 'Going through the motions'	Individual attempts to control environment Individual less able to respond to challenges – energy expended in 'looking after number 1', struggling for or protecting power base Less innovation Don't use problem-solving ability or intelligence Less appropriate 'risk taking'

Figure 11.1   Support and challenge
Source: adapted from Harrison (1995)

cess and influences whether and how the organization harnesses the learning achieved by individual members (Nutley and Davies 2001). In NHS Trusts where employees see the culture as 'low support, high challenge' (a description many doctors would give of their organizations), much work will be needed to encourage people to engage effectively in clinical governance. Clinicians may regard clinical governance as 'command and control – structures and systems' rather than as something relevant to everyday clinical work, education, training, and working relationships, which they can influence.

To embed clinical governance, NHS Trusts will need to improve their capacity for organizational learning. Senge (1990) suggests that to achieve this they must improve individual capabilities and the ability to work collaboratively in teams, question assumptions about what is current and possible within the organization, empower individuals and teams to make changes based on core values, and see the whole service rather than just the small part. The structures and processes the organization uses to deliver and monitor good governance should enhance organizational learning, helping the whole team provide the best care it can to the patient. Thus, an organization's clinical governance arrangements build on both organizational knowledge (written procedures which shape how an organization functions, communicates and analyses situations), and cultural knowledge (relating to customs, values and relationships arising from the experience of individuals).

As well as being stored and communicated, knowledge has to be used. The mechanisms whereby this happens also form an integral part of clinical governance. Organizations that are most effective at learning identify when and how they learn and when and how they fail to learn, and adapt accordingly. This learning about learning has been described as 'deutero learning' (Argyris and Schon 1978) and 'meta-learning' (Nutley and Davies 2001). The recent emphasis in the NHS is on risk management and learning from errors, single loop learning (Argyris and Schon 1978). Critical incident reviews and other risk management processes are ways of learning from errors as are clinical audit, where treatments provided are compared with evidence-based guidelines and appropriate changes are made to the service. However, such reviews are effective in improving care only if there is an evidence base to use as an authoritative comparator and changes become embedded in everyday clinical practice, not just in written protocols. When, or perhaps if, learning leads to a redefinition of policies and procedures, it is described as double loop, or generative learning. In circumstances when time, energy and leaders with change management skills are in short supply, such learning is rare unless precipitated by a crisis (Department of Health 2001b) or a review by an external body such as the Commission for Health Audit and Inspection (or its predecessor, the Commission for Health Improvement).

Much as for the medical student, where assessment (examination) drives learning, a CHAI review encourages an organization to examine its clinical governance arrangements. As well as examining policies structures and accountabilities, CHAI interviews team members from different areas and levels of the organization to see how clinical governance arrangements are used to inform daily work. It also explores the extent to which the organization makes quality improvements based on contributions to learning from all team members, including its patients, and the emphasis it places on resources and training for staff (see Box 11.6). Thus the review encourages the organization to develop behaviours that support organizational learning, and adopts an approach which empowers individuals and teams to question assumptions and make changes to everyday clinical work, education, training and working relationships.

Doctors may be seen as the natural leaders of this process as experts in delivering a key element of a health care organization's function, i.e. good medical care. But doctors do not necessarily have the skills to provide the high challenge, high support culture in which organizational and teams learn and develop and organizational excellence flourishes. Nor do many NHS organizations regard the professional development of its doctors as a key responsibility to fulfil this role.

Box 11.6   CHAI assessment of clinical governance

CHAI has identified a number of indicators of the effectiveness of an organization's clinical governance arrangements:

- Clinical effectiveness programmes
- The use of information to support clinical governance and health care delivery
- Arrangements for effective risk management
- Clinical audit arrangements
- The involvement of patients, other service users and the wider public
- Appropriate staffing and effective staff management
- Education, training and continuing professional development of the workforce
- The strategic capacity of the organization
- The patient experience

See *www.chai.nhs.uk* for further details.

Encouraging engagement with clinical governance

Scally and Donaldson (1998: 61) describe clinical governance as 'a system through which NHS organizations are accountable for continuously improving the quality of their services and safeguarding high standards of care by creating an environment in which excellence in clinical care will flourish'. But how do doctors learn to create and value this sort of working environment? What challenges do we face in trying to create this?

Considering the complexity of the phenomenon we have described, there can be no recipe for ensuring that the principles of clinical governance become integrated into the everyday practice of doctors and other health care professionals. Certainly the installation of procedures, systems and guidelines is not enough to ensure that an established culture will be replaced by significant alterations to its communities and working in ways for which, as yet, there is little evidence. Rather than look for structural or procedural solutions, it is probably better to concentrate on giving people the skills to manage change, to work with complexity and uncertainty and to understand more about the systems in which they work and appreciate the effects of their own actions on others. With these skills, health care professionals should be better equipped to think more holistically and systematically about high-quality care and the arrangements they make to bring this about.

One way in which organizations try to keep professionals engaged is by involving them in decision-making and development of strategic change. However, this assumes that those within the profession have insight into the culture in which they work. Professionals live their culture rather than ana-lyse it and, as a consequence, can themselves design systems that ignore the reasons why things work in the way that they do. Neither can one guarantee that people have the skills to perform in the ways that are essential for change or to value new ways of working because they are seen to be superior.

We suggest that senior doctors and managers need to develop their leadership skills; there should be carefully targeted action research and an increased emphasis on so-called 'non-linear' learning methods. These strate-gies are more likely to equip those working in clinical settings to contribute to organizational learning. Research should focus on the cultural imperatives that influence practice within and between professions, and systems and processes should be devised in light of these insights. Leadership and change management skills should help doctors and managers to understand more about the systems in which they work, so they can help develop an organi-zational culture in which doctors, nurses, other health care professionals and managers learn and work together, and all team members feel well supported and appropriately challenged.

Educational development should encompass the increased use of teach-ing methods that encourage individuals and teams to adapt to and learn from unfamiliar environments and contexts. Clinical educators should be con-fident in the use of non-linear approaches to learning, and constructionist as well as instructivist models. Teaching and examinations at medical school and beyond should encompass professional skills such as the ability to mo-tivate, negotiate, give constructive feedback, contribute effectively in a team, support, challenge and manage conflict. Medicine needs to develop better ways of supporting those struggling within the organization, under-performing or finding it difficult to pass exams, so that they feel confident that help will be provided.

Conclusion

Clinicians know that the values that underpin clinical governance and the principles it follows are important and morally correct. However, turning any ideology into action is fraught with difficulty. The established informal sys-tems in which doctors train and work and the culture in which these systems operate are on many levels functional for those working within it. The leg-islative rhetoric that surrounds the call for cultural change and changes in education usually ignores this reality and often grossly under-conceptualizes the workplace. Moreover, policy and organizational initiatives often fail to take into account the very complex, untidy and uncertain world which doctors and other health care professionals inhabit. And although clinicians are often the ones developing these initiatives, the outcomes of the deliberations are presented proscriptively, as the ideals of practice that can be generic and applicable in all instances.

In a search for an effective means of ensuring that doctors continue to maintain high standards of practice, validating bodies have used peer observation, case review, work with simulators as well as formal examinations. More often than not the tendency is to concentrate on what can be easily measured without understanding the nature of practice. Measuring and recording what a person 'can do' in a controlled test environment is taken to represent what he or she 'does do' in a complex clinical environment. For many clinicians, the thought of others looking over their shoulders and constantly monitoring the quality of their practice adds to further stress and places them at the centre of culpability. The government and organizational initiatives demand that learning and development continue within an already crowded practice and at times appear to ignore the functional systems that are inherent in the current culture. As a consequence these initiatives become adjuncts to practice for the individual rather than embedded within it.

The advent of clinical governance, however, presents a real opportunity for change if accompanied by changes in the approach to education and learning, a culture in which organizations as well as individuals accept responsibility, and the development of leadership capability amongst both health care professionals and managers. Both the delivery of everyday clinical care and formal clinical governance arrangements should help develop an organizational culture in which doctors, nurses, other health care professionals and managers learn and work together. With this established, the differing needs of patients can really be put at the centre of health care, resources can be managed more effectively, and the contribution of each team member can be understood and respected, consequently creating an environment in which excellence in clinical care will flourish.

12 Developing the Human Resource Dimension of Clinical Governance

Chandra Vanu Som

The clinical governance initiative may be seen as a policy response to the growing expectations of patients for better quality health care services. Through its integrated approach to quality improvement, clinical governance provides what amounts to a cultural change not least through its emphasis on multidisciplinary work, coordination, cooperation and teamwork. In this approach the role of health staff attains greater significance, because 'it is they who decide what and how much care to provide, how services will be delivered and which patients are prioritized' (Surender *et al.* 2002). Thus health care quality improvements will be crucially dependent on the knowledge, skills and motivation of health staff. In turn, the management of human resources in health care is increasingly central to the development of clinical governance.

Research and development has already supported this contention For example, a survey of 61 Trusts and in-depth analysis of 18 by West *et al.* (2002) found high associations between proactive and strategic people management and improved patient outcomes. In general, human resource practices explained 33 per cent of the variation in standardized mortality rates, comprehensive appraisal systems led to 12 per cent fewer deaths after hip fractures and Trusts with human resource directors as voting members of the Board had 7.1 per cent lower mortality rates than those without. However, the public sector in general and health service reform in particular has neglected the significance of human resource management (Fairbrother 1996; Bach 2000; Buchan 2000; West 2001; Franco *et al.* 2002). Even less attention has been paid to the human resource dimension of clinical governance. Yet, important questions arise. What are the major human resource implications of clinical governance? Is effective management of human resources essential for continuous quality improvement in health care? What kind of human resource practices would be necessary for quality improvement in health care? This chapter addresses these and related questions.

Human resource management in the NHS

Human resource management is used to refer to a philosophy of, and approach to, management of employees that is now regarded as an essential component of organizational strategy for achieving effectiveness and efficiency (Leopold *et al.* 1999). It 'encompasses issues such as organizational structure, organizational culture, personnel selection and placement, training and development, job design, and performance appraisal' (UNDP 1995: 70). In the context of health service, it involves 'the mobilization, motivation, development and deployment of human beings in and through work in the achievement of health goals, which is based on the essential value assumption that people seek ... certain satisfaction from their work' (WHO 1993). Thus an understanding of human resource is crucial to the implementation of change processes, including the introduction of new concepts through policy change and adopting new ways of working.

Successive government efforts to enhance service delivery have been accompanied increasingly by initiatives in the management of human resources. During the 1990s, for example, the creation of NHS Trusts and the internal markets were accompanied by performance-related pay and flexibility in employment practices, increased use of temporary staff, remixing of skills and grades, development of multi-skilled support workers not linked to any particular profession and other changes to working practices (Burchill and Cassey 1996). At least some NHS organizations were able to achieve significant savings in labour and administrative costs through such changes (Buchan 2000), thus justifying the adoption of proactive human resource policies and practices.

However, does the NHS have the human resource management capacity and capability to implement the further changes implied by clinical governance? The World Health Organization (WHO 2000) reports some of the consequences of inadequate attention to human resources as:

- numerical imbalances: e.g. shortages of qualified health personnel limit the capacity of the health service to improve quality of health care (recent shortages of trained nurses in the NHS are a case in point);
- training and skill mix imbalances: lack of proper training limits the ability of health staff to perform clinical tasks and a mismatch between available skills and the needs of the health care system limits continuous quality improvement;
- distribution imbalances: geographical imbalances in the management of human resources is another major problem sometimes aggravated by high cost of living (e.g. London).

How, then, could these factors be managed? The literature argues that a better understanding of the human resource management dimension will come with more research into the 'institutional processes involved in changing the culture, attitudes and practices of health care professionals' (Surender *et al.* 2002: 47) and, we could add, managers. This work is already developing. Thompson *et al.* (1999), for example, argue that comparative international research of health care organizations shows that managing the process of organizational change requires appropriate management competencies in and commitments to human resource strategies. Such strategies require first an identification of the organizational elements and its wider implications for management of staff to be addressed. The following sections of this chapter examine the human resource implications of different elements of clinical governance.

Encouraging continuing professional development

Continuing professional development (CPD) is at the heart of quality improvement initiatives. The implementation of National Service Frameworks, for example, will require new skills and knowledge through CPD (Charlton 2001). Whilst clinical governance puts responsibility on individual clinicians to take personal responsibility of CPD through revalidation (du Boulay 2000), health care organizations could use CPD to relieve stress and improve morale, job satisfaction, self-esteem and performance, not least through providing reflection and personal assessment by individual clinicians (Charlton 2001). If the greatest challenge is to manage the process through the interface between the professional bodies and the employers, managers and patients (du Boulay 2000), human resource managers can help proactively to establish effective coordination of different stakeholders.

Clearly, linking the commitment of clinical professionals to personal development and continued licence to practise would be an effective way to encourage professionals' lifelong learning (Roland *et al.* 2001). The recent General Medical Council's proposal for periodic revalidation of doctors supports the aim of continuous professional development in clinical governance. Its implementation, however, requires systematic management within individual health care organizations through the establishment and maintenance of personal learning plans and annual appraisals (Roland *et al.* 2001) and developing education and training programmes with workforce development confederations (Department of Health 2001a). Throughout, the focus should be 'problem solving, feedback through investigation results, specialist opinions, observation, reflection on difficult cases, discussion of critical incidents, and education by patients' (Charlton 2001: 3). And it is a human resource management task to manage the necessary protected time and related resources, so often the obstacles to effective CPD (Taylor *et al.* 2000, Charlton 2001).

Leadership

Strong leadership is widely identified as needed to change the existing organizational culture in favour of clinical governance. For Hackett *et al.* (1999) inspirational leadership style empowers stakeholders to accept and internalize the rationale of organizational changes of clinical governance. For others (e.g. Walshe 2000; King and Wilson 2001) transformational leadership inspires confidence among staff, challenges the status quo and initiates innovative approaches to improving the quality of care. Throughout, the leadership challenge lies in communicating the vision of clinical governance, building multidisciplinary teams, developing staff commitment and managing the change process (Hackett and Spurgeon 1996).

For Hackett *et al.* (1999) the role of chief executives in all this, as statutory guardians of clinical standards, calls for their visible and strong commitment to clinical governance principles through providing the vision for their implementation, communicating clearly their aims and objectives, encouraging participation in multidisciplinary teamwork and developing powerful mechanisms to recognize any significant achievement. Yet, clinical leadership is perhaps even more important. Through changing the local frame of reference of professional networks that influence local clinical groups and patterns of clinical decision-making, clinical leadership can inspire health professionals to accept the clinical governance agenda. In the past clinical leadership was seen almost entirely in clinical terms: active participation in Royal Colleges, in clinical specialties and so on (Hopkinson 2000). Under clinical governance, however, it includes generic leadership, communication and other human resource management skills and knowledge in multidisciplinary contexts (Donaldson 2001).

Change of culture

Attempts to change the culture through policy intervention are not new to the NHS. The reforms of the 1980s and 1990s intended to change the NHS culture but made very limited impact on the deep-seated values, beliefs, subcultures and power bases that influence clinical practice (Davies *et al.* 2000; Nicholls *et al.* 2000). Is clinical governance any different from previous reforms? Will the current initiative be able to achieve a change of culture?

Clinical governance promotes an integrated approach to quality improvement which is different from the fragmented approaches of the past. It attempts to break the barriers of differentiated cultures to forge a wide consensus on quality improvement. It also makes every health staff member individually accountable for the quality of care. In a sense it thus brings together the managerial, organizational and clinical approaches to quality improvement (Buetow and Roland 1999). Ulrich (1998) argues experience in private sector shows that proactive human resource management can drive the process of such cultural change. We might thus expect human resource management functions to help staff to develop a better understanding of how their work will contribute to meeting the overall objectives of clinical governance and provide the skills they require to perform their duties for care improvement.

Risk management

High-profile failures in health service management and the subsequent introduction of clinical governance have brought the concept of clinical risk management to the forefront of clinical care and academic discourse over recent years. Health care organizations are amongst the most complex organizations involved in service delivery and these complexities make clinical practice a high-risk job. One of the aims of clinical governance is to minimize the chances of adverse incidents by emphasizing risk management. As well as tragic costs for patients, adverse incidents bring additional costs to health organizations in the remedial care required for the patient and any legal reparations awarded as a result of negligence (Walshe and Sheldon 1998). Yet, despite safeguards, mechanisms and controls to protect the patients (Reason 2001), adverse incidents have continued to arise from technological, systems and human error.

For Gosbee and Lin (2001), clinicians and risk managers could be trained in human factor engineering (HFE) and its concern with the safe design and comfortable use of tools, machines and systems taking into account the limitations and capabilities of human being. Even one clinical staff member well trained in HFE would raise awareness and appreciation of HFE in operational decisions, minimize clinical errors from medical devices and improve outcomes of risk management initiatives. The cause of a critical incident may lie, however, in system failure (Vincent *et al.* 2000). Reason *et al.* (2000) argue that certain institutions with recurrent organizational pathologies are more vulnerable to adverse incidents than others. The authors describe this as vulnerable system syndrome (VSS) (Figure 12.1) and suggest it requires specific skills both to recognize the symptoms of VSS and prevent adverse events.

Even if some of the root causes of these incidents are associated with poor human resource management practices themselves, including the 'use of

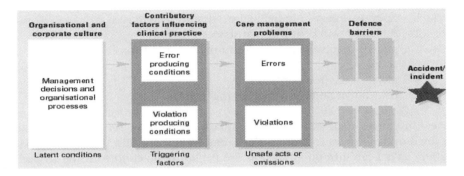

Figure 12.1 Health systems failures contributing to adverse incidents
Source: Vincent *et al.* (2000: 778)

locum doctors and agency nurses, communication and supervision problems, excessive workload, and educational and training deficiencies' (Vincent *et al.* 2000), a proactive human resource management programme is fundamental to managing risk. Formal training in the management of teams (Reason 2001) and better understanding of the implications of technology on human beings (Hackett and Spurgeon 1996) would improve the performance as well as reduce the risk of clinical errors. Individual members of the team can be trained to be aware of their collective and respective roles and responsibilities and thus enhance a team culture conducive to providing a safe environment for patients and staff (Lugon and Scally 2000). Further, amongst the requirements of the appropriate approach to risk management identified by an expert group on learning from adverse events chaired by the Chief Medical Officer (Department of Health 2000b) were a more open culture to encourage reporting and discussion of adverse incidents and mechanisms to ensure that lessons identified are put into practice.

Without an open culture it may be difficult and uncomfortable for the staff to report the clinical incidents that may have caused harm to patients (McCracken 2000). Without support through the investigation process staff will not be able to handle these situations functionally and will not have confidence in the reporting system (STHT 2002). Without either, it will not be possible to provide the necessary feedback for staff to learn from mistakes – a necessary condition for the continuous quality improvement process (Harris 2000).

Role of staff in improving patients' experience

The Department of Health (1998) highlighted some of the important aspects that influence the patient's perceptions of service delivery:

1   responsiveness to individual needs and preferences;
2   skill, care and continuity of service provision;
3   patient involvement, good information and choice;
4   access;
5   physical environment; and
6   courtesy of administrative arrangements.

New initiatives such as the Patient Advice and Liaison Service (PALS) and providing volunteers to greet patients and help them find their way (STHT 2002) have been introduced to improve patient interaction with the service. The success of such schemes requires a better understanding of these qualities of patient-focused care and the forging of genuine partnership between patients, professionals and managers.

Greco (2000) argues that at the heart of this is excellent communication between the patient and the health professional. Just as poor communication may lead to health care management problems (Vincent *et al.* 2000), good communication will contribute to improvement in service quality by improving processes such as hand-over sessions, dialogue with patients about difficult episodes of care and team reviews after clinics and surgeries (Nicholls *et al.* 2000: 175).

Promoting evidence-based practice

As we have seen in earlier chapters of this book, clinical governance stresses evidence-based practice to secure improved outcomes and consistency of quality approach and to minimize the clinical risk through the identification of effective treatments. Evidence-based practice encourages questioning, promotes a reflective approach and puts greater emphasis on lifelong learning (Glanville *et al.* 1998). The starting point for evidence-based practice is the knowledge based on sound research and development (Department of Health 1999). There are already the Cochrane Library, the Centre for Review and Dissemination (CRD), National Research Register and the National Electronic Library for Health as well as the National Institute for Clinical Excellence (NICE) to provide information on current research in medical sciences. The role of human resource management is to support this national infrastructure with local training programmes for clinical staff to develop the skills, willingness and ability to use it in clinical decision-making.

The skills required for deciding the validity and applicability of research-based evidence have important implications for identifying the training needs of the staff (Mead 2000). Multidisciplinary training and continuous professional development could be used effectively to encourage health professionals to reflect on the knowledge that underpins their practice (Ferlie

1999). Skills in presentation, persuasive communication and negotiation may be helpful in convincing the stakeholders about the benefits of the proposed change through evidence-based practice.

Some health care organizations have created new posts like the Clinical Skills Trainer (for providing inter-professional skills training) and Clinical Support Librarian (for facilitating clinicians' use of frontline electronic information). Hewitt *et al.* (2000) suggest that recruits to these posts have developed good working relationships with clinicians to secure clinical effectiveness. This is an exemplar of how the identification of human resource needs and their management in key areas of clinical governance contribute to health care improvement.

Clinical audit

Clinical audit, although preceding clinical governance, provides for it the necessary mechanism for monitoring and evaluation of quality standards (Burke and Lugon 1999). The introduction of clinical audit has changed the way clinical practitioners are expected to implement established research findings, prioritize clinical practice and use resources most effectively to improve clinical care (Pringle 1998). It not only attempts to bring patient care improvement through changes in clinical practice but also contributes to professional education, team development, enhancement of information management skills and to better management of resources (Teasdale 1996; Lord and Littlejohn 1997).

Clinical audits conducted by multidisciplinary teams need to work in partnership to improve and change practice. Opportunities for multidisciplinary skills training and a change of culture in sharing clinical information will be crucial for the success of clinical audit. However, a lack of 'ownership' necessary to bring about change or lack of motivation or commitment may lead to the failure of completion of the audit cycle. Human resource management has an important role to play in shaping the beliefs, values and perceptions of clinical audit as part of professional commitment.

Conclusion: managing human resources to support clinical governance

In any health care organization it is difficult to imagine that major changes could be implemented and high levels of performance sustained without effective human resource management. Even critics of the clinical governance initiative (e.g. Goodman 1998) recognize the importance of human relationships in the delivery of high-quality care. At its heart, clinical governance is a change process: change in the way activities are structured and processed and above all in the management of people (Garside 1998). Only good working relations will facilitate the collaboration, cooperation and communication necessary for the quality improvement that clinical governance seeks.

The central role of human resources management in the implementation of clinical governance is summarized in Figure 12.2. The human resource strategy to realize clinical governance is depicted as proactive initiatives to drive the necessary cultural change, implement evidence-based practice, develop multidisciplinary teams and forge cooperation between clinical and managerial staff. For Hackett *et al.* (1999: 101), the key aspects for this strategy include:

- *coordination*: to focus on bringing groups and teams together to develop a shared vision for clinical governance in the organization;
- *commitment*: to excite the clinicians, managers and board with the vision and develop ownership and commitment from the clinical body to the vision through approaches to improve participation, involvement and ownership;
- *competences*: to train and develop key competences amongst clinicians and managers to deliver the new clinical governance framework.

Figure 12.2 The role of human resource management in clinical governance framework

These elements are consistent with human resource management having a central responsibility for realizing clinical governance. Such a responsibility requires transforming human resourcing from a traditional reactive establishment function into a strategic facilitator that plans, programmes and delivers the human resource requirement of clinical governance. This implies restructuring the human resource management function and re-equipping its staff and infrastructure. Investment in innovative human resource practices would be one way of demonstrating the commitment of senior management to its strategic role in the implementation of clinical governance. Yet there is also a sense in which clinical governance requires reinforcement of traditional human resource management activities: recruiting appropriately qualified staff, instilling motivation and commitment, developing skills and competencies through training, empowering individuals to foster initiative, and aligning jobs with the communication and feedback mechanisms necessary for quality improvement.

The evidence cited at the beginning of this chapter (e.g. West *et al.* 2002) that suggests the benefits to health outcomes from enhanced human resource management is now being given recognition at the national level in the NHS. However, there is little evidence to suggest that the identified practices are being systematically adopted in Trusts. With so much attention to national priorities such as waiting lists it is understandable that little intellectual and organizational resource is available for restructuring human resourcing. Yet, as we have seen, clinical governance depends on it. Moreover, it is not hard to design national initiatives that could support the necessary restructuring. Most obviously, the Commission for Health Audit and Inspection (CHAI) could collect and disseminate information on innovative human resourcing practices and even the National Institute for Clinical Excellence could develop guidelines for human resourcing as it is directly related to clinical outcomes. At the local level too it is possible to envisage (with Bach 2001) the development of effective human resourcing strategies that included:

- investment in training and development of human resource specialists, general managers and professionals with human resourcing responsibilities;
- evaluation, proper audit and monitoring of human resource functions through in-house specialists or out-sourcing;
- sound human resource policies and practices developed at both operational and strategic levels.

Ultimately the effectiveness of HR practices will be reflected in reduced morbidity, lowered preventable mortality, less recurrent illness and increased health awareness. Research can make an important contribution to understanding human resource management's contribution to the effective delivery of services. So can the development of internal evaluation systems like human resource audit and human resource indicators by helping management to evaluate the effectiveness of human resourcing practices on a regular basis and in the investigation of exceptional circumstances (best practices and failures). Even if such indicators and their audit cannot encompass every single human resource activity, they may help further investigation (Tyson 1997). Human resources audit could become an integral part of the evaluation process in the proactive human resourcing strategy.

Such a human resourcing role is thus much broader than recruitment and selection and other related traditional establishment functions. It integrates the human resource strategy with the clinical governance strategy, empowers the human resource department and increases its accountability. Innovation requires greater attention to workforce planning and redesigning work in a sensitive and professional manner. However, the delivery of health care is too complex for simple solutions. Clinical governance acknowledges these complexities and attempts to address them by promoting an integrated, systematic and organization-wide approach towards continuous quality improvement. Its approach embodies cultural change as well as new ways of working. Proactive human resourcing strategies and practices are required to realize it.

13 Restructuring Clinical Governance to Maximize its Developmental Potential

Pieter Degeling, Sharyn Maxwell and Rick Iedema

As we have seen in previous chapters, clinical governance has been promoted as a medium for ensuring that clinical quality processes are integrated with the quality programme for the organization as a whole, that leadership skills are developed in clinical teams, that evidence-based practice is in day-to-day use with the infrastructure to support it and that proven good practice is systematically disseminated (Department of Health 1997). To achieve these ends, as Scally and Donaldson (1998) note, clinical governance requires structures and processes which integrate financial control, service performance and clinical quality at every level of their organization. Implementation requires an organization-wide transformation with an emphasis on local professional self-regulation.

This chapter supports these views. It argues that clinical governance provides clinicians with the opportunity to re-establish 'responsible autonomy' as a foundational principle for health care organization and management. We show how establishing such a model will require action on three fronts:

1   reorienting the operations of existing clinical governance mechanisms, for high-volume case types (patient groups), to focus on the detailed composition of clinical work;
2   institutionalizing methods and approaches that will enable clinicians prospectively to systematize the clinical work associated with these case types and review their own performance;
3   establishing structures, practices and incentives that will legitimize these processes to clinicians and underwrite the importance of 're-sponsible autonomy' as a base principle for structuring relations within clinical settings.

We project that this conception of clinical governance will have two effects. First, it will focus attention on the frontline clinical settings in which clinical work is actually performed, namely a renal unit or an orthopaedics unit and so on. Second (building on Ellis and Johnson 1999), it will highlight the benefits that will derive from utilizing clinical pathways as a basis for building multidisciplinary teams, improving the evidentiary basis of clinical practice and for setting in place processes (again at the level of individual clinical units) whereby issues of quality, safety, clinical competence, appropriateness, efficiency and effectiveness are routinely monitored, benchmarked and addressed.

The chapter opens by describing the model of clinical governance that currently prevails in most acute settings. The conceptual and hence practical shortcomings of this model are then discussed. Against this background we examine methods, structures and practices that would characterize an alternative approach. This new approach seeks to maximize clinician engagement by, first, focusing on the specifics of clinical work for high-volume patient types, second, engendering multidisciplinary self-governance, and third, re-establishing responsible autonomy as a foundation principle of health care organization and management.

Implementation of clinical governance

Scally and Donaldson note that clinical governance was 'a big idea that has shown that it can inspire and enthuse' and that 'the challenge for the NHS – health professionals and managers alike – is to turn this new concept into reality' (Scally and Donaldson 1998). That the reference to 'challenge' here masks as much as it evokes may be attributed in part to the countervailing expectations that have been held of clinical governance. At one and the same time, it is construed as a vehicle for giving local effect to centrally determined regulatory processes and for engendering bottom-up change and development. As illustrated in Figure 13.1, in support of its modernization agenda, the Blair government established an implementation structure that envisaged activity at national and local levels. The national activity has focused on developing clear standards for service provision and establishing mechanisms for monitoring their implementation. Responsibility for standard setting lies with the National Institute for Clinical Excellence (NICE) and National Collaboratives in clinical specialties such as cancer and chronic heart disease. Responsibility for performance monitoring lies now with the Commission for Health Audit and Inspection (CHAI), formerly the Commission for Health Improvement (CHI), and through mechanisms such as National Performance Framework and a National Patient and User Survey.

Details on how local clinical government arrangements 'fitted into' this structure were provided in a number of consultation documents. For example, chief executives of Trusts were informed that, in addition to their

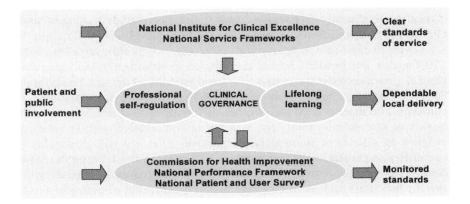

Figure 13.1 Clinical improvement structures

Source: Department of Health (1998)

accountability for corporate governance, they now would have to account for: the presence or absence of clearly defined lines of accountability for the overall quality of clinical care, comprehensive quality improvement activities, risk management policies, and procedures for all professional groups to identify and remedy poor performance (Department of Health 1998).

On a somewhat different tack, the same circular emphasized the developmental nature of clinical governance. Thus, 'Clinical governance provides NHS organizations and individual health professions with a framework within which to build a single, coherent, local programme for quality improvement' (Department of Health 1998: para. 3.3). To this end Trusts were informed that by April 2000 they would need to have:

- established leadership, accountability and working arrangements;
- carried out a baseline assessment on capacity and capability;
- formulated and agreed a development plan in the light of this assessment; and
- clarified reporting arrangements for clinical governance within board and annual reports.

(NHS Executive 1999: para. 7)

This developmental thrust was assessed and supported by CHI, now CHAI, whose activities have complemented its advisory and regulatory functions with respect to the implementation of National Service Frameworks for specific conditions and NICE guidance. The Commission for Health Improvement (CHI) provided very detailed advice on the individual aspects of clinical governance that it regarded as important such as risk management, clinical audit, clinical effectiveness, quality assurance, staff development, and clinical governance's formal arrangements at board level.

Given its dual role as adviser and regulator, it is hardly surprising that CHI's advice was heeded and has contributed to striking similarities in the clinical governance structures that have been established in most Trusts (as in Figure 13.2). It is a model that emphasizes the top-down accountability of clinicians and managers for issues variously identified as affecting the overall quality of care. Responsibility for monitoring and addressing these issues is assigned to a series of stand-alone committees (that is a risk management committee, a clinical audit committee and so on). In most hospitals, these committees are supported by 'specialist staff' designated as attending to specific functions such as risk management, clinical audit or pathway development. The work of these staff is to gather data on the issue falling within their particular committee's remit and ensure that committee decisions are implemented within clinical settings. Each issue-based committee is expected to report routinely to the Trust's clinical governance committee which itself reports to the Trust board.

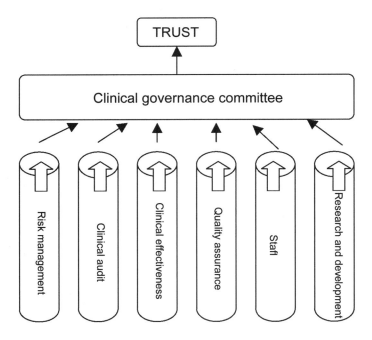

Figure 13.2 'Silo' organizational structure of clinical governance

How form has dominated substance in clinical governance implementation

Whilst the model of clinical governance being implemented in most Trusts meets the formal requirements now placed on them, it is ill-suited to setting in train developmental processes to change substantively the organization and performance of clinical work along lines consistent with the intention of reform. Noteworthy here is the lack of discussion and guidance on what can and needs to be done to encourage and support doctors, nurses, allied health workers and managers to:

- accept interconnections between clinical and resource dimensions of care;
- recognize the need to balance clinical autonomy with transparent accountability;
- support the systemization of clinical work; and
- subscribe to the power-sharing implications of more integrated and team-based approaches to clinical work performance and evaluation.

The contrast between a model of clinical governance capable of giving effect to these principles and the model in place in most Trusts becomes clearer when we consider how implementation was conceived by both outside commentators and by 'on the ground' managers. For example, at the same time that central policy authorities were outlining their expectations of clinical governance, commentators associated with the British Association of Medical Managers noted that many Trusts had already established internal systems that variously focused on clinical audit, risk management and quality improvement (see, for example, BAMM 1998; Scotland 1998).

Whilst the reach and formalization of these stand-alone systems varied between Trusts, most boards found that they could meet the requirements now placed on them by strengthening existing systems that dealt with matters such as clinical audit, introducing additional systems to cover the full gamut of issues on which they now needed to report, and establishing the required committee structure that would signify the presence of a co-ordinated approach. This structure would also enable the Trust board to be accountable for the nominated aspects of clinical performance. In summary, Trust boards found, and were being told, that implementing government policy on clinical governance did not require wholesale change but could be achieved, largely, by strengthening existing reporting mechanisms and ensuring that these were linked and coordinated at the top levels of the Trust.

The adoption of this approach produced three effects counterproductive to the developmental potential of clinical governance. First, a Trust's clinical work continues to be conceived and spoken about as an undifferentiated aggregate. The resulting failure to disaggregate care into different patient categories has meant that efforts to improve quality, clinical effectiveness and efficiency can only be pursued via a number of top-down initiatives and related reporting structures that retrospectively gather data on generic issues such as quality, risk, safety and patient satisfaction. The abstracted and fragmented depictions of care that result, by their nature, cannot encompass the diversity of clinical work entailed in, for example, treating a patient with a fracture or, alternatively, via a primary care team, supporting a patient in self-managing his or her asthma. These shortcomings, in turn, undermine the relevance of clinical governance for many medical, nursing and allied health staff and lead them to regard it as doing little more than adding to their paperwork whilst simultaneously bolstering the inspectorial character of management's interest in clinical work.

The second effect derives from the way that the silo model supports the hesitancy of many clinician managers about change initiatives that transgress what some of their erstwhilst medical colleagues regard as their right to self-define, self-describe and self-validate their own work. Noteworthy here is the silence of bodies such as CHI and the NHS Modernization Agency about what can and needs to be done to ground and integrate the constituent silos of clinical governance at the level where clinical work is performed. For example, how can clinical governance be made to focus on how an orthopaedics unit 'does' hip replacements or how a primary health care team provides 'a year of care' for a patient with diabetes? Inevitably efforts to answer questions such as these raise a further set of questions about how systematization of clinical work in each of these patient categories would contribute to clinical skills development as well as improving the safety, quality and appropriateness of care and, with that, patients' experience of care.

In contrast with the change-oriented approach to clinical unit management that would result from the routine occurrence of conversations of this kind, conventional conceptions of clinical unit management emphasize 'managing up' on resource acquisition and 'managing down' on budgetary and waiting lists targets. Moreover, as efforts are focused upon avoiding and/or containing medical resistance on these limited objectives, the potential contributions of nurses (particularly nurse managers) to a more developmental model of clinical governance is neither recognized nor tapped. Under these circumstances there is a real risk that clinical governance remains an exercise in which a concern to meet formal reporting requirements overrides the opportunity for substantive change.

This outcome, paradoxically, also provides grounds for the view that clinical governance is nothing more than another wrong-headed attempt by central policy players to extend their control over what takes place in front-line service provision. People of this persuasion argue that the prominence given in past CHI inspections to the detailed reporting requirements associated with each of the silos, and the growing number of other inspectorial bodies such as the Audit Commission, Health Service Ombudsman and professional regulatory bodies, are all manifestations of the top-down surveillance orientations of central policy authorities. In somewhat the same vein, other clinicians and managers view clinical governance in terms of the way that it has extended the targets and measures against which the performance of Trust senior managers are judged.

Such negative depictions of clinical governance, again, provide the motive force for a downward spiral that ultimately is deleterious to its developmental potential. For many doctors, for example, the perceived emphasis on outside surveillance and performance management justifies their indifferent engagement with if not their resistance to clinical governance. In turn, this lacklustre engagement of medicine (as with earlier reform initiatives on resource management and clinical audit) has tended to reinforce the scepticism of general managers about the possibility of engendering clinician-led bottom-up change, particularly in the organization and performance of clinical work. This assessment reinforces the erroneous belief that the most effective levers for change are those that are external to clinical settings such as budgetary constraints and more closely targeted performance monitoring systems. And the (to be) expected medical response to these top-down (and ultimately) ineffective efforts to generate change will set in motion yet a further iteration of the downward spiral.

An alternative model of clinical governance

To realize its developmental potential we require a model of clinical governance that is integrated with other initiatives on the agenda of reform and grounded in a recognition of the centrality of clinician involvement in the design, provision and improvement of care. These requirements can be met by establishing structures and methods that, by design, engender conversations that focus on the *detailed composition of clinical work* in ways that render its performance and organization available to *self-governance by multi-disciplinary teams*.

The reference to *the detailed composition of clinical work* foreshadows benefits that would derive from adopting methods and approaches that (for high-volume case types) will enable clinicians prospectively to systematize their clinical work. The aim here is to establish and reinforce practices that are consistent with both the overall agenda of reform and the particular concerns of clinical governance, and which will encourage multidisciplinary clinical teams to review their performance through structured conversations around questions such as:

- Are we doing the right things? (Given assessed health needs and existing resource constraints, are we delivering value for money? On a (high volume) condition-by-condition basis, how appropriate and effective are the services we offer?)
- Are we doing things right? (Are we managing clinical performance according to national codes of clinical practice? For high-volume case types (on a condition-by-condition basis) how systematized are our care processes and how are we performing on risk, safety, quality, patient evaluation and clinical outcomes?)
- Are we are keeping up with new developments and what are we doing to extend our capacity to undertake clinical work in these areas? (On a condition-by-condition basis, what strategies are in place for service and professional development? What are we doing about clinical mentoring, leadership development, staff appraisal and review?)

The reference to *self-governance by multidisciplinary teams* foreshadows the importance of structures, practices and incentives that will underwrite the centrality of 'responsible autonomy' as a base principle for structuring relations within clinical settings. Two elements are central here. First, the conjunction of 'responsibility' and 'autonomy' points to the benefits that will derive (to clinicians, patients and the system as whole) from clinicians taking the lead in systematizing clinical work in ways that strike a balance between their clinical autonomy and their accountability for quality, effectiveness and efficiency. Second, the conjunction of 'responsibility' and 'autonomy' highlights the importance of bottom-up and clinically informed approaches to organizing, managing and reviewing clinical work that, given their focus on the composition of clinical work, render its performance transparent and available to 'collective self-control'.

Recognition of the importance of such multidisciplinary conversations, however, begs a number of questions about the organizational level at which these conversations should occur, who should be involved, who should be responsible for generating and facilitating these conversations, what structural and resource support these people will require, what methods they might use and what can and needs to be done to encourage clinician engagement. On the last of these questions, the literature on the diffusion of clinical innovations shows that clinicians' response to change depends, in part, on how far the proposed change is perceived as being distanced from their day-to-day clinical interest and experience (Gosling *et al.* 2003a, 2003b). Findings such as these reinforce the importance of a clinical work-centred model of clinical governance, i.e. one that can encompass the detailed composition of the treatment regimens that clinicians in nominated clinical units or care settings (for example an orthopaedics unit, a birth unit or a primary care team) render to their high-volume case types. In an orthopaedics unit, for example, these case types usually include treatments for patients undergoing a hip or knee replacement, or who are being treated for a fractured neck of femur. Once identified, these case types become focal points for developing multidisciplinary integrated care pathways (ICPs) that are designed prospectively to integrate clinical work and improve quality, clinical effectiveness and efficiency.

Integrated care pathways (ICPs) as base building blocks for an alternative model of clinical governance

Following, amongst others, Lomas (1989); Leape (1990); Thomson *et al.* (1995); Holt *et al.* (1996); and Hindle (2001), ICPs are defined as systematically developed written statements of the agreed sequence of multidisciplinary diagnostic and therapeutic processes which, in light of available evidence, stated resource constraints and the experience of patients and carers, prospectively:

- describe the composition and timing (and therefore sequencing) of the range of multidisciplinary activities that are needed to treat the specified condition;
- identify the events in this sequence whose occurrence or non-occurrence will significantly affect clinical quality, patient experience and technical efficiency; and
- define the indicators that will be used to assess performance with respect to cost, clinical effectiveness, patient and provider safety, adverse events, patient/carer involvement, satisfaction, complaints and claims.

These attributes, in turn, provide the basis for recording and analysing variance within and between clinical settings and routinely generating multidisciplinary discussions on how the effectiveness and efficiency of condition-specific care processes can be improved.

In this regard, an accumulating body of evidence points to the way that ICPs can contribute to improving the evidentiary basis of clinical practice (Turley *et al.* 1994; Gottlieb *et al.* 1996; Gregory *et al.* 1996; Collier 1997), interdisciplinary communication and service integration (Hart 1992), relations between professions and team satisfaction (Johnson 1994), clinicians' sense of care continuity (Flynn 1993), discharge planning (Guiliano and Poirier 1991), awareness of the impact of 'foibles' on team members (Poole 1994), and reduced isolation of clinicians in specialized practice (Guiliano and Poirier 1991). Equally there is evidence about how ICPs enable patients and their families to understand and influence what is involved in the full scope of their treatment in ways that benefits both clinical effectiveness and patient satisfaction (Guiliano and Poirier 1991; Woodyard and Sheetz 1993; Borokowski 1994; Johnson 1994; Poole 1994). Moreover, there is evidence that ICPs improve work flows, flexibility and problem-solving (Flynn 1993) and interdepartmental relations (Johnson 1994), reduce inappropriate admissions (Becker *et al.* 1997) and resource use (Gallagher 1994; Calligaro 1996) as well as reducing unnecessary lengths of stay (Archer *et al.* 1997) and clinical risk (Ellis 1997). On more general levels, Del Togno-Armansco (1993) reported that the net financial gains generated by ICPs are substantial even for allowing for high costs during the planning and 'set-up' periods (during which little or no financial benefit is realized), and Degeling *et al.* (2000) pointed to the importance of systematized forms of care such as ICPs for maintaining quality in situations of financial stringency.

In summary, the literature suggests that multidisciplinary ICPs provide means for systematizing care in ways that will: extend its evidentiary basis, strengthen service integration, improve clinical effectiveness, quality and technical efficiency as well as improve patient and clinician satisfaction. These attributes, in combination, allow the method simultaneously to address both the technical efficiency and clinical improvement orientations of recent health care reforms.

The foregoing does not mean, however, that individual service settings should develop and implement ICPs for all the treatments they perform. The range of conditions treated and procedures performed within a hospital means that it is neither realistic nor useful to consider systematizing all its clinical work. It is also the case that about 50 per cent of a hospital's clinical work is high-volume, routine, predictable and clearly amenable to systematization. For example, a recent study that utilized two consecutive years of hospital discharge data from four acute Trusts showed that emergency admissions accounted for 83 per cent and in-patient elective episodes accounted for 17 per cent of all bed days consumed within the Trusts (Degeling and Kennedy 2004). Broken down by admission type the data show that for *emergency admissions*:

- 30 Health Resource Groups (HRGs) (out of 547) accounted for 46 per cent of all emergency in-patient episodes and these HRGs accounted for 39 per cent of all emergency generated bed days;
- 18 of these HRGs referenced conditions (usually chronic) with a high risk of repeated emergency admission; these patients tended to account for 33 per cent of all emergency patient episodes and 18 per cent of all bed days.

And for *in-patient elective admissions*:

- 30 HRGs accounted for 53 per cent of in-patient elective episodes and 47 per cent of elective bed-days; and
- 333 HRGs involved fewer than 40 episodes across all Trusts.

For *day-only elective admissions*:

- 30 HRGs accounted for 75 per cent of day elective episodes (excluding unclassified and psychiatric HRGs); and
- 398 HRGs involved fewer than 40 episodes across all Trusts.

Clinicians and managers derive a number of benefits from disaggregating a hospital's mix of patients in this way. First, with low-volume case types the data should stimulate clinicians to examine the quality and risk implications of some of their units' clinical activity. For example, in the case of in-patient and day-case elective admissions mentioned above, the relatively high number of HRGs with low-volume case types raises questions about whether units undertaking this work have (and are retaining) the requisite clinical experience and skills to do so. Second, the data on high-volume case types, when further disaggregated to the level of individual disease codes within the International Classification of Diseases Version 10 (ICD10), would provide clinicians with a basis for identifying case types for which ICPs can be developed and implemented to the benefit of systematizing clinical work along lines described above. These ICPs, in turn, will provide the focal points for collecting data that will inform structured multidisciplinary conversations about: safety, risk, quality, care integration, clinical appropriateness, effectiveness and technical efficiency of individual care processes (for example a hip replacement, a normal delivery, or a year of care for a patient with chronic obstructive pulmonary disease (COPD)). The same data can also be used to meet reporting requirements of central policy authorities on clinical governance and performance management. Finally, systematizing clinical work for high-volume case types may produce a 'virtuous spillover' effect in ways that will improve quality in other less frequently performed treatment modalities.

In summary, the systematization of clinical work that will emerge from developing and implementing ICPs for high-volume case types will enable clinicians to specify the information they require to give substance and form to *responsible autonomy* as the foundational principle of a system of *clinical self-governance*. This will occur as medical, nursing and allied health staff directly involved in the care of specific high-volume case types utilize the methodology of pathways to reflect collectively on their joint work and ask questions along the following lines:

- Does our clinical practice incorporate the perspectives of patients and all treating health professionals and have we incorporated these perspectives into a clinical pathway?
- Is our clinical practice informed by evidence, national guidelines and protocols? What issues does this pose for us clinically, professionally and organizationally and how are we resolving these?
- At what points and to what extent does the care we provide for this condition vary from that outlined in the clinical pathway?
- To what extent (and in what direction: viz. better vs. worse) have these variations affected: service integration, the experience of patients, quality, safety, risk, clinical effectiveness and technical efficiency?
- What clinical, organizational and behavioural factors have produced these variations? Can we change these factors or do we need to change the pathway?

Construed in these terms it is apparent that developing, implementing and reviewing ICPs (that is 'pathwaying') is both a structured and an ongoing process. A number of elements are important here. First, ICPs are not immutable documents setting out inviolable treatment regimens. Second, the existence of a pathway does not obviate clinicians' responsibility to make clinical judgements and to tailor care according to their assessment of the clinical needs of individual patients. In other words, clinical variation remains a 'to be expected' (in the sense of an often required) feature of clinical practice. The matter at issue is what a clinical team can learn from these variations and how they can systematize this learning. Accordingly, under a pathway-based system of care, when the care process varies from that described in the pathway, the reasons for the variance are recorded and, in part, become the focus of structured across-profession conversations along lines described above.

The benefits derived from these conversations will occur at three levels. First, the fact that the conversations are grounded in the detailed clinical work entailed in treating identifiable patient groups (patients undergoing a normal birth or patients undergoing a hip replacement) will ensure their relevance to clinicians and hence strengthen clinician engagement. Second, in their occurrence, the conversations will integrate the constituent elements of clinical governance in ways that significantly extend its developmental potential. For example, as medical, nursing and allied health clinicians use pathway(ing) methodologies to reflect on how, for example, 'they do' hip replacements, knee replacement and fractures, they also will clarify the elements that are critical for determining the stability, appropriateness and clinical effectiveness of each procedure as well as specifying the measures they need to judge their own performance. The pathways that result can then be used to compare the unit's clinical production processes across time to the benefit of reducing risk and improving safety, service integration, clinical effectiveness as well as the evidentiary basis of clinical practice, the quality of care and patients' experience of the care they have received. Finally, as clinicians routinely reconsider the utility and validity of individual pathways they also substantiate their collective control over how these are comprised.

An implementation structure

Recognition of the benefits that would flow from clinicians taking the lead in systematizing and reviewing their collective performance will not, however, guarantee the method's adoption in all clinical settings. Extrapolating from findings in a growing literature on clinical practice change (Stocking 1992; Bero *et al.* 1998; Grol and Grimshaw 1999; Wallace *et al.* 2001a), it is clear that a clinical staff's willingness to use pathway-based approaches to organizing, monitoring and remediating their collective clinical performance will be influenced by the extent to which:

- clinical work systemization is integral to the organization's *accountability structure* with respect to both its clinical and managerial performance;
- the Trust has *integrated developmental* efforts on evidence-based clinical practice, quality improvement service integration and technical efficiency and the extent to which these efforts are specifically directed at systematizing the performance and review of clinical work on high-volume case types;
- frontline clinical units (for example an orthopaedics unit, an obstetrics unit or a primary care team) are *supported with the resources* (i.e. authority, staff, information and the attention of senior clinicians and managers) they require to implement the multidisciplinary pathwaying processes described above.

In other words, clinician engagement with pathway-based clinical work systematization in part depends on the extent to which clinicians believe that their organization's operational and developmental structures and strategies are consistent with and hence supportive of their adoption of this approach. Accordingly, efforts to promote a more developmental model of clinical governance would be assisted greatly by pursuing initiatives at two related levels. *At the level of the Trust as a whole*, it requires setting in place structures and practices specifically focused on monitoring and improving condition- and/or treatment-specific clinical 'production' processes along lines displayed in Figure 13.3.

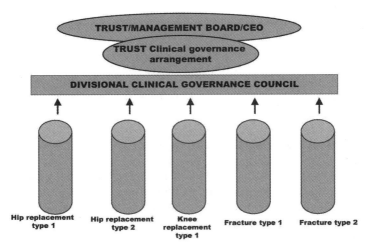

Each condition-treatment specific report includes data on evidence, cost outcomes, clinical effectiveness, quality, safety, adverse events, variance, complaints/claims

A similar structure could operate within Primary Care Trusts. In these cases, general practices and community-based services (the individual clinical units) would report on the 'Year of Care' (pathway-based) they provide for patients with specific chronic conditions such as COPD, diabetes, coronary heart disease or asthma.

Figure 13.3 Pathway-focused clinical governance – acute settings

When constituted along these lines, clinical governance mechanisms and processes will provide authoritative backing for the pathway-based approach to clinical organization and management outlined above. In very important ways, the model signals a shift in emphasis from generic issues to the pathway-based performance of individual clinical units. In the example illustrated in Figure 13.3, an orthopaedic unit is reporting its pathway-based performance on its high-volume case types with respect to their evidence base, cost, outcomes, clinical effectiveness, quality, safety, adverse events, variance and complaints and/or claims.

At the level of *individual clinical units* (e.g. an orthopaedics unit, a paediatric unit or primary care team) pathway-based clinical governance arrangements would need to be complemented by processes that, for high-volume treatments and/or conditions, integrate decisions about all these aspects of care. Responsibility for developing these processes (through the structured cross-professional conversations described earlier) would be assigned to clinical managers within individual units. Their work in this regard will be to support multidisciplinary teams in designing, monitoring and managing the detailed composition of clinical work in their units. In turn, specification of the tasks of clinician managers will provide a basis both for describing the position of 'clinician manager' and for emphasizing its importance.

Discussion

The differences between the clinical governance arrangements displayed in Figures 13.2 and 13.3 are found in the processes that each engenders and the types of conversations they are structured to produce. In the case of Figure 13.2, the clinical work of a Trust is conceived and talked about as an undifferentiated aggregate. Whilst it is accepted that there are differences in what individual specialties do to and with their patients, the detailed composition of clinical work is regarded, in the main, as something that, of its nature, largely lies within the sole purview of the clinicians immediately involved. General acceptance of this opaque and ultimately privileged conception of clinical work reinforces the dichotomization between clinical and managerial domains that plagues the day-to-day operation of all too many health care organizations. This dichotomization occurs in a number of forms, the most pervasive of which is cultural. Research evidence shows how, in support of separations between clinical and managerial domains, many clinicians:

- construe the relationship between autonomy and accountability in zero sum terms with an increase in one being the paired opposite of a decrease in the other. In this regard, recent efforts to increase the scope, reach and transparency of accountability systems are regarded as government-sponsored, baleful management intrusions into the clinical domain;
- deny interconnections between the clinical and resource dimensions of care in ways that cast clinicians as morally driven patient advocates and managers as bureaucratically driven controllers and resources rationers;
- reject clinical work systematization as a managerially driven project that denies both the clinical and personal individuality of patients as well as threatening the expert basis of clinical judgement and practice to the detriment of both patients and care innovation; and
- deny the power-sharing implications of clinical practice and consider efforts in this regard as undermining well established, and clinically and operationally required, relations of authority as between, for example, medicine and nursing as well as flying in the face of legal requirements and patient expectations (Degeling *et al.* 2001, 2002, 2003).

Consistent with such purist depictions of clinical work, general management is variously cast as being responsible for orchestrating the acquisition, deployment and maintenance of the resources (such as staff, supplies, technology and capital) that clinicians require to undertake their work. On a broader front, clinicians expect managers to protect their organization from outside interference by, for example, 'satisfying' its reporting requirements to central policy authorities on budgetary matters, activity levels, waiting lists and a range of other centrally imposed performance indicators. Under these circumstances it is hardly surprising that the model of clinical governance implemented by the management of most Trusts has comprised a number of stand-alone monitoring activities that, utilizing bureaucratically determined categories and indicators, gather, review and audit data on generic issues such as adverse events, near-misses, infection rates, staff and patient complaints. The matters identified are then retrospectively 'managed', often in ways that leave their systemic causes (located more often than not within the clinical domain) unaddressed.

In contrast, pathway-based clinical governance (Figure 13.3) embodies a new stance on performance improvement that goes beyond the issues that are the focus of, for example, designated clinical auditors, quality coordinators and risk managers. Based in a disaggregated and condition-specific conception of the work of a hospital or a primary care unit, it invites the people *who perform clinical work* to define, describe and validate what *they do as teams*. By explicitly recognizing clinicians' centrality to the *organization and performance* of clinical work, a pathway-based system of clinical governance ensures that *(clinical) management* is 'distributed throughout the system, and not centered in any "centre" that monopolizes power, knowledge or control' (Gee *et al.* 1996).

The institutionalization of pathways that will result from a pathway-based approach to clinical governance will expand the work of clinicians from thinking and talking solely about the *expert-clinical* dimensions of care to include also its *cross-disciplinary and organizational* aspects, including finance, logic of service, staff skill mixes, resource management and so on. Moreover, as clinicians collectively accept and acquire the skills needed to undertake this new way of managing and doing clinical work they will become 'professionals-cum-managers' (Dent and Whitehead 2002).

Under these circumstances the relationship between managers and clinicians becomes a 'symbiotic relationship that is mediated and facilitated by a "leader" who cannot control or fully understand the local units but can assist their learning, organization, combination and adaption' (Gee *et al.* 1996). Moreover, as clinicians intertwine their knowledge and understandings into an agreed pathway and (by way of variance analysis and ongoing negotiations with other clinical stakeholders, funders, informal carers and patients) over time modify pathways, they also enact and hence reinforce their ownership of these pathways.

In other words, a pathway-based model of clinical governance does not presage a 'taylorization' of clinical work (Storey 1985; Knights 1990; Wilmott 1990; Harrison 2002) in which a detailed knowledge of the 'what' and 'how to' clinical processes is extracted from clinicians and placed within the purview and control of managers. Rather, the pathwaying engendered by our preferred model of clinical governance embodies a *dispersal* of knowledge among clinicians. This occurs as, for example, doctors, nurses, allied health staff and patients continually network and redefine their knowledges and expertises about the specifics of the care processes that are entailed in treating nominated patient case types.

On a broader front, we project that relations resulting from the adoption of our model of clinical governance will exhibit two features. First, as care providers continually renegotiate 'the what and how' of clinical pathways across professional identities and boundaries (Degeling *et al.* 1998; Degeling 2000; Iedema 2003), their modes of conduct will come to exhibit features reminiscent of what Habermas has termed 'ideal speech situations' (Habermas 1984, 1987). Second, following Rose (1996), as people routinely enact the methods, structures and processes outlined above they will enfold the authority of a system of clinical *self*-governance 'into the soul'. And in doing so they will realize the developmental potential of clinical governance (Donaldson 1998).

14 Governing Medicine: Governance, Science and Practice

Stephen Harrison

'Clinical governance' has never been a clearly defined entity. As Andrew Gray notes in his Introduction to this book, official definitions have been both vague and varied, whilst even supporters in the field have held markedly different conceptions. As Gray also notes, in the technical discourse of academic politics, the term 'governance' is commonly used to contrast with the term 'government', often to signify a mode of coordination based on networks rather than on hierarchy. But that has not transpired to be the character of clinical governance. The degree of interpretative flexibility left by official anodyne formulations has not left the contributors to this book in any doubt that clinical governance entails a variety of mechanisms aimed at securing greater managerial control of the health professions, most obviously medicine: in Gray's terms, a shift from governance based on 'communion' to governance based on 'command'.

The substantive content of clinical governance has developed pragmatically since its invention in the late 1990s, and might now be characterized as including the following elements, some organizational, others philosophical, but all of which are clearly discernible in the contributions to this book. First, a key element in the new arrangements is that chief executives are now responsible for the clinical, as well as the financial performance of their institutions. This is not merely symbolic, but implies that top managers need to be prepared to challenge doctors in order to retain their jobs. Second, clinical governance cannot be understood other than in relation to the activities of new external institutions of standard-setting, inspection and surveillance developed since 1999, of which the National Institute for Clinical Excellence (NICE), the Commission for Health Improvement (CHI) and its successor the Commission for Health Audit and Inspection (CHAI) and the NHS Modernization Agency are perhaps the most prominent examples. Third, the development of these new institutions has proceeded in parallel with an attenuation of medical self-regulation as it had existed for a century; doctors must periodically revalidate their General Medical Council (GMC) registration, and the GMC (along with other health professional registration bodies) is subject to supervision by the new Council for the Regulation of Health Care

Professionals. Fourth, unsurprisingly given the very limited clinical expertise amongst the most senior NHS managers, the implementation of clinical governance is very much based on explicit policies and procedures, an approach that is carried through into the inspection criteria employed by the regulatory agencies mentioned above. Finally, there is a strong philosophical link between clinical governance and the outputs of the 'evidence-based medicine' movement, though these phenomena are by no means identical.

Themes and contributions

The contributors to Part 1 of this book have analysed this substantive phenomenon in various, though largely complementary, ways. Rob Flynn approaches the task through contemporary sociological theory, specifically Foucault's notion of 'governmentality'. In this view, liberal societies are increasingly characterized by systems of audit that encourage individuals both to internalize managerial rationalities and to engage in self-surveillance. The result, when applied to a complex and uncertain endeavour such as medicine, is a complex hybrid of 'soft' and 'hard' methods of control, perhaps moving increasingly towards 'machine bureaucracy'.

Whereas Flynn's analysis is placed in a wider *social* context, Mick Moran's analysis of the rupture of a system of medical self-regulation that persisted for more than a century is placed in a wider *political and economic* context. According to this, medicine has simply been a specific manifestation of the British tendency to 'club government', in which elite actors operated largely informally on the basis of mutual trust. Although some medicine-specific factors (notably a series of scandals) have been at work, the decline of medical self-regulation is mainly the result of the more general decline of club government as a part of governments' attempts to reconstruct the British economy.

The next two chapters are in part concerned with *historical* context. Steve Watkins sees clinical governance as an implicit trade of loss of autonomy in return for increased NHS funding. He combines a historical account of medical perceptions of state–medicine relations with a clear sense of disappointment that contemporary UK governments seem unwilling to enter into a genuine partnership with medicine, preferring (in his memorable phrase) to pursue a perhaps incoherent 'triple way' of central control, devolution to primary care commissioners and privatization of health care provision. My own offering (Chapter 5) begins with a historical sketch that confirms Moran's assessment of the relative recency of substantive medical–managerial conflict in the NHS, in this case by comparing the 1960s 'golden age' of medicine with developments over the last twenty years, of which clinical governance is the culmination. This analysis generally concurs with

Flynn's view of the trend towards 'harder' forms of bureaucratic rule, though preferring the term 'neo-bureaucracy' as a recognition that much rule-enforcement derives from the activities of regulatory agencies rather than from the activities of line management. Such forms of bureaucracy, it is argued, risk a series of undesired consequences, including a number touched on by other contributors.

Finally in Part 1, Pieter Degeling and his colleagues place clinical governance in the context of comparative *professional perceptions*, revealing some very different underlying assumptions about the kinds of quality improvement systems that it might employ, along with a striking demonstration of the extent to which the key philosophical feature of systematization has been differentially internalized by nurse managers.

The contributors to Part 2 provide a series of critical perspectives on the nature and role of evidence, which (as was noted above) is often treated as a key element of clinical governance. It is a truism that we value evidence-based clinical practice for, after all, the alternatives (random practice, prejudice-based practice or ignorance-based practice) can barely be contemplated. But there exist genuinely important disputes about what constitutes valid evidence. Dave Byrne explores a central, but rarely observed difficulty with contemporary notions that the randomized controlled trial (RCT) offers a gold standard of research validity in terms of individual patients. Byrne's point is that, although RCTs should provide valid evidence about probable outcomes *in populations*, there are no logical grounds on which a clinician can transfer such probabilities to the expected outcome for a specific patient. If drug X improves the condition of 50 per cent of patients with disease Y, kills 2 per cent, and leaves 48 per cent unchanged, it does not follow that Mrs Smith's personal chances of experiencing these events if treated with the drug are 50:2:48 respectively. Indeed, it seems to follow (though Byrne himself does not enter into ethical questions) that if a clinician were to employ, or advise a patient to employ, population probabilities in an individual case, he or she would be implicitly following utilitarian ethics, that is pursuing the benefit of the population rather than the individual.

Sue White and Andy Bilson offer a different critique; a great deal of the output of the evidence-based medicine movement relies on the assumption that knowledge is, or can be made *explicit*. It is assumed, for instance, that research evidence can be translated into clinical guidelines that instruct clinicians what to do in specified contingencies. But White's research in children's services indicates both that a great deal of professional knowledge is *tacit* (we know more than we can tell) and that the processes of diagnosis and treatment are often *non-linear*. The same themes are evident in the much more high-technology area of telemedicine studied by Maggie Mort and her colleagues, who also suggest, crucially, that the actors furthest away from the technology (such as policy-makers) are most likely to hold inflated certainties about it.

Finally in Part 2, Marian Barnes takes up the question of service users' views. As contemporary conflicts in respect of Beta Interferon for multiple sclerosis patients and the Measles–Mumps–Rubella triple vaccine have shown, there is no reason to expect that services users (or indeed the public) will simply acquiesce in the findings of research. Barnes notes that the kind of participatory democracy that characterizes New Labour rhetoric of citizenship implies open debate amongst equals. Accordance of legitimacy to the stories and emotions that can determine user views is therefore a necessary condition of genuine participatory democracy in the NHS.

Despite all the critiques and qualifications offered in Parts 1 and 2, clinical governance is being realized day by day in the NHS. The contributors to Part 3 are all concerned with various aspects of this realization, yet raise many of the themes discussed by earlier contributors. Nancy Redfern and Jane Stewart are involved in postgraduate medical education and are fully aware of both the importance of clinical uncertainty, of tacit knowledge and of professional collegiality as a means of allowing the latter to be acquired. They also point to significant tensions between short-term efficiency in terms of getting the immediate job done and longer-term effectiveness in ensuring that doctors possess essential skills for later use. Like Barnes, they note that doctors and patients may disagree over what is best, but are further concerned that the latter may be wrong.

Chandra Som is concerned with wider human resources policies for clinical governance, noting an empirical link between progressive policies and improvement in patient outcomes. Though committed to inspirational and 'transformational' leadership at the top, he asserts that multidisciplinary leadership at the more micro, clinical level is most important.

Finally in Part 3, Pieter Degeling and his colleagues provide a detailed organizational proposal for how clinical governance might be implemented in the future. These proposals take account of a number of the observations made by other contributors. First, they identify a need for work to be organized as 'clinical production processes' at a micro level at which actors have a technical understanding of types of patients and interventions. Second, they propose a framework of systematization of common case types (which certainly exist) into integrated care pathways (ICPs), but without the expectation that these are inviolable. Third, they stress a need for ICPs to be legitimized by the multidisciplinary teams that will operate them. Fourth, they are somewhat hostile to the brand of top-down control and obsessive formal reporting that characterizes current policy. Rather radically (since it entails a high degree of trust in professionals), they advocate in its place a system of 'local professional self-regulation' apparently based on currently unfashionable ideals of 'reflective practice' (Schon 1983) and the Habermasian 'ideal speech situation' (Habermas 1984, 1987).

Towards a new model of medical professionalism?

We can begin to sum up by noting that clinical governance to date represents a clear direction of travel for medical professionalism. First, there has been significant attenuation in the degree of professional self-regulation at national level. The corporatist arrangement whereby the state ceded substantial powers to occupational groups in return for their disciplining their own members (Cawson 1982, 1985) is moribund. Governments can defeat the medical profession on major matters of principle. Second, medical work at the grassroots level is subject to parallel pressures from regulatory agencies and from local managers. It does not follow that professional defeats at macro level necessarily lead to professional weakness at micro level (Annandale 1989; Harrison *et al.* 1990). The outcome at micro level is as yet unclear, though (as noted in Chapter 5) there is some evidence of professional resignation in the face of regulatory and managerial activity. Third, however, there are a number of NHS organizational changes that are outside the scope of this book but which are highly consonant with the trends towards bureaucratization identified here. Principal amongst these are plans for PCT commissioning of secondary care services to take place in the 'currency' of casemix measures (Healthcare Resource Groups: HRGs) at nationally fixed prices (Department of Health 2002). It is clear from experience in the United States that the scope for systematic control of medical work goes well beyond anything yet attempted in the UK (Robinson 1999), yet it remains unlikely that it will ever be 'proletarianized' or routinized completely (Freidson 2001: 212–13).

Taken together, these and other changes outlined by the contributors to this book suggest that the UK may be moving towards a new model of medical professionalism along the lines sketched out in Table 14.1. (For a fuller discussion of some of the elements of the model, see Harrison and McDonald 2003.) Each model is defined in terms of seven elements, though these are not wholly independent of each other.

First, rationality: the observation here, deriving from remarks of Weber (1947, 1948), was made originally in connection with medicine in the USA (Ritzer and Walcak 1988). The implication is that medical practice is increasingly based on rules whose adherence is based on expected outcomes for populations and which may conflict with desired outcomes for individual patients. Clinical guidelines and protocols are obvious examples of such rules. Second, professional knowledge: since the mid-twentieth century science has provided a background that has *informed* the practice of clinical medicine,

Table 14.1 Changing models of medical professionalism

Dimension	Traditional model	Bureaucratized model
Rationality	Substantive: based on treatment objectives for specific patients	Formal: based on rules for treating classes of patients
Knowledge	Professional empiricism and tacit knowledge against background of scientific research	Explicit cumulative scientific evidence in foreground, e.g. hierarchy of evidence
Application of knowledge	'Embedded' and 'embodied': ideal of reflective practice and open communication with peers	'Embrained' and 'encoded': increasingly explicit, and bureaucratized, e.g. in protocols and clinical guidelines
Identification of patient needs	Retrospective or emergent through professional interpretation	Prospective: increasingly bureaucratized
Resource limitations	Professional pragmatism: implicit rationing	Explicit cost-effectiveness and cost-utility analysis
Regulation basis	Trust and 'communion': professional self-regulation	Confidence and 'command': increasingly via formal systems and external regulation
Professional social ideal	Collegial: ideology of basic equality of practitioners	Stratified: explicit recognition of elites based on medical research and medically qualified management

Source: adapted from Harrison and McDonald (2003)

rather than an authoritative body of knowledge that has *determined* such practice. Thus much clinical practice has been 'empirical' (in the sense of based on trial-and-error), based on 'tacit knowledge' derived from the physician's personal experience, and often described as an 'art' as much as a science. Clinical governance's connection to evidence-based medicine privileges explicit research evidence derived from RCTs. Third, the application of knowledge: the traditional approach to the application of medical knowledge is *reflective practice*. It centres on the notion that since much knowledge is tacit ('embodied' is the term employed in Chapter 2) and/or based on shared professional culture ('embedded'), an individual professional should be constantly self-critical of his or her own practice. Such assumptions have now largely given way to the routinization of practice as prescribed by rules, along with the use of rule-following as a key element of performance management.

Fourth, the identification of patient needs: health care for individuals has in the past been treated as a predesigned commodity. The traditional conceptualization of patient needs is that they emerge and are modified in the course of ongoing clinician/patient interaction. Whilst the physician is legally and ethically obliged to seek the patient's consent to treatment and is ethically obliged to act in the patient's best interests, the long-standing assumption has been that the professional interpretation of these matters should be dominant. Increasingly, however, patients are regarded as members of a class or population whose needs can be prospectively specified (as outlined in Chapter 13).

Fifth, coping with resource limitations: historically, a great deal of such rationing in the NHS has been implicit so far as patients have been concerned. In particular, hospital waiting lists and the doctrine of professional autonomy for clinicians have provided an important safety valve for allowing rationing decisions to take place virtually invisibly (Harrison and Hunter 1994). In their place, the political control of waiting lists and the creation of NICE has crystallized and institutionalized a more explicit approach, based largely on microeconomic appraisal.

Sixth, professional regulation: medical knowledge is somewhat esoteric, so that it is self-evident that patients need to be protected from incompetents and charlatans. The same considerations imply that physicians cannot effectively be regulated by non-physicians, so that the long-standing traditional model of professional regulation is *self*-regulation ('communion' in the terms of Chapter 1), predominantly through apparatuses of state licensure, centring on the General Medical Council, dominated for much of its history by senior physicians (Stacey 1992), with important contributions from the medical Royal Colleges. These institutions have historically been very much concerned with medical education and (in the case of the GMC) standards of non-clinical behaviour, with the consequence that fully trained physicians have been subject to little scrutiny in their clinical work. This traditional model is currently under challenge both at national level (as outlined in Chapter 5) and at the level of the daily work of physicians, which has become subject to inspection, the results of which may have important consequences for the hospitals and clinics that employ them, and 'command'.

Finally, the professional social ideal: medicine has for the last century maintained at least the appearance of collegiality, or equal status of members, within itself, an appearance that has perhaps served the twin purposes of socializing members into an attitude of loyalty to colleagues, and of presenting to the outside world an image of an occupation all of whose members are competent and trustworthy (Freidson 1984). It is now arguable that medicine is explicitly stratified into elites based on research and on management, leaving a clearer rank-and-file to be controlled and managed.

We began this book with the question 'what does clinical governance mean in theory and practice?' Table 14.1 is as near as we can get to a single answer, but of course some *caveats* are in order. First, the models are presented here as Weberian 'ideal types', that is as hypothetical constructions whose elements help us to analyse observations rather than representing precise empirical descriptions. (The term 'ideal type' does not normally carry any normative connotation from the perspective of the analyst, but in the present case it does carry the additional inference that contemporary policy-makers have a preference for the newer 'bureaucratized' model.) Second, although we present this as the general direction in which the professional world of medicine seems to be moving, not all possible futures for medicine necessarily entail movement along all the dimensions in Table 14.1; the proposals in Chapter 13, for instance, entail a substantial degree of trust and reflective practice. Third, it is not the purpose of this book to adopt a normative stance on these changes, though the normative positions of some of our contributors can perhaps be discerned beneath their dispassionate prose. Readers must reach their own conclusions, perhaps pausing to reflect on the near-intractability of the policy puzzle faced by any state that wishes to ensure the provision of good medical services for its subjects:

> How to [both] nurture and control occupations with complex, esoteric knowledge and skill ... which provide us with critical personal services.
>
> (Freidson 2001: 220)

References

Aaron, H.J. and Schwartz, W.B. (1982) *The Painful Prescription: Rationing Hospital Care*. Washington, DC: Brookings Institution.

Abbott, A. (1988) *The System of Professions*. London: University of Chicago Press.

Annandale, E. (1989) Proletarianization or restratification of the medical profession? The case of obstetrics, *International Journal of Health Services*, 19(4): 611–34.

Anspach, R. (1988) Notes on the sociology of medical discourse: the language of case presentation, *Journal of Health and Social Behaviour*, 29: 357–75.

Archer, S. B., Burnett, R.J., Flesch, L.V. *et al.* (1997) Implementation of a clinical pathway decreases length of stay and hospital charges for patients undergoing total Colectomy and Ileal Pounch/Anal Anastomosis, *Surgery*, 122(4): 699–703.

Argyris, C. and Schon, D.A. (1978) *Organizational Learning: A Theory of Action Perspective*. Reading, MA: Addison-Wesley.

Armstrong, J.S. (1982) Strategies for implementing change: an experiential approach, *Group and Organization Studies*, 7(4): 457–75.

Ashmore, M., Mulkay, M. and Pinch, T. (1989) *Health and Efficiency: A Sociology of Health Economics*. Buckingham: Open University Press.

Atkinson, B.J. and Heath, A.W. (1987) Beyond objectivism and relativism: implications for family therapy research, *Journal of Strategic and Systemic Therapies*, 1: 8–17.

Atkinson, P. (1995) *Medical Talk and Medical Work*. London: Sage Publications.

Bach, S. (2000) Health sector reform and human resource management: Britain in comparative perspective, *International Journal of Human Resource Management*, (11)5: 925–42.

Bach, S. (2001) *HR and New Approaches to Public Sector Management: Improving HRM Capacity*. Geneva: World Health Organization.

BAMM (British Association of Medical Managers) (1998) *Clinical Governance in the NHS*. Stockport: BAMM.

Barker, P., Campbell, P. and Davidson, B. (eds) (1999) *From the Ashes of Experience. Reflections on Madness, Survival and Growth*. London: Whurr Publishers.

Barnes, M. (1999a) Users as citizens: collective action and the local governance of welfare, *Social Policy and Administration*, 33(1): 73–90.

Barnes, M. (1999b) *Building a Deliberative Democracy: An Evaluation of Two Citizens' Juries*. London: Institute for Public Policy Research.

Barnes, M. and Bennett, G. (1998) Frail bodies, courageous voices: older people influencing community care, *Health and Social Care in the Community*, 6(2): 102–11.

Barnes, M. and Cormie, J. (1995) On the panel – good hospital discharge, *Health Service Journal*, 2 March: 30–1.

Barnes, M. and Prior, D. (2000) *Private Lives as Public Policy*. Birmingham: Venture Press.

Barnes, M. and Shardlow, P. (1997) From passive recipient to active citizen. Participation in mental health user groups, *Journal of Mental Health*, 6(3): 275–86.

Barnes, M. and Wistow, G. (1993) *Gaining Influence, Gaining Support: Working with Carers in Research and Practice*. Working Paper No. 8, Nuffield Institute for Health, University of Leeds.

Barnes, M. and Wistow, G. (1994) Learning to hear voices: listening to users of mental health services, *Journal of Mental Health*, 3: 525–40.

Barnes, M., Newman, J., Knops, A. and Sullivan, H. (2003) Constituting the public for public participation, *Public Administration*, 81(2): 379–99.

Bartley, M. (1990) Do we need a strong programme in medical sociology? *Sociology of Health and Illness*, 12(4): 371–90.

Bateson, G. and Bateson, M.C. (1988) *Angels Fear: An Investigation into the Nature and the Meaning of the Sacred*. London: Rider.

Beck, U. (1992) *Risk Society: Towards a New Modernity*. London: Sage Publications.

Becker, B.N., Breiterman-White, R., Nylander, W. *et al* (1997) Care pathway reduces hospitalizations and cost for Haemodialysis Vascular Access Surgery, *American Journal of Kidney Disease*, 30(4): 525–31.

Benger, J. (2001) Standards, effectiveness and costs of telemedicine. Paper presented to Department of Health ICT Research Initiative Workshop on *ICT to Change Practice*, Open University, Milton Keynes, 15 June.

Berlant, J. (1975) *Profession and Monopoly: A Study of Medicine in the United States and Great Britain*. Berkeley, CA: University of California Press.

Bero, L., Grilli, R., Grimshaw, J. *et al.* (1998) Getting research findings into practice: closing the gap between research and practice: an overview of systematic reviews of interventions to promote the implementation of research findings, *British Medical Journal*, 317(7156): 465.

Bilson, A. (1997) Guidelines for a constructivist approach: steps towards the adaptation of ideas from family therapy for use in organizations, *Systems Practice*, 10(2): 153–78.

Bilson, A. and Barker, R. (1994) Siblings of children in care or accommodation: a neglected area of practice, *Practice*, 6(4): 226–35.

Bilson, A. and Barker, R. (1995) Parental contact in foster care and residential care after the Children Act, *British Journal of Social Work*, 25(3): 367–81.

Bilson, A. and Barker, R. (1998) Looked after children and contact: reassessing the social work task, *Research, Policy and Planning*, 16(1): 20–7.

Bilson, A. and Ross, S. (1999) *Social Work Management and Practice: Systems Principles*, second edition. London: Jessica Kingsley Publishers.

Black, N. (1998) Clinical governance: fine words or action? *British Medical Journal*, January, 316: 297–8.

Blair, T. (1998) Address to Conference on *All Our Tomorrows*, Earls Court, London, July.

Blalock, H.M. (1982) *Conceptualization and Measurement in the Social Sciences*. London: Sage Publications.

Blau, P.M. (1955) *The Dynamics of Bureaucracy*. Chicago, IL: University of Chicago Press.

Bloor, D. (1976) *Knowledge and Social Imagery*. London: Routledge.

Bloor, M. (1976) Bishop Berkeley and the Adeno-Tonsillectomy Enigma: an exploration of variation in the social construction of medical disposal, *Sociology*, 10: 43–61.

Booth, T. and Booth, W. (1994) *Parenting under Pressure. Mothers and Fathers with Learning Difficulties*. Buckingham: Open University Press.

Borokowski, V. (1994) Implementation of a managed care model in an acute care setting, *Journal of Healthcare Quality*, 16(2): 25–7, 30.

Brearley, S. (2001) What is evidence based medicine? *Radiography*, 7(1): 7–10.

Brindle, D. (2002) The big picture, *NHS Primary Care Magazine*, February: 16–17.

Brown, B. and Crawford, P. (2003) The clinical governance of the soul: 'deep management' and the self-regulating subject, *Social Science and Medicine*, 56(1): 67–81.

Buchan, J. (2000) Health sector reform and human resources: lessons from the United Kingdom, *Health Policy and Planning*, 15(3): 319–25.

Buetow, S.A. and Roland, M. (1999) Clinical governance: bridging the gap between managerial and clinical approaches to quality of care, *Quality in Health Care*, 8: 184–90.

Burchill, F. and Cassey, A. (1996) *Human Resource Management: The NHS – A case Study*. Basingstoke: Macmillan.

Burke, C. and Lugon, M. (1999) Clinical audit and clinical governance, in M. Lugon and J. Secker-Walker (eds) *Clinical Governance: Making it Happen*. London: The Royal Society of Medicine Press.

Burns, T. and Stalker, G.M. (1961) *The Management of Innovation*. London: Tavistock.

Burrell, G. (1998) Modernism, postmodernism and organizational analysis: the contribution of Michel Foucault, in A. McKinlay and K. Starkey (eds) *Foucault, Management and Organization Theory*. London: Sage Publications.

Byrne, D. (2002) *Interpreting Quantitative Data*. London: Sage Publications.

Byrne, D.S. (1998) *Complexity Theory and the Social Sciences*. London: Routledge.

Calabresi, G. and Bobbitt, P. (1978) *Tragic Choices*. New York, NY: Norton.

Calligaro, K.D. (1996) Role of nursing personnel in implementing clinical pathways and decreasing hospital costs for major vascular surgery, *Journal of Vascular Nursing*, 14(3): 57–61.

Callon, M., Law, J. and Rip, A. (1986) *Mapping the Dynamics of Science and Technology*. London: Macmillan.

Caporaso, J. (1996) The European Union and forms of state: Westphalian, regulatory or post-modern? *Journal of Common Market Studies*, 34(1): 29–52.

Cawson, A. (1982) *Corporatism and Welfare: Social Policy and State Intervention in Britain*. London: Heinemann.

Cawson, A. (ed.) (1985) *Organized Interests and the State: Studies in Meso-Corporatism*. London: Sage Publications.

Charlton, R. (2001) Continuing professional development (CPD) and training, *British Medical Journal*, 323: 2–3.

Church, K. (1996) Beyond 'bad manners': the power relations of 'consumer participation' in Ontario's community mental health system, *Canadian Journal of Community Mental Health*, 15(2): 27–44.

Cilliers, P. (1998) *Complexity and Postmodernism*. London: Routledge.

Clarke, J., Cochrane, A. and Mcloughlin, E. (1994) Mission accomplished or unfinished business? The impact of managerialization, in J. Clarke, A. Cochrane and E. McLoughlin (eds) *Managing Social Policy*. London: Sage Publications.

Clegg, S. (1998) Foucault, power and organizations, in A. McKinlay and K. Starkey (eds) *Foucault Management and Organization Theory*. London: Sage Publications.

Coburn, D., Torrance, G.M. and Kaufert, J.M. (1983) Medical dominance in Canada in historical perspective: the rise and fall of medicine? *International Journal of Health Services*, 13(3): 407–32.

Collier, P.E. (1997) Do clinical pathways for major vascular surgery improve outcomes and reduce cost? *Journal of Vascular Surgery*, 26(2): 179–85.

Coote, A. and Lenaghan, J. (1997) *Citizens' Juries: Theory into Practice*. London: Institute for Public Policy Research.

Cormie, J. (1999) The Fife User Panels Project: empowering older people, in M. Barnes and L. Warren (eds) *Paths to Empowerment*. Bristol: The Policy Press.

Courpasson, D. (2000) Managerial strategies of domination: power in soft bureaucracies, *Organization Studies*, 21(1): 141–61.

Crompton, R. (1990) Professions in the current context, *Work, Employment and Society*, Special Issue, May: 147–66.

Crosby, N. (1996) Creating an authentic voice of the people. Paper presented at the annual meeting of the Midwest Political Science Association.

Damasio, A.R. (1994) *Descartes' Error: Emotion, Reason and the Human Brain*. New York, NY: Avon Books.

Dandeker, C. (1990) *Surveillance, Power and Modernity*. Cambridge: Polity Press.

Davies, H.T.O. (1999) Falling public trust in health services: implications for accountability, *Journal of Health Services Research and Policy*, 4(4): 193–4.

Davies, H.T.O. and Nutley, S.M. (1999) The rise and rise of evidence in health care, *Public Money and Management*, 19(1): 9–16.

Davies, H.T.O. and Nutley, S.M. (2000) Healthcare: evidence to the fore, in H.T.O. Davies, S.M. Nutley, and P.C. Smith, (eds) *What Works? Evidence-based Policy and Practice in Public Services*. Bristol: The Policy Press.

Davies, T.O., Nutley, S.M. and Mannion, R. (2000) Organizational culture and quality of health care, *Quality in Health Care*, 9: 111–19.

Dean, M. (1999) *Governmentality: Power and Rule in Modern Society*. London: Sage Publications.

Deetz, S. (1992) Disciplinary power in the modern corporation, in M. Alvesson and H. Willmott (eds) *Critical Management Studies*. London: Sage Publications.

Deetz, S. (1998) Discursive formations, strategized subordination and self-surveillance, in A. McKinlay and K. Starkey (eds) *Foucault, Management and Organization Theory*. London: Sage Publications.

Degeling, P. (2000) Reconsidering clinical accountability: an examination of some dilemmas inherent in efforts to bolster clinician accountability, *International Journal of Health Planning and Management*, 15(1): 3–16.

Degeling, P. and Kennedy, J. (2004) What is the work? An analysis of activity in four NHS Trusts in northern England. Durham: Centre for Clinical Management Development, University of Durham.

Degeling, P., Kennedy, J., Hill, M., Carnegie, M. and Holt, J. (1998) *Professional Subcultures and Hospital Reform*. Sydney: Centre for Hospital Management and Information Systems Research, University of New South Wales.

Degeling, P., Sorensen, R., Maxwell, S. *et al* (2000) *The Organization of Hospital Care and its Effects*. Sydney: Centre for Clinical Governance Research, University of New South Wales.

Degeling, P., Kennedy, J. and Hill, M. (2001) Mediating the cultural boundaries between medicine, nursing and management: the central challenge in hospital reform, *Health Services Management Research*, 14(1): 36–48.

Degeling, P., Macbeth, F., Kennedy, J. *et al* (2002) *Professional Subcultures and Clinical Governance Implementation in NHS Wales: A Report to the National Assembly for Wales*. Durham: University of Durham.

Degeling, P., Maxwell, S., Kennedy, J. and Coyle, B. (2003) Medicine, management and modernization: a 'danse macabre'? *British Medical Journal*, 326: 649–52.

Del Togno-Armansco, V. (1993) *Collaborative Nursing Case Management: A Handbook for Development and Implementation*. New York, NY: Springer Publication Co. Inc.

Dent, M. (1995) Doctors, peer review and quality assurance, in T. Johnson, G. Larkin and M. Saks (eds) *Health Professions and the State in Europe*. London: Routledge.

Dent, M. and Whitehead, S. (2002) *Managing Professional Identities: Knowledge Performativity and the New Professional*. London: Routledge.

Department of Health (1997) *The New NHS: Modern. Dependable*, Cm. 3807. London: The Stationery Office.

Department of Health (1998) *A First Class Service: Quality in the New NHS*. London: Department of Health.

Department of Health (1999) *Supporting Doctors, Protecting Patients*. London: Department of Health.

Department of Health (2000a) *The NHS Plan*, Cm. 4818. London: The Stationery Office.

Department of Health (2000b) *An Organization with a Memory. Report of an Expert Group on Learning from Adverse Events in the NHS* (Chairman: Chief Medical Officer). London: The Stationery Office.

Department of Health (2001a) *Improving Working Lives for Doctors*. London: Department of Health.

Department of Health (2001b) *Learning from Bristol: The Report of the Public Inquiry into Children's Heart Surgery at Bristol Royal Infirmary 1984–1995* (Chairman: Ian Kennedy). London: Department of Health.

Department of Health (2001c) *Modernising Regulation in the Health Professions: Consultation Document*. London: Department of Health.

Department of Health (2002) *Reforming NHS Financial Flows: Introducing Payment by Results*. London: Department of Health.

Department of Health and Social Security (1983) *NHS Management Inquiry* (Chairman: Sir Roy Griffiths). London: Department of Health and Social Security.

Department of Health and Social Security and Welsh Office (1979) *Patients First: Consultative Paper on the Structure and Management of the National Health Service in England and Wales*. London: HMSO.

Department of Health, Welsh Office, Scottish Home and Health Department, and Northern Ireland Office (1989) *Working for Patients*, Cm 555. London: HMSO.

Desrosières, A. (1998) *The Politics of Large Numbers*. Cambridge, MA: Harvard University Press.

Dingwall, R. (1999) Professions and social order in a global society, *International Review of Sociology*, 9: 131–40.

Donaldson, L.J. (1998) Clinical governance and service failure in the NHS, *Public Money and Management*, 18(4): 10–11.

Donaldson, L.J. (2000) Clinical governance: a mission to improve, *British Journal of Clinical Governance*, 5: 1–8.

Donaldson, L.J. (2001) Safe high quality health care: investing in tomorrow's leaders, *Quality in Health Care*, 10 (Supplement II): ii8–ii12.

Dowswell, G., Harrison, S. and Wright, J. (2002) The early days of primary care groups: general practitioners' perceptions, *Health and Social Care in the Community*, 10(1): 46–54.

Dryzek, J.S. (1994) *Discursive Democracy. Politics, Policy and Political Science*. Cambridge: Cambridge University Press.

du Boulay, C. (2000) From CME to CPD: getting better at getting better? *British Medical Journal*, 320: 393–4.

Du Gay, P. (1993) Enterprising management in the public sector, *Work, Employment and Society*, 7: 643–8.

Du Gay, P. (1996) *Consumption and Identity at Work*. London: Sage Publications.

Du Gay, P. (2000) *In Praise of Bureaucracy: Weber, Organization, Ethics*. London: Sage Publications.

Dunkerley, D. and Glasner, P. (1998) Empowering the public? Citizens' juries and the new genetic technologies, *Critical Public Health*, 8(3): 181–92.

Dunleavy, P. (1981) Professions and policy charge: some notes towards a model of ideological corporatism, *Public Administration Bulletin*, 36: 3–16.

Dunsire, A. (1978) *Implementation in a Bureaucracy: The Executive Process, Part 1*. London: Martin Robertson and Oxford University Press.

Dyer, W. (2001) The identification of the careers of mentally disordered offenders using cluster analysis in a complex realist framework. Unpublished Ph.D. thesis, University of Durham.

Edwards, N. and Marshall, M. (2003) Doctors and managers. A constructive dialogue has to replace mutual suspicion, *British Medical Journal*, 326: 116–17.

Edwards, N., Kornacki, M. and Silversin, J. (2002) Unhappy doctors: what are the causes and what can be done? *British Medical Journal*, 324: 835–8.

Egan, G. (1993) *Adding Value*. San Francisco, CA: Jossey-Bass.

Ellis, B. (1997) Integrated care pathways: implications for clinical risk management, *Health Care Risk Report*, 3(6): 13–15.

Ellis, B. and Johnson, S. (1999) The care pathway: a tool to enhance clinical governance, *British Journal of Clinical Governance*, 4(2): 61–7.

Ellis, N.D. and Chisholm, J. (1993) *Making Sense of the Red Book*, second edition. London: Routledge.

Elston, M. (1991) The politics of professional power: medicine in a changing health service, in J. Gabe, M. Calnan and M. Bury (eds) *The Sociology of the Health Service*. London: Routledge.

Eraut, M. (1996) *Developing Professional Knowledge and Competence*. London: Falmer Press.

Etherington, K. (2000) *Narrative Approaches to Working with Adult Male Survivors of Child Sexual Abuse*. London: Jessica Kingsley.

Fairbrother, P. (1996) Trade unions and human resource management in Britain: case study evidence from the public sector, utilities and manufacturing, *Employee Relations*, 18(6): 10–27.

Ferlie, E. (1999) Clinical effectiveness and evidence based medicine: some implementation issues, in M. Lugon and J. Secker-Walker (eds) *Clinical Governance: Making It Happen*. London: The Royal Society of Medicine Press.

Fielding, N.G. and Lee, R.M. (1998) *Computer Analysis and Qualitative Research*. London: Sage Publications.

Firth-Cozens, J. and Payne, R. (1999) *Stress in Healthcare Professions*. Chichester: John Wiley and Sons.

Fishkin, J.S. (1991) *Democracy and Deliberation*. New Haven, CT: Yale University Press.

Flynn, A.M. (1993) Case management: a multi-disciplinary approach to the evaluation of cost and quality standards, *Journal of Nursing Care Quality*, 8(1): 58–66.

Flynn, R. (1992) *Structures of Control in Health Management*. London: Routledge.

Flynn, R. (1999) Managerialism, professionalism and quasi-markets, in M. Exworthy and S. Halford (eds) *Professionals and the New Managerialism in the Public Sector*. Buckingham: Open University Press.

Flynn, R. (2002) Clinical governance and governmentality. *Health, Risk and Society*, 4(2): 155–73.

Flynn, R. and Williams, G. (eds) (1997) *Contracting for Health: Quasi-Markets and the National Health Service*. Oxford: Oxford University Press.

Flynn, R., Williams, G. and Pickard, S. (1996) *Markets and Networks: Contracting in Community Health Services*. Buckingham: Open University Press.

Foley, M. (1989) *The Silence of Constitutions*. London: Routledge.

Forsyth, G. (1966) *Doctors and State Medicine: A Study of the British National Health Service*. London: Pitman Medical.

Foster, P. and Wilding, P. (2000) Whither welfare professionalism? *Social Policy and Administration*, 34(2): 143–59.

Foucault, M. (1991) [original in French, 1978] Governmentality, in G. Burchill, C. Gordon and P. Miller, *The Foucault Effect*. London: Harvester Wheatsheaf.

Fox, A. (1974a) *Man Mismanagement*. London: Hutchinson.

Fox, A. (1974b) *Beyond Contract*, London: Faber and Faber.

Franco, L.M., Bennett, S. and Kanfer, R. (2002) Health sector reform and public sector health worker motivation: a conceptual framework, *Social Science and Medicine*, 54: 1255–66.

Fraser, S.W. and Greenhalgh, T. (2001) Coping with complexity: educating for capability, *British Medical Journal*, 323: 799–803.

Freidson, E. (1970) *Professional Dominance*. New York, NY: Atherton Press.

Freidson, E. (1984) The changing nature of professional control, *Annual Review of Sociology*, 10: 1–20.

Freidson, E. (1985) The reorganization of the medical profession, *Medical Care Review*, 42(1): 11–35.

Freidson, E. (1986) *Professional Powers*. Chicago, IL: University of Chicago Press.

Freidson, E. (1994) *Professionalism Reborn*. Oxford: Polity Press.

Freidson, E. (2001) *Professionalism: The Third Logic*. Cambridge: Polity Press.

Fukuyama, F. (1995) *Trust: The Social Virtues and the Creation of Prosperity*. London: Hamish Hamilton.

Gabe, J., Calnan, M. and Bury, M. (1991) Introduction, in J. Gabe, M. Calnan and M. Bury (eds) *The Sociology of the Health Service*. London: Routledge.

Gallagher, C. (1994) Applying quality improvement tools to quality planning:

paediatric femur fracture clinical path development, *Journal for Healthcare Quality*, 16(3): 6–14.

Garside, P. (1998) Organisational context for quality: lessons from the fields of organisational development and change management, *Quality in Health Care*, 7 (Supplement): S8–S15.

Gee, J., Hull, G. and Lankshear, C. (1996) *The New Work Order: Behind the Language of the New Capitalism*. Sydney: Allen and Unwin.

Giddens, A. (1991) *Consequences of Modernity*. Cambridge: Polity Press.

Glanville, J., Haines, M. and Auston, I. (1998) Finding information on clinical effectiveness, *British Medical Journal*, 317: 200–3.

GMC (General Medical Council) (1993) *Tomorrow's Doctors*. London: General Medical Council.

GMC (2001) *Good Medical Practice*. London: General Medical Council.

Goodman, N.W. (1998) Clinical governance, *British Medical Journal*, 317: 1725–7.

Goodman, N.W., O'Kelly, S.W. and Maxwell, R. (2001) Implementing clinical governance, *British Medical Journal*, 323: 753a.

Gosbee, J. and Lin, L. (2001) The role of human factors engineering in medical device and medical errors, in C. Vincent (ed.) *Understanding Clinical Risk Management: Enhancing Patient Safety*, second edition. London: BMJ Publishing Group.

Gosling, A., Westbrook, J. and Braithwaite, J. (2003a) Clinical team functioning and IT innovation: a study of the diffusion of a point-of-care online evidence system, *Journal of the American Medical Informatics Association*, 10(3): 244–51.

Gosling, A., Westbrook, J. and Coiera, E. (2003b) Variation in the use of online clinical evidence: a qualitative analysis, *International Journal of Medical Informatics*, 69(1): 1–16.

Gottlieb, L.D., Roer, D., Jega, K. *et al.* (1996) Clinical pathway for pneumonia: development, implementation and initial experience, *Best Practices and Benchmarking in Healthcare*, 1(5): 262–5.

Gray, A.G. (1998) *Business Like but Not Like a Business: The Challenge for Public Sector Management*. London: Public Finance Foundation/CIPFA.

Gray, A.G. and Jenkins, W.I. (1993) Markets, managers and the public service: the changing of a culture, in P. Taylor-Gooby and R. Lawson (eds) *Markets and Managers*. Buckingham: Open University Press.

Greco, M. (2000) Assessing the quality of communication using patient feedback, *Clinical Governance Bulletin*, 1(3): 4–5.

Green, J. (2000) Epistemology, evidence and experience: evidence based health care in the work of accident alliances, *Sociology of Health and Illness*, 22(4): 453–76.

Greenaway, D. (2001) Chair of UK Telemedicine Association presentation to the House of Commons Select Committee on Health, 26 April. London: HMSO.

Gregory, C., Pope, S., Werry, D. and Dobek, P. (1996) Reduced length of stay and improved appropriateness of care with a clinical path for total knee or hip arthroplasty, *Journal on Quality Improvement*, 22(9): 617–27.

Grey Turner, E. (1982) *The History of the British Medical Association. Volume II: 1932–81*. London: British Medical Association.

Grol, R. and Grimshaw, J. (1999) Evidence-based implementation of evidence-based medicine, *The Joint Commission Journal on Quality Improvement*, 25(10): 503–13.

Guiliano, K.K. and Poirier, C.E. (1991) Nursing case management: critical pathways to desirable outcomes, *Nursing Management*, 22(3): 52–5.

Gutmann, A. and Thompson, D. (1996) *Democracy and Disagreement*. Cambridge, MA: Harvard University Press.

Habermas, J. (1984) *Theory of Communicative Action, Vol. 1: Reason and the Rationalization of Society*, Boston, MA: Beacon Press.

Habermas, J. (1987) *Theory of Communicative Action, Vol. 2: Lifeworld and System – A Critique of Functionalist Reason*. Boston, MA: Beacon Press.

Hackett, M.C. (1999) Implementing clinical governance in Trusts, *International Journal of Health Care Quality Assurance*, 12: 210–13.

Hackett, M. and Spurgeon, P. (1996) Leadership and vision in the NHS: how do we create the 'vision thing'? *Health Manpower Management*, 22(1): 5–9.

Hackett, M., Lilford, R. and Jordan, J. (1999) Clinical governance: culture, leadership and power the key to changing attitudes and behaviours in trusts, *International Journal of Health Care Quality Assurance*, 12(3): 98–104.

Hall, C. (1997) *Social Work as Narrative: Storytelling and Persuasion in Professional Texts*. Aldershot: Ashgate.

Ham, C.J. (1981) *Policy Making in the National Health Service*. London: Macmillan.

Ham, C. (1999) *Health Policy in Britain*, fourth edition. Houndsmill and London: Macmillan.

Ham, C. and Hill, M. (1993) *The Policy Process in the Modern Capitalist State*, second edition. Hemel Hempstead: Harvester Wheatsheaf.

Hanley, B., Bradburn, J., Gorin, S. *et al.* (2000) *Involving Consumers in Research and Development in the NHS: Briefing Notes for Researchers*. Winchester: Consumers in the NHS Research Support Unit, Help for Health Trust.

Harris, A. (2000) Risk management in practice: how are we managing? *British Journal of Clinical Governance*, 5(3): 142–9.

Harrison, R. (1995) Organization culture and quality of service, in *Collected Papers of Roger Harrison*. Maidenhead: McGraw-Hill.

Harrison, S. (1981) The politics of health manpower, in A.F. Long and G. Mercer (eds) *Manpower Planning in the National Health Service*. Farnborough: Gower Press.

Harrison, S. (1982) Consensus decision making in the National Health Service: a review, *Journal of Management Studies*, 19(4): 337–94.

Harrison, S. (1988) *Managing the National Health Service: Shifting the Frontier?* London: Chapman and Hall.

Harrison, S. (1998) The politics of evidence based medicine in the UK, *Policy and Politics*, 26(1): 15–31.

Harrison, S. (1999a) Clinical autonomy and health policy: past and futures, in M. Exworthy and S. Halford (eds) *Professionals and the New Managerialism in the Public Sector*. Buckingham: Open University Press.

Harrison, S. (1999b) New Labour, modernization and health care governance. Paper presented at the Political Studies Association/Social Policy Association conference, *New Labour, New Health*, London, September.

Harrison, S. (2001) Reforming the medical profession in the United Kingdom 1989–97: structural interests in health care, in M. Bovens, B.G. Peters and P. t'Hart (eds) *Success and Failure in Public Governance*. Aldershot: Edward Elgar.

Harrison, S. (2002) New Labour, modernization and the medical labour process, *Journal of Social Policy*, 31(3): 465–85.

Harrison, S. (2003) Health policy, in M. Kogan and M. Hawksworth (eds) *The Routledge Encyclopaedia of Government and Politics*, second edition. London: Routledge.

Harrison, S. and Ahmad, W.I.U. (2000) Medical autonomy and the UK state 1975 to 2025, *Sociology*, 34(1): 129–46.

Harrison, S. and Dowswell, G. (2002) Autonomy and bureaucratic accountability in primary care: what English general practitioners say, *Sociology of Health and Illness*, 24(2): 208–26.

Harrison, S. and Gray, A.G. (2000) *Governing Medicine – Clinical Governance in UK Health Institutions*. Briefing for ESRC Seminar Series. Leeds: Nuffield Institute for Health, University of Leeds.

Harrison, S. and Hunter, D.J. (1994) *Rationing Health Care*. London: Institute for Public Policy Research.

Harrison, S. and Lim, J. (2000) Clinical governance and primary care in the English National Health Service: some issues of organization and rules, *Critical Public Health*, 10(3): 321–9.

Harrison, S. and Lim, J. (2003) The frontier of control: doctors and managers in the NHS 1966 to 1997, *Clinical Governance*, 8(2): 13–17.

Harrison, S. and McDonald, R. (2003) Science, consumerism and bureaucracy: new legitimations of medical professionalism, *International Journal of Public Sector Management*, 16(2): 110–21.

Harrison, S. and Pollitt, C. (1994) *Controlling Health Professionals*, Buckingham: Open University Press.

Harrison, S., Hunter, D. and Pollitt, C. (1990) *The Dynamics of British Health Policy*. London: Routledge.

Harrison, S., Hunter, D.J., Marnoch, G. and Pollitt, C. (1992) *Just Managing: Power and Culture in the National Health Service*. London: Macmillan.

Hart, R. (1992) MD-directed critical pathways: it's time. *Hospitals*, 5 (December).

Hayles, K. (1999) *How We Became Posthuman*. Chicago, IL: University of Chicago Press.

Heller, T., Heller, D. and Pattison, S. (2001) Vaccination against mumps, measles and rubella: is there a case for deepening the debate? *British Medical Journal*, 323: 838–40.

Hewitt, J., Watson, J.A. and Weist, A. (2000) Working together to improve patient care: the clinical skills trainer and the clinical support librarian, *Clinical Governance Bulletin*, 1(3): 9–10.

Hicks, A. (1994) Qualitative analytical comparison and analytical induction: the case of the emergence of the social security state, *Sociological Methods and Research*, 23(1): 86–113.

Hindle, D. (2001) Caring about carepaths in Queensland and Bulgaria: a commentary, *Australian Health Review*, 24(4): 15–17.

Hoggett, P. (1994) The politics of the modernization of the UK welfare state, in R. Burrows and B. Loader (eds) *Towards a Post-Fordist Welfare State?* London: Routledge.

Hoggett, P. (1996) New modes of control in the public service, *Public Administration*, 74(1): 9–32.

Holt, P., Wilson, A. and Ward, J. (1996) *Clinical Practice Guidelines and Critical Pathways: A Status Report on National and NSW Development and Implementation Activity*. Sydney: New South Wales Health Department.

Hood, C. (1995a) The 'new public management' in the 1980s, *Accounting, Organizations and Society*, 20: 93–109.

Hood, C. (1995b) Contemporary public management: a new global paradigm?, *Public Policy and Administration*, 10(2): 104–17.

Hood, C., Rothstein, H., Baldwin, R., Rees, J. and Spackman, M. (1999) Where risk society meets the regulatory state, *Risk Management*, 1: 21–34.

Hopkinson, R.B. (2000) Clinical leadership in practice – wearing many hats, *Health Care Review Online*, 4(9).

Huber, G.L. and Garcia, C.M. (1991) Computer assistance for testing hypotheses about qualitative data: the software package AQUAD 3.0, *Qualitative Sociology*, 14: 325–48.

Iedema, R. (2003) *Discourses of Post-bureaucratic Organization*. Amsterdam and Philadelphia, PA: John Benjamin's Publishing Company.

Iliffe, S. and Gordon, H. (1976) *Pickets in White*. London: MPU Publications.

Jankowski, R. (2001) Implementing national guidelines at local level, *British Medical Journal*, 322: 1258–9.

Jessop, B. (1994) The transition to post-Fordism and the Schumpeterian workfare state, in R. Burrows and B. Loader (eds) *Towards a Post-Fordist Welfare State?* London: Routledge.

Johnson, S. (1994) Patient-focussed care without the upheaval, *Nursing Standard*, 8(29): 20–1.

Johnson, T. (1972) *Professions and Power*. London: Macmillan.

Johnson, T. (1995) 'Governmentality and the institutionalization of expertise', in

T. Johnson, G. Larkin and M. Saks (eds) *Health Professions and the State in Europe*. London: Routledge.

Kelleher, D., Gabe, J. and Williams, G. (1994) Understanding medical dominance in the modern world, in J. Gabe, D. Kelleher and G. Williams (eds) *Challenging Medicine*. London: Routledge.

Kemshall, H. (2000) Conflicting knowledges on risk, *Health, Risk and Society*, 2: 143–58.

Kendall, E. (2001) *The Future Patient*. London: IPPR.

Khalil, E.L. (1996) Social theory and naturalism, in E.L. Khalil and K. Boulding (eds) *Evolution, Order and Complexity*. London: Routledge.

King, J. and Wilson, M. (2001) *General Practice: Building on Quality: Identifying Potential Models for Primary Clinical Care for Australia*. Monash Institute of Public Health.

Kirsch, G. (2001) Inventing the future of eHealth. Video Address to *eHealth: a futurescope*, City University, London, April.

Klein, R. (1990) The state and the profession: the politics of the double bed, *British Medical Journal*, 301: 700–2.

Knights, D. (1990) Subjectivity, power and the labour process, in D. Knights and H. Wilmott (eds) *Labour Process Theory*. Basingstoke: Macmillan.

Knights, D. and McCabe, D. (2000) Ain't misbehavin? Opportunities for resistance under new forms of quality management, *Sociology*, 34: 421–36.

Kooiman, J. (1993) Social-political governance: an introduction, in J. Kooiman (ed.) *Modern Governance*. London: Sage Publications.

Lam, A. (2000) Tacit knowledge, organizational learning and societal institutions – an integrated framework, *Organization Studies*, 21: 487–513.

Latham, L., Freeman, T., Walshe, K. and Spurgeon, P. (1999) *The Early Development of Clinical Governance: A Survey of NHS Trusts in the West Midlands*. Birmingham: Health Services Management Centre, University of Birmingham.

Latimer, J. (2000) *The Conduct of Care: Understanding Nursing Practice*. Oxford: Blackwell.

Latour, B. (1987) *Science in Action: How to Follow Scientists and Engineers Through Society*. Cambridge, MA: Harvard University Press.

Lave, J. and Wenger, E. (1995) *Situated Learning. Legitimate Peripheral Participation*. Cambridge: Cambridge University Press.

Law, J. (1989) Technology and heterogeneous engineering: the case of Portuguese expansion, in W. Bijker, T. Hughes and T. Pinch (eds) *The Social Construction of Technological Systems: New Directions in the Sociology and History of Technology*. Cambridge, MA: MIT Press.

Lawson, H. (1984) *Reflexivity: The Postmodern Predicament*. London: Hutchinson.

Leape, L.L. (1990) Practice guidelines and standards: an overview, *Quality Review Bulletin*, February: 42–9.

Leibrich, J. (1999) *A Gift of Stories. Discovering How to Deal with Mental Illness*. Dunedin: University of Otago Press.

Leopold, J., Harris, L. and Watson, T. (1999) *Strategic Human Resourcing: Principles, Perspectives and Practices.* London: Financial Times–Pitman Publishing.

LGMB (Local Government Management Board) (1996) *Citizens' Juries in Local Government: Report for LGMB on the Pilot Projects.* London: Local Government Management Board.

Light, D.W. (1995) Countervailing powers: a framework for professions in transition, in T.J. Johnson, G. Larkin and M. Saks (eds) *Health Professions and the State in Europe.* London: Routledge.

Lipsky, M. (1980) *Street-Level Bureaucracy: Dilemmas of the Individual in Public Services.* New York, NY: Sage Publications.

Llewellyn, S. (2001) Two-way windows: clinicians as medical managers, *Organization Studies*, 22: 593–623.

Lomas, J. (1989) Do practice guidelines guide practice? *New England Journal of Medicine*, 321: 1306–11.

Lord, J. and Littlejohns, P. (1997) Evaluating healthcare policies: the case of clinical audit, *British Medical Journal*, 315: 668–71.

Lugon, M. and Scally, G. (2000) Risk management (Editorial), *Clinical Governance Bulletin*, 1(2): 1–2.

Lugon, M. and Secker-Walker, J. (eds) (1999) *Clinical Governance: Making it Happen.* London: Royal Society of Medicine Press.

Luhmann, N. (1979) *Trust and Power.* Chichester: John Wiley.

McCracken, M. (2000) Developing risk reporting in a hospital trust, *Clinical Governance Bulletin*, 1(2): 7–8.

McIntyre, S. and Pettigrew, M. (2000) Good intentions are not enough, *Journal of Epistemiology and Community Health*, 54: 802–3.

McIver, S. (1997) *An Evaluation of the Kings Fund Citizens' Juries Programme.* Birmingham: University of Birmingham, Health Services Management Centre.

MacKenzie, D. (1990) *Inventing Accuracy.* Cambridge, MA: MIT Press.

McKinlay, J. and Arches, J. (1985) Towards the proletarianization of physicians, *International Journal of Health Services*, 15: 161–95.

McKinlay, J.B. and Marceau, L. (2002) The end of the golden age of doctoring, *International Journal of Health Services*, 32(2): 379–416.

McKinlay, A. and Starkey, K. (1998) Managing Foucault: Foucault, management and organization theory, in A. McKinlay and K. Starkey (eds) *Foucault, Management and Organization Theory.* London: Sage Publications.

McLaren, P. (2001) *Telemed 2001: from research to service delivery.* Conference, Royal Society of Medicine, 15–16 January, London.

Mahmood, K. (2003) The implementation of a local primary care incentive scheme: medical versus management priorities. *Clinical Governance*, 8(2): 19–25.

Mair, F. and Whitten, P. (2000) Systematic review of studies of patient satisfaction with telemedicine, *British Medical Journal*, 320: 1517–20.

Majone, G. (1986) Mutual adjustment by debate and persuasion, in F.X. Kaufman,

G. Majone and V. Ostrom (eds) *Guidance, Control and Evaluation in the Public Sector: The Bielefeld Interdisciplinary Project*. Berlin: De Gruyter.

Marquand, D. (1988) *The Unprincipled Society: New Demands and Old Politics*. London: Jonathan Cape.

Marris, P. and Rein, M. (1967) *Dilemmas of Social Reform*. London: Routledge and Kegan Paul.

Marshall, M., Sheaff, R., Rogers, A. *et al.* (2002) A qualitative study of the cultural changes in primary care organizations needed to implement clinical governance, *British Journal of General Practice*, 52: 641–5.

Mattingly, C. (1998) *Healing Dramas and Clinical Plots: The Narrative Structure of Experience*. Cambridge: Cambridge University Press.

May, C. and Ellis, N.T. (2001) When protocols fail: technical evaluation, biomedical knowledge, and the social construction of facts about a telemedicine clinic, *Social Science and Medicine*, 53: 989–1002.

Maynard, A. (1999) Clinical governance – an economic perspective, *British Journal of Clinical Governance*, 4: 4–6.

Mea, V. Della (2001) What is e-Health (2): the death of telemedicine? *Journal of Medical Internet Research*, 3(2): e22.

Mead, P. (2000) Clinical guidelines: promoting clinical effectiveness or a professional minefield? *Journal of Advanced Nursing*, 31(1): 110–16.

Merrison Committee (1975) *Report of the Committee of Inquiry into the regulation of the medical profession* (Chairman: A.W. Merrison), Cmnd. 6018. London: HMSO.

Middleton, D. and Hewitt, H. (2000) Biography and identity: life story work in transitions of care for people with learning difficulties, in P. Chamberlayne, J. Bornat and T. Wengraf (eds) *The Turn to Biographical Methods in Social Sciences*. London: Routledge.

Midwinter, A. and McGarvey, N. (2001) In search of the regulatory state: evidence from Scotland, *Public Administration*, 79(4): 825–49.

Mizrahi, T. (1985) Getting rid of patients: contradictions in the socialization of internists to the doctor–patient relationship, *Sociology of Health and Illness*, 7(2): 214–35.

Moran, M. (1999) *Governing the Health Care State*. Manchester: Manchester University Press.

Moran, M. and Wood, B. (1993) *States, Regulation and the Medical Profession*. Buckingham: Open University Press.

Mort, M., May, C. and Williams, T. (2003) Remote doctors and absent patients: acting at a distance in telemedicine? *Science, Technology and Human Values*, 28(2): 274–95.

Mowatt, G., Bower, D.J., Brebner, J.A. *et al.* (1997) When and how to assess fast changing technologies: a comparative study of four generic technologies, *Health Technology Assessment*, 1(14): 1–151.

Muirhead Little, E. (1932) *The History of the British Medical Association 1832–1932*. London: British Medical Association.

Navarro, V. (1988) Professional dominance or proletarianization? Neither, *Millbank Quarterly*, 66 (supp. 2): 57–75.

NHS (National Health Service) Executive (1998) *Information for Health: An Information Strategy for the Modern NHS, 1998–2001*. London: Department of Health.

NHS Executive (1999) *Clinical Governance in the New NHS*, Health Service Circular 1999/45. London: Department of Health.

Nicholls, S., Cullen, R., O'Neill, S. and Halligan, A. (2000) Clinical governance: its origins and its foundations, *British Journal of Clinical Governance*, 5(3): 172–8.

Nutley, S.M. and Davies, H.T.O. (2001) Developing organizational learning in the NHS, *Medical Education*, 35: 35–41.

Oakley, A. (2000) *Experiments in Knowing*. Cambridge: Polity Press.

O'Neill, O. (2002) *A Question of Trust: The BBC Reith Lectures 2002*. Cambridge: Cambridge University Press.

Osborne, D. and Gaebler, T. (1992) *Reinventing Government: How the Entrepreneurial Spirit is Transforming the Public Sector*. Reading, MA: Addison-Wesley.

Osborne, T. (1993) On liberalism, neo-liberalism and the 'liberal profession' of medicine, *Economy and Society*, 22: 345–56.

Patterson, L. (2002) The role of CHI in monitoring the development of clinical governance in Trusts, *British Journal of Clinical Governance*, 7(3): 147–9.

Pawson, R. and Tilley, N. (1997) *Realistic Evaluation*. London: Sage Publications.

Pedler, M., Burgoyne, J. and Boydell, T. (1995) *A Manager's Guide to Self Development*. Maidenhead: McGraw-Hill.

Perkin, H. (1990) *The Rise of Professional Society: England since 1880*. London: Routledge.

Peters, T.J. and Waterman, R.H. (1982) *In Search of Excellence*. New York, NY: Harper & Row.

Petts, J. (1997) The public–expert interface in local waste management decisions: expertise, credibility and process, *Public Understanding of Science*, 6: 359–81.

Petts, J. (2001) Evaluating the effectiveness of deliberative processes: waste management case studies, *Journal of Environmental Planning and Management*, 44(2): 207–26.

Phillips, A. (1995) *The Politics of Presence*. Oxford: Oxford University Press.

Pithouse, A. (1987) *Social Work: The Social Organization of an Invisible Trade*. Aldershot: Avebury Gower.

Polanyi, M. (1967) *The Tacit Dimension*. London: Routledge and Kegan Paul.

Pollitt, C. (1990) *Managerialism and the Public Services*. Oxford: Blackwell.

Poole, D.G. (1994) *Industrial Process Control*. Albany: Delmar.

Power, M. (1997) *The Audit Society*. Oxford: Oxford University Press.

Pringle, M. (1998) Preventing ischaemic heart disease in one general practice: from one patient, through clinical audit, needs assessment, and commissioning into quality improvement, *British Medical Journal*, 317: 1120–3.

Putnam, L.L. and Mumby, D.K. (1993) Organizations, emotions and the myth of rationality, in S. Fineman (ed.) *Emotions in Organizations*. London: Sage Publications.

Quennell, P. (2003) Getting a word in edgeways? Patient group participation in the appraisal process of the National Institute for Clinical Excellence, *Clinical Governance*, 8(2): 39–45.

Ragin, C.C. (1987) *The Comparative Method: Moving beyond Qualitative and Quantitative Strategies*. Berkeley, CA: University of California Press.

Ragin, C.C. (1994) *Constructing Social Research*. Thousand Oaks, CA: Pine Forge Press.

Rao, N. (ed.) (2000) *Representation and Community in Western Democracies*. Basingstoke: Macmillan.

Ray, L.J. and Reed, M. (1994) Weber, organizations and modernity: an introduction, in L.J. Ray and M. Reed (eds) *Organizing Modernity*. London: Routledge.

Reason, J.T. (2001) Understanding adverse events: the human factor, in C. Vincent (ed.) *Understanding Clinical Risk Management: Enhancing Patient Safety*, second edition. London: BMJ Publishing Group.

Reason, J.T., Carthey, J. and de Laval, M.R. (2000) Diagnosing 'vulnerable system syndrome': an essential prerequisite to effective risk management, *Quality in Health Care*, 10 (Supplement II): ii21–ii25.

Redfern, N., Bynoe, A.G., O'Halloran, C., Pokora, J. and Connor, M.P. (2000) Individual doctors and clinical governance: achieving an appropriate balance of support and challenge in hospital medicine, *Clinician in Management*, 9: 169–76.

Renn, O., Webler, T., Rakel, H., Dienel, P. and Johnson, B. (1993) Public participation in decision making: a three step procedure, *Policy Sciences*, 26: 189–214.

Rhodes, R.A.W. (1997) *Understanding Governance: Policy Networks, Governance, Reflexivity and Accountability*. Buckingham: Open University Press.

Ritzer, G. and Walcak, D. (1988) Rationalization and deprofessionalization of physicians, *Social Forces*, 67: 1–22.

Roberts, J. (2000) From know-how to show-how? Questioning the role of information and communication technologies in knowledge transfer, *Technology Analysis and Strategic Management*, 12(4): 429–43.

Robinson, J.C. (1999) *The Corporate Practice of Medicine: Competition and Innovation in Health Care*. Berkeley, CA: University of California Press.

Roland, M., Campbell, S. and Wilkin, D. (2001) Clinical governance: a convincing strategy for quality improvement? *Journal of Management in Medicine*, 15(3): 188–201.

Rose, N. (1993) Government, authority and expertise in advanced liberalism, *Economy and Society*, 22: 283–99.

Rose, N. (1996) Identity, genealogy, history, in P. Du Gay (ed.) *Questions of Cultural Identity*. London: Sage Publications.

Rose, N. (1999) *Powers of Freedom*. Cambridge: Cambridge University Press.

Rose, N. and Miller, P. (1992) Political power beyond the state: problematics of governmentality, *British Journal of Sociology*, 43: 173–205.

Rowland, H. (2003) Janus – the two faces of the Commission for Health Improvement, *Clinical Governance*, 8(1): 33–8.

Sacks, O. (1995) *An anthropologist on Mars*. New York, NY: Alfred Knopf.

Salter, B. (2001) Who rules? The new politics of medical regulation, *Social Science and Medicine*, 52: 871–83.

Scally, G. and Donaldson, L. (1998) Clinical governance and the drive for quality improvement in the new NHS in England, *British Medical Journal*, 317: 61–5.

Scase, R. (2001) Why we're so clock wise, *Observer*, 26 August.

Schon, D.A. (1983) *The Reflective Practitioner: How Professionals Think in Action*. Aldershot: Ashgate and Basic Books.

Schon, D.A. (1988) From technical rationality to reflection-in-action, in J. Dowie and A. Elstein, *Professional Judgement: A Reader in Clinical Decision Making*. Cambridge: Cambridge University Press.

Schulz, R.I. and Harrison, S. (1986) Physician autonomy in the Federal Republic of Germany, Great Britain and the United States, *International Journal of Health Planning and Management*, 1(5): 1213–28.

Scotland, A. (1998) Clinical governance in the new NHS: an agenda for personal and organizational development, *Clinician in Management*, 7(3): 138–41.

Scott, J. (1998) *Seeing Like a State: How Certain Schemes to Improve the Human Condition Have Failed*. New Haven, CT: Yale University Press.

Senge, P.M. (1990) *The Fifth Discipline: The Art and Practice of the Learning Organization*. New York, NY: Doubleday Currency.

Sibeon, R. (1997) *Contemporary Sociology and Policy Analysis*. Eastham and London: Tudor.

Sinclair, S. (1997) *Making Doctors: An Institutional Apprenticeship*. Oxford: Berg.

Singleton, V. and Michael, M. (1993) Actor-networks and ambivalence: general practitioners in the cervical screening programme, *Social Studies of Science*, 23: 227–64.

Smith, C. (2001) Trust and confidence: possibilities for social work in 'high modernity', *British Journal of Social Work*, 31: 287–305.

Smith, R. (1989) Discipline 1: the hordes at the gate, *British Medical Journal*, 298: 1502–5.

Smith, R. (2001) Why are doctors so unhappy?, *British Medical Journal*, 322: 1073–4.

Stacey, M. (1989a) The General Medical Council and professional accountability, *Public Policy and Administration*, 4(1): 12–27.

Stacey, M. (1989b) A sociologist looks at the GMC, *The Lancet*, 1 April: 713–14.

Stacey, M. (1992) *Regulating British Medicine: The General Medical Council*. Chichester: Wiley.

Stewart, R. (1979) *The Reality of Management*. Harmondsworth: Penguin.

STHT (Sheffield Teaching Hospitals NHS Trust) (2002) *Clinical Governance Annual Report 2001–2002: Quality is Everyone's Business – Innovating – Learning – Improving*. Sheffield: Sheffield Teaching Hospitals NHS Trust.

Stocking, B. (1992) Promoting change in clinical care, *Quality in Health Care*, 1: 56–60.

Storey, J. (1985) The means of management control, *Sociology*, 9: 193–211.

Surender, R., Locock, L., Chambers, D., Dopson, S. and Gabby, J. (2002) Closing the gap between research and practice in health: lessons from a clinical effectiveness initiative, *Public Management Review*, 4(1): 45–61.

Swage, T. (2000) *Clinical Governance in Health Care Practice*. Oxford: Butterworth-Heinemann.

Tannenbaum, S.J. (1994) Knowing and acting in medical practice, *Journal of Health Politics, Policy and Law*, 19(1): 27–44.

Taylor, C. and White, S. (2000) *Practising Reflexivity in Health and Welfare: Making Knowledge*. Buckingham: Open University Press.

Taylor, P., Pocklington, S., Barrett, S., Jolley, P. and Baker, A. (2000) Implementing clinical governance – getting the skills into practice, *Clinical Governance Bulletin*, 1(3): 5–6.

Teasdale, S. (1996) The future of clinical audit: learning to work together, *British Medical Journal*, 313: 574.

Thagard, P. (2000) *How Scientists Explain Disease*. Princeton, NJ: Princeton University Press.

Thompson, S. and Hoggett, P. (2001) The emotional dynamics of deliberative democracy, *Policy and Politics*, 29(3): 351–64.

Thompson, D., Snape, E. and Stokes, C. (1999) Health service reform and human resource management in Hong Kong public hospitals, *International Journal of Health Planning and Management*, 14: 19–39.

Thomson, R., Lavender, M. and Madhok, R. (1995) How to ensure that guidelines are effective, *British Medical Journal*, 311: 237–42.

Turley, K., Tyndall, M., Roge, C. *et al.* (1994) Critical pathway methodology: effectiveness in congenital heart surgery, *Annals of Thoracic Surgery*, 58(1): 57–63.

Turner, B.S. (1995) *Medical Power and Social Knowledge*, second edition. London: Sage Publications.

Turner, B.S. (1997) From governmentality to risk: some reflections on Foucault's contribution to medical sociology, in A. Peterson and R. Bunton (eds) *Foucault, Health and Medicine*. London: Routledge.

Tyson, S. (1997) Human resource strategy: a process for managing the contribution of HRM to organizational performance, *The International Journal of Human Resource Management*, 8(3): 227–90.

Ulanowicz, R.E. (1996) The propensities of evolving systems, in E.L. Khalil and K. Boulding (eds) *Evolution, Order and Complexity*. London: Routledge.

Ulrich, D. (1998) A new mandate for human resources, *Harvard Business Review*, 76(1): 124–34.

UNDP (United Nations Development Programme) (1995) *Public Sector Management, Governance, and Sustainable Human Development*, Discussion Paper. New York, NY: Management Development and Governance Division, Bureau for Policy and Programme Support, United Nations Development Programme.

Varela, F.J. (1992) *Ethical Know-How: Action, Wisdom and Cognition*. Stanford, CA: Stanford University Press.

Vincent, C., Taylor-Adams, S., Chapman, E.J. *et al.* (2000) How to investigate and analyse clinical incidents: Clinical Risk Unit and Association of Litigation and Risk Management protocol, *British Medical Journal*, 320: 777–81.

Vogel, D. (1986) *National Styles of Regulation: Environmental Policy in Great Britain and the United States*. Ithaca, NY: Cornell University Press.

Waddington, I. (1984) *The Medical Profession in the Industrial Revolution*. Dublin: Gill and Macmillan.

Waddington, I. (1990) The movement towards the professionalization of medicine, *British Medical Journal*, 301: 688–90.

Wakeford, T. (1999) *Citizen Foresight: A Tool to Enhance Democratic Policy Making: 1. The Future of Food and Agriculture*. London: Centre for Governance Innovation and Science.

Wallace, L., Freeman, T., Latham, L., *et. al.*, (2001a) Organizational strategies for changing clinical practice, *Quality in Health Care*, 10(2): 77–82.

Wallace, L., Spurgeon, P., Latham, L., *et al.*, (2001b) Clinical governance, organizational culture and change management in the new NHS, *Clinician in Management*, 10: 23–31.

Walshe, K. (2000) *Clinical Governance: A Review of the Evidence*. Birmingham: Health Services Management Centre, University of Birmingham.

Walshe, K. and Sheldon, T.A. (1998) Dealing with clinical risk: implications of the rise of evidence-based health care, *Public Money and Management*, 18(4): 15–20.

Walshe, K., Freeman, T., Latham, L., *et al.*, (2000) *Clinical Governance: From Policy to Practice*. Birmingham: Health Services Management Centre, University of Birmingham.

Watkins, S. (1982) Occupational health services: part of the health care system? MSc thesis, University of Manchester.

Watkins, S. (1987) *Medicine and Labour: The Politics of a Profession*. London: Lawrence and Wishart.

Watkins, S. and Iliffe, S. (1989) Unpack the package, *Health Service Journal*, 4 May: 546.

Webb, J. (1999) Work and the new public service class, *Sociology*, 33: 747–66.

Weber, M. (1947) *The Theory of Social and Economic Organisation.* Trans. A.M. Henderson and T. Parsons. New York, NY: Free Press.

Weber, M. (1948) *From Max Weber: Essays in Sociology,* H.H. Gerth and C.W. Mills (eds). London: Routledge.

Webler, T. (1995) 'Right' discourse in citizen participation: an evaluative yardstick, in O. Renn, T. Webler and P. Wiedemann (eds) *Fairness and Competence in Citizen Participation.* Dordrecht: Kluwer.

Webster, C. (1988) *The Health Services since the War, Vol. 1: Problems of Health Care: The National Health Service before 1959.* London: HMSO.

West, E. (2001) Management matters: the link between hospital organization and quality of patient care, *Quality in Health Care,* 10: 40–8.

West, M.A., Borrill, C., Dawson, J. *et al.* (2002) The link between the management of employees and patient mortality in acute hospitals, *International Journal of Human Resource Management,* 13(8): 1299–310.

White, S. (1998) Examining the artfulness of risk talk, in A. Jokinen, K. Juhila and T. Poso (eds) *Constructing Social Work Practices.* Aldershot: Ashgate.

White, S. (2002) Accomplishing the case in paediatrics and child health: medicine and morality in inter-professional talk, *Sociology of Health and Illness,* 24(4): 409–35.

White, S. and Stancombe, J. (2003) *Clinical Judgement in the Health and Welfare Professions: Extending the Evidence Base.* Maidenhead: Open University Press.

Williams, M. (1999) Single case probabilities in the social world, *Journal for the Theory of Social Behaviour,* 29(2): 187–201.

Wilmott, H.C. (1990) Subjectivity: the dialectics of praxis: opening up the core of labour process analysis, in D. Knights and H. Wilmott (eds) *Labour Process Theory.* Basingtoke: Macmillan.

Woodyard, L.W. and Sheetz, J.E. (1993) Critical pathway patient outcomes: the missing standard, *Journal of Nursing Care Quality,* 8(1): 51–7.

Woolgar, S. (1988) *Science: The Very Idea.* London: Tavistock.

WHO (World Health Organization) (1993) *WHO Training Manual on Management of Human Resources for Health.* Geneva: World Health Organization.

WHO (2000) *The World Health Report, 2000.* Geneva: World Health Organization.

Young, I.M. (1990) *Justice and the Politics of Difference.* Princeton, NJ: Princeton University Press.

Young, I.M. (2000) *Inclusion and Democracy.* Oxford: Oxford University Press.

Znaniecki, F. (1934) *The Method of Sociology.* New York, NY: Farrar and Rinehart.

Index

Page numbers in *italics* refer to boxes and tables; *passim* indicates frequent intermittent references.